2024 Joint International Conference on Computational Linguistics, Language Resources and Evaluation (LREC-COLING 2024)

Tutorial Summaries

Torino, Italy
20-25 May 2024

Editors:

Roman Klinger
Naoaki Okazaki

ISBN: 978-1-7138-9761-3

Printed from e-media with permission by:

Curran Associates, Inc.
57 Morehouse Lane
Red Hook, NY 12571

Printed with permission by Curran Associates, Inc. (2025)

For permission requests, please contact the Association for Computational Linguistics at the address below.

Association for Computational Linguistics
209 N. Eighth Street
Stroudsburg, Pennsylvania 18360

Phone: 1-570-476-8006
Fax: 1-570-476-0860

acl@aclweb.org

Additional copies of this publication are available from:

Curran Associates, Inc.
57 Morehouse Lane
Red Hook, NY 12571 USA
Phone: 845-758-0400
Fax: 845-758-2633
Email: curran@proceedings.com
Web: www.proceedings.com

LREC-COLING 2024

The 2024 Joint International Conference on Computational Linguistics, Language Resources and Evaluation (LREC-COLING 2024)

Tutorial Summaries

Editors
Roman Klinger and Naoaki Okazaki

20-25 May, 2024
Torino, Italy

Proceedings of the 2024 Joint International Conference on Computational Linguistics, Language Resources and Evaluation (LREC-COLING 2024): Tutorial Summaries

ISSN 2951-2093 (COLING); 2522-2686 (LREC)

Jointly organized by the ELRA Language Resources Association
and the International Committee on Computational Linguistics

Message from the Tutorial Chairs

Welcome to the Tutorials Session of LREC–COLING 2024.

The tutorials are organized to give conference attendees a comprehensive overview by experts on topics relevant to our field. As a novelty, we did not only ask for proposals that are cutting edge or introductory to a topic, but also requested proposals for adjacent research areas in recognition of the interdisciplinary nature of the field.

We received 20 submissions from which we selected 13 to be taught at the conference. Out of those three are introductory (one to an adjacent topic), and the majority present cutting-edge topics. Unsurprisingly, a popular topic is large-language models, which are covered by multiple tutorials with varying perspectives on multimodality, evaluation, knowledge editing and control, hallucination, and bias. Other tutorials cover argument mining, semantic web, dialogue systems, semantic parsing, inclusion in NLP systems, and applications in chemistry.

Our thanks go to the conference organizers for effective collaboration, and in particular to the general chairs Nicoletta Calzolari and Min-Yen Kan and the publication chairs Francis Bond and Alexandre Rademaker.

We hope you enjoy the tutorials.

LREC–COLING 2024 Tutorial Co-chairs

- Naoaki Okazaki
- Roman Klinger

Table of Contents

From Multimodal LLM to Human-level AI: Modality, Instruction, Reasoning, Efficiency and Beyond

Hao Fei[♣] Yuan Yao[♣] Zhuosheng Zhang[♡] Fuxiao Liu[♠] Ao Zhang[♣] Tat-seng Chua[♣]
[♣]National University of Singapore
[♡]Shanghai Jiao Tong University
[♠]University of Maryland, College Park
haofei37@nus.edu.sg, yaoyuanthu@gmail.com, zhangzs@sjtu.edu.cn,
fl3es@umd.edu, aozhang@u.nus.edu, dcscts@nus.edu.sg

Abstract

Artificial intelligence (AI) encompasses knowledge acquisition and real-world grounding across various modalities. As a multidisciplinary research field, multimodal large language models (MLLMs) have recently garnered growing interest in both academia and industry, showing an unprecedented trend to achieve human-level AI via MLLMs. These large models offer an effective vehicle for understanding, reasoning, and planning by integrating and modeling diverse information modalities, including language, visual, auditory, and sensory data. This tutorial aims to deliver a comprehensive review of cutting-edge research in MLLMs, focusing on four key areas: MLLM architecture design, instructional learning, multimodal reasoning, and the efficiency of MLLMs. We will explore technical advancements, synthesize key challenges, and discuss potential avenues for future research. All the resources and materials are available at `https://mllm2024.github.io/COLING2024`

Keywords: Large Language Model, Artificial Intelligence, Multimodal Learning, Instruction Tuning, Reasoning, Efficiency Learning

1. Introduction

This year, the whole world has witnessed astonishing advancements in artificial intelligence (AI) to date due to the emergence of large language models (LLMs), such as OpenAI's ChatGPT (OpenAI, 2022b) and GPT-4 (OpenAI, 2022a). LLMs have showcased remarkable capabilities in understanding language, hinting at the not-so-distant arrival of true AGI. Following ChatGPT, a series of open-source LLMs have been published, e.g., Flan-T5 (Chung et al., 2022), Vicuna (Chiang et al., 2023), LLaMA (Touvron et al., 2023a) and Alpaca (Taori et al., 2023), sparking a surge in research revolving around LLMs. The advent of LLMs has also profoundly changed the way tasks are modeled within the NLP community. Human interactions with NLP models have shifted from traditional methods like classification and sequence labeling to a unified 'query-answer' paradigm between user and agent with natural prompt texts (Lester et al., 2021). LLMs have demonstrated promising results in both zero-shot and few-shot settings across various NLP and CV tasks, even with some existing benchmarks being well solved.

However, in reality, we humans inhabit a world where various modalities of information coexist, including visual, auditory, sensory and more, beyond pure language. This realization underscores the necessity of endowing LLMs with multimodal perception and comprehension capabilities to achieve human-level AI, i.e., AGI. This endeavor has given rise to an emerging topic of Multimodal LLMs (MLLMs). MLLMs offer a compelling argument for enhancing the robustness of LLMs by enabling multisensory learning, with each sensory modality complementing the others. Researchers devise additional encoders in front of textual LLMs for receiving inputs in other modalities, leading to the development of MLLMs, such as BLIP-2 (Li et al., 2023), Flamingo (Alayrac et al., 2022a), MiniGPT-4 (Zhu et al., 2023), Video-LLaMA (Zhang et al., 2023c), LLaVA (Liu et al., 2023e), PandaGPT (Su et al., 2023), SpeechGPT (Zhang et al., 2023b) and NExT-GPT (Wu et al., 2023b).

As the manner of interactions with LLMs has been shifted into a more human-centric 'query-answer' style, the learning of LLMs has also been changed. Different from the typical training of deep models, e.g., masked language modeling (Devlin et al., 2019), instruction tuning has been introduced as a major approach for LLMs/MLLMs' tuning (Yin et al., 2023; Su et al., 2023). With sufficient instruction tuning, LLMs/MLLMs are taught to faithfully follow human instructions. Also, it is critical to fully exploit the potential of LLMs/MLLMs for achieving human-level reasoning. Correspondingly, researchers have designed the Chain-of-Thought (CoT) concept (Wei et al., 2022b), which offers a solution enabling LLMs with complex problem-solving abilities on language (Wang et al., 2023; Fei et al., 2023a) or multimodal data (Zhang et al., 2023d; Zhang and Zhang, 2023). Simultaneously, it has been demonstrated that the larger the model

LREC-COLING 2024 Tutorials, pages 1–8

sizes and parameters, the more evident the emergence of capabilities in LLMs/MLLMs (Wei et al., 2022a). However, constructing and training extremely large-scale LLMs come at a significant cost, which poses a great challenge for widespread research in this field. Consequently, the efficient development of models becomes a crucial aspect of MLLM's progress.

In this **cutting-edge tutorial**, we aim to offer a comprehensive introduction to techniques for building MLLMs that contribute to achieving stronger, more efficient and more human-level AI. We will delve into recent progress in the realm of MLLMs under four parts, which also are the key components of the topic of MLLMs. **First, multi-modality architecture design**, we elaborate on the cutting-edge approaches to designing architectures that seamlessly integrate multiple modalities, enabling MLLMs to process a variety of sensory inputs effectively. **Second, instruction learning**, we delve into the intricacies of instruction learning, where we discuss the methods and strategies used to train models to follow human instructions under multi-modalities accurately. **Third, multimodal reasoning**, we will present the techniques and methodologies behind multimodal reasoning, which empowers MLLMs to perform intricate reasoning tasks across different modalities with their cognitive capabilities. **Finally, efficiency of MLLMs**, we will give a brief overview of efficient model development, exploring strategies to construct MLLMs that balance performance with computational resources, making them accessible for a wider range of research applications. For each part of the components, we survey the progress and elaborate all the existing techniques on the track, and finally shed light on the future possible directions.

2. Tutorial Outline

This **half-day** (3.5 hours) tutorial presents a systematic overview of recent advancements, trends, resources and also emerging challenges that cover the following topics.

Part 1: Introduction and Overview (10 mins) We begin motivating the topic of MLLMs with the current progress in both academia and industry for achieving the goal of human-level AI. And then we place the emphasis on the key aspects of building successful MLLMs, which bring out the following tutorial content.

Part 2: MLLM Architecture Design (80 mins) We start with the introduction of pre-training language models (Devlin et al., 2019; Radford et al., 2019; Brown et al., 2020), and then transit to the LLMs of pure languages (OpenAI, 2022a; Touvron et al., 2023b), e.g., ChatGPT. Key techniques of LLMs will be highlighted. Then, we delve into the development of MLLMs based on the success of textual LLMs. We will review the architecture design and training techniques of existing popular MLLMs from two main aspects. (1) First, we will summarize vanilla MLLM architectures that integrate LLMs with different modality information (Alayrac et al., 2022b; Li et al., 2023; Liu et al., 2023e), including multimodal encoding, fusion and generation. (2) Second, we will review the pretraining techniques to learn foundational MLLM capabilities from large-scale multimodal data (Alayrac et al., 2022b; Hu et al., 2023; Radford et al., 2021).

We humans consistently keep engaging in the process of receiving and producing multimodal content every minute and hour, e.g., language, visual, sound, touch and smell. Thus, building MLLMs that only can understand multimodal information is never enough to achieve the goal of human-level AI. In this sub-topic, we further introduce the current progress in developing unified multimodal agents that are able to perceive inputs and generate outputs in arbitrary combinations of text, images, videos, audio, and beyond (Wu et al., 2023a; Shen et al., 2023; Tang et al., 2023; Wu et al., 2023b). We present the existing popular modeling architectures of the any-to-any MLLMs, as well as the discussion in terms of their pros and cons. And finally we shed light on the key points in realizing the more human-like MLLMs, such as the concept of world knowledge modeling, and end-to-end unified agents.

Part 3: Multimodal Instruction Tuning (40 mins) Multimodal instruction tuning typically refers to the process of optimizing instructions or guidance for a system or model that can understand and process multiple types of inputs, such as text, images, audio, etc. Recent open-source instruction-tuned MLLMs including Alayrac et al. (2022a); Zhu et al. (2023); Zhang et al. (2023c); Liu et al. (2023e); Su et al. (2023); Liu et al. (2023b); Zhang et al. (2023b); Wu et al. (2023b); Liu et al. (2023b,d) have shown remarkable performance. In this part, we will delve into how to build instruction-tuned MLLMs step by step. This session is structured as follows. (1) First, we will introduce the construction of visual instruction data and how to improve data quantity and quality. (2) Second, We will engage in the intricate details of the architecture and training strategies of current MLLMs, like MiniGPT4 (Zhu et al., 2023), LLaVA (Liu et al., 2023e) and etc. (3) Third, we will discuss the challenges in this domain, including parameter-efficient training and relieving hallucination issues (Liu et al., 2023c,a).

Part 4: Multimodal Reasoning (40 mins) Imagine trying to study a textbook without any figures, diagrams, or tables. Multimodal reasoning is a rapidly evolving research field that aims to enhance deep learning models by enabling them to learn from information gathered from various sources and engage in complex reasoning (Hu et al., 2017; Alayrac et al., 2022b; Lu et al., 2022; Yang et al., 2023; Driess et al., 2023). In this section, we will delve into the techniques and methodologies that form the foundation of multimodal reasoning. These techniques empower MLLMs to perform intricate reasoning tasks across different modalities, drawing upon their cognitive abilities. This session is structured as follows. (1) First, we will introduce benchmark datasets and assess the performance of MLLMs on these benchmarks. (2) Second, we will engage in a detailed discussion exploring key research topics, including multimodal chain-of-thought reasoning (Zhang et al., 2023d), multimodal in-context learning (Zhao et al., 2023b), and compositional reasoning (Lu et al., 2023). (3) Third, we will address the challenges faced in this area and discuss future research directions, including multimodal tool learning and multimodal autonomous agents.

Part 5: Efficient MLLM Development (40 mins) MLLM construction (Alayrac et al., 2022b; OpenAI, 2022a) is typically costful, which usually takes thousands of GPU hours and causes severe carbon emissions. In this condition, efficient MLLM development aims at training MLLMs with reduced training cost, while still ensuring excellent multimodal understanding ability. In this section, we will make a systematical review of the techniques that contribute to training efficiency from 3 aspects: (1) First of all, to reduce the training cost, parameter-efficient tuning like LoRA (Hu et al., 2021) is usually employed. We will introduce several parameter-efficient tuning methods (Hu et al., 2021; Dettmers et al., 2023) and corresponding examples. (2) Secondly, using the high-quality training data (Liu et al., 2023e; Li et al., 2023) is essential to boost the training efficiency. We list the widely used databases and make a discussion on their effects. (3) Thirdly, we will introduce how to organize the above mentioned techniques by using different training paradigms. For example, VPG-Trans (Zhang et al., 2023a) propose a two-stage transfer learning framework to realize MLLM construction with around 10% cost. After reviewing existing techniques, we will discuss the challenges and future directions, including how to decide the optimal corpus composition and search for the most efficient training paradigm.

3. Reading List

LLMs and MLLMs. GPT-3 (Brown et al., 2020); GPT-4 (OpenAI, 2022a); Flamingo (Alayrac et al., 2022b); BLIP-2 (Li et al., 2023); LLaVA (Liu et al., 2023e); Visual ChatGPT (Wu et al., 2023a); HuggingGPT (Shen et al., 2023); CoDi (Tang et al., 2023); ImageBind (Girdhar et al., 2023); NExT-GPT (Wu et al., 2023b); AnyMAL (Moon et al., 2023); VisCPM (Hu et al., 2023); Muffin (Yu et al., 2023); Qwen-VL (Bai et al., 2023); KOSMOS-2 (Peng et al., 2023).

Instruction Tuning. MiniGPT4 (Zhu et al., 2023); LLaVA (Liu et al., 2023e); LRV-Instruction (Liu et al., 2023b); Llama-adapter v2: (Gao et al., 2023); SVIT (Zhao et al., 2023a); mplug-owl (Ye et al., 2023).

Reasoning with LLM. Multimodal-CoT (Zhang et al., 2023d); MMICL (Zhao et al., 2023b); Chameleon (Lu et al., 2023); Auto-UI (Zhang and Zhang, 2023).

Efficient Learning. LoRA (Hu et al., 2021), QLoRA (Dettmers et al., 2023), LLaVA (Liu et al., 2023e), LaVIN (Luo et al., 2023), VPGTrans (Zhang et al., 2023a).

4. Presenters

Hao Fei (`https://haofei.vip`). He is currently a research fellow in the School of Computing, National University of Singapore; and also an associate researcher at Sea AI Lab, Singapore. His research interests cover NLP and multimodal learning, with specific interests in structural learning and LLMs. Over 40 of his research papers have been published at top-tier venues, *e.g.*, ICML, NeurIPS, ACL, ACM MM, AAAI, SIGIR, IJCAI, WWW, EMNLP, TOIS, TNNLS. He won the Paper Award Nomination at ACL 2023. He co-organized the Workshop on Deep Multimodal Learning for Information Retrieval at ACM MM 2023. He has been the co-organizer of top-tier conferences, such as Workshop Chair and Volunteer Chair in EMNLP, WSDM and ACL. He served as Area Chair and Senior Program Committee in relevant multiple conferences, such as EMNLP, WSDM, AAAI, IJCAI and ACL.

Yuan Yao (`https://yaoyuanthu.github.io/`). He is currently a research fellow in the School of Computing, National University of Singapore. His research interests include MLLMs and information extraction. He has published over 20 papers in top-tier conferences and journals, including ACL, EMNLP, NAACL, COLING, ICCV, ECCV, NeurIPS, AAAI, and Nature Communications. He has served as a PC member for ARR, ACL, EMNLP, NeurIPS, AAAI, WWW, etc.

Zhuosheng Zhang (`https://bcmi.sjtu.edu.cn/~zhangzs/`). He is currently an Assistant Professor at Shanghai Jiao Tong University, China. His research interests include NLP, LLMs, and multimodal autonomous agents. He has published over 50 papers in top-tier conferences and journals, including TPAMI, ICLR, ACL, AAAI, EMNLP, TNNLS, TASLP, and COLING. He has won 1st place in various language understanding and reasoning leaderboards, such as HellaSwag, SQuAD2.0, MuTual, RACE, ShARC, and CMRC. He has several tutorials at conferences, including IJCAI 2021 and IJCNLP-AACL 2023.

Fuxiao Liu (https://fuxiaoliu.github.io). He is currently a PhD student in the school of Computer Science, University of Maryland, College Park. His research interests cover multiple vision and language tasks, including image/video captioning, multimodal semantic alignment, fact-checking, document understanding. His recent focus is on building customizable large models that follow humans' intent. His research has been published at top-tier venues, *e.g.*, EMNLP, ICLR, EACL, COLING. He has ever interned multiple companies, including Nvidia, Adobe, Microsoft and Tencent.

Ao Zhang (https://waxnkw.github.io). He is currently a PhD student in the School of Computing, National University of Singapore. His research interests mainly lies on multimodal large language model, multimodal prompt learning and structured scene understanding. He has published several papers on top-tier conferences including ICCV, ECCV, ACL, EMNLP, AAAI, and NeurIPS.

Tat-seng Chua (https://chuatatseng.com). He is the KITHCT Chair Professor with the School of Computing, National University of Singapore, where he was the Acting and Founding Dean of the School from 1998 to 2000. His main research interests include multimedia learning and social media analytics. He is the Co-Director of NExT++, a joint center between NUS and Tsinghua University, to develop technologies for live social media search. He is the 2015 winner of the prestigious ACM SIGMM Technical Achievement Award and has received the best papers (or candidates) over 10 times in top conferences (SIGIR, WWW, MM, etc). He serves as the General Chair of top conferences multiple times (MM 2005, SIGIR 2008, WSDM 2023, etc), and the chief editors of multiple journals (TOIS, TMM, etc). He has given invited keynote talks at multiple top conferences, including the recent one on the topic of large language models.

5. Other Information

Type of Tutorial: Cutting-edge.

Past Tutorials: To our knowledge, there is no prior tutorial for delivering comprehensive instruction on the topic of multimodal LLMs.

Target Audience: Our tutorial is targeted at members of a broad range of relevant communities, e.g., NLP, CV and broad AI, who have interests in building LLMs and applying LLMs to achieve stronger task performances. This includes researchers, students of both academia and industry, as well as practitioners wishing to make use of LLMs in their learning pipelines. We expect that participants are comfortable with the basic foundations of both NLP and multimodal learning tasks, as well as the basic knowledge of standard generative models e.g., transformers. While we do not require any readings, we recommend reviewing the works cited in this proposal, especially the reading list.

Prerequisites: Following knowledge is assumed:

- Machine Learning: basic probability theory, supervised learning, transformer models
- NLP: Familiarity with LLMs; prompt tuning technique, generative NLP, etc.
- Multimodal Learning: Familiarity with multimodal modeling, e.g., visual, video, audio; diffusion models, etc.

Estimated Participant Number: 200.

Breadth: We estimate that approximately 30% of the tutorial will center around work done by the presenters. This tutorial categorizes the goal of developing successful MLLMs into several sub-topics, and each of the sub-topics includes a significant amount of other researchers' works.

Open Access: We make all teaching material available online, and we agree to allow the publication of slides and video recordings in the LREC-COLING 2024.

Diversity Considerations: The content and methods in this tutorial broadly cover the key common knowledge from NLP, CV and machine learning fields. Thus, this tutorial will facilitate a wide range of communities in diverse topics and domains. The speakers are from diversified academic institutions with different backgrounds and regions, e.g., including both professors, research fellows and Ph.D. students, and from Sinagpore, China and USA. We will reach out to academic communities to encourage them to attend our tutorial for the participation of diverse audiences.

6. Ethics Statement

Our tutorial is committed to promoting the research and responsible AI development. All the materials cited, occurred and presented in this tutorial strictly follow the corresponding regulations and licenses. We emphasize the importance of respecting user privacy, ensuring fairness in LLM systems, and advocating addressing potential biases across modalities. We encourage participants to consider the societal impact of their work and prioritize transparency, accountability, and inclusivity in their research. Together, we aim to advance multimodal AI technologies while upholding the highest ethical standards.

7. Bibliographical References

Jean-Baptiste Alayrac, Jeff Donahue, Pauline Luc, Antoine Miech, Iain Barr, Yana Hasson, Karel Lenc, Arthur Mensch, Katherine Millican, Malcolm Reynolds, Roman Ring, Eliza Rutherford, Serkan Cabi, Tengda Han, Zhitao Gong, Sina Samangooei, Marianne Monteiro, Jacob L. Menick, Sebastian Borgeaud, Andy Brock, Aida Nematzadeh, Sahand Sharifzadeh, Mikolaj Binkowski, Ricardo Barreira, Oriol Vinyals, Andrew Zisserman, and Karén Simonyan. 2022a. Flamingo: a visual language model for few-shot learning. In *Proceedings of the NeurIPS*.

Jean-Baptiste Alayrac, Jeff Donahue, Pauline Luc, Antoine Miech, Iain Barr, Yana Hasson, Karel Lenc, Arthur Mensch, Katherine Millican, Malcolm Reynolds, et al. 2022b. Flamingo: a visual language model for few-shot learning. *Advances in Neural Information Processing Systems*, 35:23716–23736.

Jinze Bai, Shuai Bai, Shusheng Yang, Shijie Wang, Sinan Tan, Peng Wang, Junyang Lin, Chang Zhou, and Jingren Zhou. 2023. Qwen-vl: A frontier large vision-language model with versatile abilities. *arXiv preprint arXiv:2308.12966*.

Tom Brown, Benjamin Mann, Nick Ryder, Melanie Subbiah, Jared D Kaplan, Prafulla Dhariwal, Arvind Neelakantan, Pranav Shyam, Girish Sastry, Amanda Askell, et al. 2020. Language models are few-shot learners. *Advances in neural information processing systems*, 33:1877–1901.

Sijin Chen, Xin Chen, Chi Zhang, Mingsheng Li, Gang Yu, Hao Fei, Hongyuan Zhu, Jiayuan Fan, and Tao Chen. 2023. Ll3da: Visual interactive instruction tuning for omni-3d understanding, reasoning, and planning. *arXiv preprint arXiv:2311.18651*.

Wei-Lin Chiang, Zhuohan Li, Zi Lin, Ying Sheng, Zhanghao Wu, Hao Zhang, Lianmin Zheng, Siyuan Zhuang, Yonghao Zhuang, Joseph E. Gonzalez, Ion Stoica, and Eric P. Xing. 2023. Vicuna: An open-source chatbot impressing gpt-4 with 90

Hyung Won Chung, Le Hou, Shayne Longpre, Barret Zoph, Yi Tay, William Fedus, Eric Li, Xuezhi Wang, Mostafa Dehghani, Siddhartha Brahma, Albert Webson, Shixiang Shane Gu, Zhuyun Dai, Mirac Suzgun, Xinyun Chen, Aakanksha Chowdhery, Sharan Narang, Gaurav Mishra, Adams Yu, Vincent Y. Zhao, Yanping Huang, Andrew M. Dai, Hongkun Yu, Slav Petrov, Ed H. Chi, Jeff Dean, Jacob Devlin, Adam Roberts, Denny Zhou, Quoc V. Le, and Jason Wei. 2022. Scaling instruction-finetuned language models. *CoRR*, abs/2210.11416.

Tim Dettmers, Artidoro Pagnoni, Ari Holtzman, and Luke Zettlemoyer. 2023. Qlora: Efficient finetuning of quantized llms. *arXiv preprint arXiv:2305.14314*.

Jacob Devlin, Ming-Wei Chang, Kenton Lee, and Kristina Toutanova. 2019. BERT: Pre-training of deep bidirectional transformers for language understanding. In *Proceedings of the 2019 Conference of the North American Chapter of the Association for Computational Linguistics: Human Language Technologies, Volume 1 (Long and Short Papers)*, pages 4171–4186.

Danny Driess, Fei Xia, Mehdi SM Sajjadi, Corey Lynch, Aakanksha Chowdhery, Brian Ichter, Ayzaan Wahid, Jonathan Tompson, Quan Vuong, Tianhe Yu, et al. 2023. Palm-e: An embodied multimodal language model. *arXiv preprint arXiv:2303.03378*.

Hao Fei, Bobo Li, Qian Liu, Lidong Bing, Fei Li, and Tat-Seng Chua. 2023a. Reasoning implicit sentiment with chain-of-thought prompting. In *Proceedings of the 61st Annual Meeting of the Association for Computational Linguistics*, pages 1171–1182.

Hao Fei, Qian Liu, Meishan Zhang, Min Zhang, and Tat-Seng Chua. 2023b. Scene graph as pivoting: Inference-time image-free unsupervised multimodal machine translation with visual scene hallucination. In *Proceedings of the 61st Annual Meeting of the Association for Computational Linguistics*, pages 5980–5994.

Hao Fei, Shengqiong Wu, Wei Ji, Hanwang Zhang, and Tat-Seng Chua. 2023c. Empowering dynamics-aware text-to-video diffusion with large language models. *arXiv preprint arXiv:2308.13812*.

Peng Gao, Jiaming Han, Renrui Zhang, Ziyi Lin, Shijie Geng, Aojun Zhou, Wei Zhang, Pan Lu, Conghui He, Xiangyu Yue, et al. 2023. Llama-adapter v2: Parameter-efficient visual instruction model. *arXiv preprint arXiv:2304.15010*.

Rohit Girdhar, Alaaeldin El-Nouby, Zhuang Liu, Mannat Singh, Kalyan Vasudev Alwala, Armand Joulin, and Ishan Misra. 2023. Imagebind: One embedding space to bind them all. In *Proceedings of the IEEE/CVF Conference on Computer Vision and Pattern Recognition*, pages 15180–15190.

Edward J Hu, Yelong Shen, Phillip Wallis, Zeyuan Allen-Zhu, Yuanzhi Li, Shean Wang, Lu Wang, and Weizhu Chen. 2021. Lora: Low-rank adaptation of large language models. *arXiv preprint arXiv:2106.09685*.

Jinyi Hu, Yuan Yao, Chongyi Wang, Shan Wang, Yinxu Pan, Qianyu Chen, Tianyu Yu, Hanghao Wu, Yue Zhao, Haoye Zhang, et al. 2023. Large multilingual models pivot zero-shot multimodal learning across languages. *arXiv preprint arXiv:2308.12038*.

Ronghang Hu, Jacob Andreas, Marcus Rohrbach, Trevor Darrell, and Kate Saenko. 2017. Learning to reason: End-to-end module networks for visual question answering. In *Proceedings of the IEEE international conference on computer vision*, pages 804–813.

Brian Lester, Rami Al-Rfou, and Noah Constant. 2021. The power of scale for parameter-efficient prompt tuning. In *Proceedings of the 2021 Conference on Empirical Methods in Natural Language Processing*, pages 3045–3059.

Junnan Li, Dongxu Li, Silvio Savarese, and Steven C. H. Hoi. 2023. BLIP-2: bootstrapping language-image pre-training with frozen image encoders and large language models. In *Proceedings of the ICML*, pages 19730–19742.

Fuxiao Liu, Tianrui Guan, Zongxia Li, Lichang Chen, Yaser Yacoob, Dinesh Manocha, and Tianyi Zhou. 2023a. Hallusionbench: You see what you think? or you think what you see? an image-context reasoning benchmark challenging for gpt-4v (ision), llava-1.5, and other multi-modality models. *arXiv preprint arXiv:2310.14566*.

Fuxiao Liu, Kevin Lin, Linjie Li, Jianfeng Wang, Yaser Yacoob, and Lijuan Wang. 2023b. Aligning large multi-modal model with robust instruction tuning. *arXiv preprint arXiv:2306.14565*.

Fuxiao Liu, Kevin Lin, Linjie Li, Jianfeng Wang, Yaser Yacoob, and Lijuan Wang. 2023c. Mitigating hallucination in large multi-modal models via robust instruction tuning. In *The Twelfth International Conference on Learning Representations*.

Fuxiao Liu, Xiaoyang Wang, Wenlin Yao, Jianshu Chen, Kaiqiang Song, Sangwoo Cho, Yaser Yacoob, and Dong Yu. 2023d. Mmc: Advancing multimodal chart understanding with large-scale instruction tuning. *arXiv preprint arXiv:2311.10774*.

Haotian Liu, Chunyuan Li, Qingyang Wu, and Yong Jae Lee. 2023e. Visual instruction tuning. *CoRR*, abs/2304.08485.

Zhiyuan Liu, Sihang Li, Yanchen Luo, Hao Fei, Yixin Cao, Kenji Kawaguchi, Xiang Wang, and Tat-Seng Chua. 2023f. Molca: Molecular graph-language modeling with cross-modal projector and uni-modal adapter. In *Proceedings of the 2023 Conference on Empirical Methods in Natural Language Processing*, pages 15623–15638.

Pan Lu, Swaroop Mishra, Tanglin Xia, Liang Qiu, Kai-Wei Chang, Song-Chun Zhu, Oyvind Tafjord, Peter Clark, and Ashwin Kalyan. 2022. Learn to explain: Multimodal reasoning via thought chains for science question answering. *Advances in Neural Information Processing Systems*, 35:2507–2521.

Pan Lu, Baolin Peng, Hao Cheng, Michel Galley, Kai-Wei Chang, Ying Nian Wu, Song-Chun Zhu, and Jianfeng Gao. 2023. Chameleon: Plug-and-play compositional reasoning with large language models. *arXiv preprint arXiv:2304.09842*.

Gen Luo, Yiyi Zhou, Tianhe Ren, Shengxin Chen, Xiaoshuai Sun, and Rongrong Ji. 2023. Cheap and quick: Efficient vision-language instruction tuning for large language models. *arXiv preprint arXiv:2305.15023*.

Seungwhan Moon, Andrea Madotto, Zhaojiang Lin, Tushar Nagarajan, Matt Smith, Shashank Jain, Chun-Fu Yeh, Prakash Murugesan, Peyman Heidari, Yue Liu, et al. 2023. Anymal: An efficient and scalable any-modality augmented language model. *arXiv preprint arXiv:2309.16058*.

OpenAI. 2022a. Gpt-4 technical report.

OpenAI. 2022b. Introducing chatgpt.

Zhiliang Peng, Wenhui Wang, Li Dong, Yaru Hao, Shaohan Huang, Shuming Ma, and Furu Wei. 2023. Kosmos-2: Grounding multimodal large language models to the world. *arXiv preprint arXiv:2306.14824*.

Long Qian, Juncheng Li, Yu Wu, Yaobo Ye, Hao Fei, Tat-Seng Chua, Yueting Zhuang, and Siliang Tang. 2024. Momentor: Advancing video large language model with fine-grained temporal reasoning. *arXiv preprint arXiv:2402.11435*.

Leigang Qu, Shengqiong Wu, Hao Fei, Liqiang Nie, and Tat-Seng Chua. 2023. Layoutllm-t2i: Eliciting layout guidance from llm for text-to-image generation. In *Proceedings of the 31st ACM International Conference on Multimedia*, pages 643–654.

Alec Radford, Jong Wook Kim, Chris Hallacy, Aditya Ramesh, Gabriel Goh, Sandhini Agarwal, Girish Sastry, Amanda Askell, Pamela Mishkin, Jack Clark, et al. 2021. Learning transferable visual models from natural language supervision. In *International conference on machine learning*, pages 8748–8763. PMLR.

Alec Radford, Jeffrey Wu, Rewon Child, David Luan, Dario Amodei, Ilya Sutskever, et al. 2019. Language models are unsupervised multitask learners. *OpenAI blog*, 1(8):9.

Yongliang Shen, Kaitao Song, Xu Tan, Dongsheng Li, Weiming Lu, and Yueting Zhuang. 2023. Hugginggpt: Solving AI tasks with chatgpt and its friends in huggingface. *CoRR*, abs/2303.17580.

Yixuan Su, Tian Lan, Huayang Li, Jialu Xu, Yan Wang, and Deng Cai. 2023. Pandagpt: One model to instruction-follow them all. *CoRR*, abs/2305.16355.

Zineng Tang, Ziyi Yang, Chenguang Zhu, Michael Zeng, and Mohit Bansal. 2023. Any-to-any generation via composable diffusion. *arXiv preprint arXiv:2305.11846*.

Rohan Taori, Ishaan Gulrajani, Tianyi Zhang, Yann Dubois, Xuechen Li, Carlos Guestrin, Percy Liang, and Tatsunori B. Hashimoto. 2023. Stanford alpaca: An instruction-following llama model.

Hugo Touvron, Thibaut Lavril, Gautier Izacard, Xavier Martinet, Marie-Anne Lachaux, Timothée Lacroix, Baptiste Rozière, Naman Goyal, Eric Hambro, Faisal Azhar, Aurélien Rodriguez, Armand Joulin, Edouard Grave, and Guillaume Lample. 2023a. Llama: Open and efficient foundation language models. *CoRR*, abs/2302.13971.

Hugo Touvron, Thibaut Lavril, Gautier Izacard, Xavier Martinet, Marie-Anne Lachaux, Timothée Lacroix, Baptiste Rozière, Naman Goyal, Eric Hambro, Faisal Azhar, et al. 2023b. Llama: Open and efficient foundation language models. *arXiv preprint arXiv:2302.13971*.

Lei Wang, Wanyu Xu, Yihuai Lan, Zhiqiang Hu, Yunshi Lan, Roy Ka-Wei Lee, and Ee-Peng Lim. 2023. Plan-and-solve prompting: Improving zero-shot chain-of-thought reasoning by large language models. In *Proceedings of the 61st Annual Meeting of the Association for Computational Linguistics*, pages 2609–2634.

Jason Wei, Yi Tay, Rishi Bommasani, Colin Raffel, Barret Zoph, Sebastian Borgeaud, Dani Yogatama, Maarten Bosma, Denny Zhou, Donald Metzler, Ed H. Chi, Tatsunori Hashimoto, Oriol Vinyals, Percy Liang, Jeff Dean, and William Fedus. 2022a. Emergent abilities of large language models. *Trans. Mach. Learn. Res.*, 2022.

Jason Wei, Xuezhi Wang, Dale Schuurmans, Maarten Bosma, Fei Xia, Ed Chi, Quoc V Le, Denny Zhou, et al. 2022b. Chain-of-thought prompting elicits reasoning in large language models. *Advances in Neural Information Processing Systems*, 35:24824–24837.

Chenfei Wu, Shengming Yin, Weizhen Qi, Xiaodong Wang, Zecheng Tang, and Nan Duan. 2023a. Visual chatgpt: Talking, drawing and editing with visual foundation models. *CoRR*, abs/2303.04671.

Shengqiong Wu, Hao Fei, Leigang Qu, Wei Ji, and Tat-Seng Chua. 2023b. Next-gpt: Any-to-any multimodal llm. *CoRR*, abs/2309.05519.

Zhengyuan Yang, Linjie Li, Jianfeng Wang, Kevin Lin, Ehsan Azarnasab, Faisal Ahmed, Zicheng Liu, Ce Liu, Michael Zeng, and Lijuan Wang. 2023. Mm-react: Prompting chatgpt for multimodal reasoning and action. *arXiv preprint arXiv:2303.11381*.

Qinghao Ye, Haiyang Xu, Guohai Xu, Jiabo Ye, Ming Yan, Yiyang Zhou, Junyang Wang, Anwen Hu, Pengcheng Shi, Yaya Shi, et al. 2023. mplug-owl: Modularization empowers large language models with multimodality. *arXiv preprint arXiv:2304.14178*.

Zhenfei Yin, Jiong Wang, Jianjian Cao, Zhelun Shi, Dingning Liu, Mukai Li, Lu Sheng, Lei Bai, Xiaoshui Huang, Zhiyong Wang, Jing Shao, and Wanli Ouyang. 2023. LAMM: language-assisted multi-modal instruction-tuning dataset, framework, and benchmark. *CoRR*, abs/2306.06687.

Tianyu Yu, Jinyi Hu, Yuan Yao, Haoye Zhang, Yue Zhao, Chongyi Wang, Shan Wang, Yinxv Pan, Jiao Xue, Dahai Li, et al. 2023. Reformulating vision-language foundation models and datasets towards universal multimodal assistants. *arXiv preprint arXiv:2310.00653*.

Ao Zhang, Hao Fei, Yuan Yao, Wei Ji, Li Li, Zhiyuan Liu, and Tat-Seng Chua. 2023a. Transfer visual prompt generator across llms. *Proceedings of the NeurIPS*.

Dong Zhang, Shimin Li, Xin Zhang, Jun Zhan, Pengyu Wang, Yaqian Zhou, and Xipeng Qiu. 2023b. Speechgpt: Empowering large language models with intrinsic cross-modal conversational abilities. *CoRR*, abs/2305.11000.

Hang Zhang, Xin Li, and Lidong Bing. 2023c. Video-llama: An instruction-tuned audio-visual language model for video understanding. *CoRR*, abs/2306.02858.

Zhuosheng Zhang and Aston Zhang. 2023. You only look at screens: Multimodal chain-of-action agents. *ArXiv preprint*, abs/2309.11436.

Zhuosheng Zhang, Aston Zhang, Mu Li, Hai Zhao, George Karypis, and Alex Smola. 2023d. Multimodal chain-of-thought reasoning in language models. *arXiv preprint arXiv:2302.00923*.

Bo Zhao, Boya Wu, and Tiejun Huang. 2023a. Svit: Scaling up visual instruction tuning. *arXiv preprint arXiv:2307.04087*.

Haozhe Zhao, Zefan Cai, Shuzheng Si, Xiaojian Ma, Kaikai An, Liang Chen, Zixuan Liu, Sheng Wang, Wenjuan Han, and Baobao Chang. 2023b. Mmicl: Empowering vision-language model with multi-modal in-context learning. *arXiv preprint arXiv:2309.07915*.

Li Zheng, Hao Fei, Fei Li, Bobo Li, Lizi Liao, Donghong Ji, and Chong Teng. 2023. Reverse multi-choice dialogue commonsense inference with graph-of-thought. *arXiv preprint arXiv:2312.15291*.

Deyao Zhu, Jun Chen, Xiaoqian Shen, Xiang Li, and Mohamed Elhoseiny. 2023. Minigpt-4: Enhancing vision-language understanding with advanced large language models. *CoRR*, abs/2304.10592.

Geo-Cultural Representation and Inclusion in Language Technologies

Sunipa Dev
Google Research
sunipadev@google.com

Rida Qadri
Google Research
ridaqadri@google.com

Abstract

Training and evaluation of language models are increasingly relying on annotations by humans to judge questions of representation and safety. While techniques such as RLHF are being broadly applied, there is less consideration of how socio-cultural identity and positionality of the annotators involved in this process play a key role in what is taken as ground truth by our models. Yet, we currently do not have ways to integrate rich and diverse community perspectives into our language technologies.

Accounting for such cross-cultural differences in interacting with technology is an increasingly crucial step for evaluating AI harms holistically. Without this, the state of the art of the AI models being deployed is at risk of causing unprecedented biases at a global scale. This tutorial uses interactive exercises to illustrate how cultural identity of annotators and varying methods of human feedback influence evaluations of appropriate representations of global concepts.

1 Introduction

Increasingly, researchers and engineers are relying on human annotation to train, develop, and shape language models. However, as language models are being integrated into global systems of social and cultural importance such as search, education, and even creativity, the annotation tasks veer into increasingly culturally subjective questions of evaluating representation, toxicity, abusive language, stereotyping, and more. Measuring such representational quality of generated content requires significant culturally situated expertise and nuanced judgment on specific signifiers and social connotations of language (Qadri et al., 2023). Who you ask and how you ask them also changes the content of such subjective evaluations(Denton et al., 2021; Dev et al., 2023). To highlight this contingency of our existing evaluation methods, in this tutorial we will work through the following questions together:

1. How do we account for socio-cultural identities and perspectives of the annotators training our models?
2. How do we resolve disagreements in annotations when they come from culturally different raters for a subjective task?
3. What do qualitative and open-ended methods offer us as a mode of evaluation?
4. How can new research on understanding socially subjective data annotation tasks help build more robust, generalizable, and safe models?

1.1 Relevance at LREC-COLING

NLP research and development has seen immense, fast-paced progress in recent years, with a large growth in generative language models both in size, and number. Their capabilities have also increased and diversified, making their evaluations that much harder, but also more critical. However, as has been seen, these evaluations of models mostly focus on Western perspectives across a board of tasks from language fluency to NER. When we consider tasks closely related to experienced biases and harms, this concern magnifies (Davani et al., 2023). Harms faced by people in different parts of the world goes unchecked, and populations are often misrepresented or not represented at all in the model outputs. This major gap hints at a need for advancements in existing evaluation paradigms, and a recalibration of the approaches towards data annotation and aggregation.

We will discuss this pressing topic through emerging, state-of-the-art research in the area. With methodologies such as RLHF, and human centered AI fast developing, and cutting edge AI technologies being integrated into lives globally, these discussions at computational linguistics venues will be imperative towards fostering inclusive practices

LREC-COLING 2024 Tutorials, pages 9–12

around data resource creation, model building, and evaluations.

2 Outline

2.1 Tutorial Content

This tutorial will adopt three interactive annotation exercises and discuss approaches and the results obtained from them. All participants will together rate some sample questions in each exercise.

The first two exercises will ask for binary or categorical answers in response to first, a culturally under-specified question for instance quality of a response on music or film without a cultural locale specified, and then a statement with cultural specificity, such as a text quality of a model generated paragraph about people from a nationality or culturally specific facts about an area or population. These two exercises will open space for discussion on the varying forms of expertise annotations require and whether binary or closed-ended questions capture this cultural expertise

The third exercise will pair up individuals of different cultural backgrounds to evaluate generated text from each other's cultural background. The mode of evalution will be open ended.

The tutorial will the discuss the pros and cons of these approaches, the subjectivity of annotations, and ways to incorporate them into our NLP pipelines. In doing so, it will demonstrate the importance of culturally situated, and deeply engaged strategies of data collection and annotation. It will discuss the need for well documented, distributed, and diversely annotated data for ensuring data (for both training and measurement) quality.

3 Tutorial Structure

We have structured the tutorial into the following parts. Each part will be interactive and we will encourage questions throughout the tutorial. We will also keep aside at least the last 7 minutes of each of the following sessions to be just for Q/A.

Part 1 - Context and Motivation [45 mins] We will begin with a short, introductory talk by the presenters where we will motivate the problem setup and give examples of how cultural subjectivity and expertise can shape evaluation outcomes. We will also demonstrate how these differences impact what is treated as 'ground truth' by our AI pipelines. Specifically, in tasks that check for model safety and beneficence, these discrepancies can lead to representational as well as quality of service harms.

Part 2: Live rater annotation [45 mins] This segment of the tutorial will be extremely hands on, and aimed at investigating together how our experiences shape the way we annotate presence or absence of certain features in text or image data points. The task will be shared through a web link during the tutorial.
The total time for this segment will be split in the following way:

- Annotation [15 mins] Introduce text snippets and do two exercises to have the audience evaluate the two types of generated text : culturally under specified and culturally specified.
- Review of what was annotated [30 mins] Collective review of results of annotation exercise to discuss what kinds of knowledge did the person leverage to answer and if a binary rating was able to capture their feedback?

Coffee Break: 30 mins

Part 3: Cross-Cultural Annotation [45 mins]

- Annotation [15 mins] Cross Open ended questions on cultural quality of the text and explanations of what the models did well what it did poorly
- Discussion of the specificity of cultural expertise needed to evaluate text and what annotators of other identities missed or picked up on[30 mins]

Discussion and Closing [30 mins] We will spend the last 30 minutes summarizing the tutorial and answering any additional questions.

4 Target Audience

The target audience for this could be NLP researchers, engineers, and practitioners at any career stage. They could be actively using annotated data to rain or evaluate models, or creating the datasets for these purposes. With the discussions and exercises at the tutorial, they will collectively reflect on the range of impacts each rater assumption and rating task structure choice has.

Prerequisite Knowledge: No specific prerequisite knowledge is needed. However, a general knowledge of data annotations and/or evaluation tasks in NLP could be helpful.

Equipment needed: Venue with wifi so participants can engage with material.
Attendees are recommended to bring their laptops for better experience.

5 Diversity Statement

The topic of the tutorial is very tightly linked with the mission of diverse representation of people in NLP. The tutorial highlights how differing lived experiences across the globe impact what is 'ground truth' in data annotations for different people. Unilateral decisions or tasks only considering majority over categorical ratings do not do justice to the subjective tasks that LLMs built on these datasets perform. Through this tutorial we will elaborate the importance of global inclusion into NLP technologies for equitable model development and deployment.

6 Other Information

The presenters have experience introducing and leading discussions on cultural considerations in AI pipelines. Some other venues where we have co-organized and conducted tutorials and workshops with a similar goals include FAccT 2023 (Tutorial on Cross Cultural Considerations in AI; 50 attendees), EACL 2023 (Cross Cultural Considerations in NLP Workshop; 75 attendees), NeurIPS 2022 (Cultures in AI Workshop; 50 attendees), CVPR 2023 (Ethical Considerations in Creative Applications of Computer Vision).

With this track record of successful events on this theme at multiple venues, we expect a similar range of attendees at COLING. We will also be advertising the tutorial through multiple channels including social media, and mailing lists.

7 Reading List

1. Whose Ground Truth? Accounting for Individual and Collective Identities Underlying Dataset Annotation; Emily Denton, Mark Díaz, Ian Kivlichan, Vinodkumar Prabhakaran, Rachel Rosen; Data Centric AI Workshop at NeurIPS 2021 ((Denton et al., 2021))

2. SeeGULL: A Stereotype Benchmark with Broad Geo-Cultural Coverage Leveraging Generative Models; Akshita Jha, Aida Mostafazadeh Davani, Chandan K Reddy, Shachi Dave, Vinodkumar Prabhakaran, Sunipa Dev; ACL 2023 ((Jha et al., 2023))

3. Probing pre-trained language models for cross-cultural differences in values; Arnav Arora, Lucie-Aimée Kaffee, Isabelle Augenstein; Proceedings of the First Workshop on Cross-Cultural Considerations in NLP (C3NLP) at EACL 2023 ((Arora et al., 2023))

4. Cultural Incongruencies in Artificial Intelligence; Vinodkumar Prabhakaran, Rida Qadri, Ben Hutchinson; Cultures and AI Workshop at NeurIPS 2022 ((Prabhakaran et al., 2022))

5. Assessing cross-cultural alignment between ChatGPT and human societies: An empirical study; Yong Cao, Li Zhou, Seolhwa Lee, Laura Cabello, Min Chen, Daniel Hershcovich; Proceedings of the First Workshop on Cross-Cultural Considerations in NLP (C3NLP) at EACL 2023 ((Cao et al., 2023))

8 Presenter Bios

Sunipa Dev (she/her, Google Research, `sunipadev@google.com`) is a Senior Research Scientist at Google Research working towards fair, inclusive, and socio-culturally aware NLP. Her research centers around inclusion of global perspectives in different pipelines in NLP, particularly in model evaluations to better understand and mitigate potential risks and harms. Prior to this, she was an NSF Computing Innovation Fellow at UCLA, before which she was awarded her PhD at the School of Computing at the University of Utah.

She has taught guest lectures and given talks centered on inclusive NLP at multiple places including University of Utah (2023), University of Southern California (2023), University of Bocconi (2021), and a keynote at TrustNLP Workshop (ACL 2023). She is currently a program chair for WINLP (organizing across different NLP venues including NAACL, ACL, and EMNLP), and was the affinity workshop chair at NeurIPS 2022 and a workflow chair for AAAI 2022. She has also co-organized tutorials and workshops at various venues including KDD 2021, NeurIPS 2022, EACL 2023, and FAccT 2023.

Rida Qadri (she/her, Google Research, `ridaqadri@google.com`) Rida Qadri is a Senior Research Scientist at Google Research.

Her research interrogates the cultural assumptions underpinning the design and deployment of generative AI systems. She specifically focuses on the harms produced by culturally inappropriate AI design choices and documents how communities resist and repair these technologies.

She has given guest lectures on cultural failures of AI at MIT, University of North Carolina, Maastricht University and spoken on keynote panels at FAccT 2022 and IEEE world AI IOT Congress. She has co-organized workshops at the intersection of AI and Culture at NeurIPS 2022, CHI 2021 and CVPR 2023. She has a PhD in Computational Urban Studies from the Massachusetts Institute of Technology.

9 Ethics Statement

This workshop will help draw attention towards the ethics of globally deploying models which incorporate world views of only few parts of the world, both in its training and evaluations. It will urge deeper reflections of how each data instance that we use to build or evaluate a model can have different interpretations by different people and communities globally. By doing so, this tutorial will be actively fighting against further marginalizations or erasure of people from different communities and cultures.

References

Arnav Arora, Lucie-aimée Kaffee, and Isabelle Augenstein. 2023. Probing pre-trained language models for cross-cultural differences in values. In *Proceedings of the First Workshop on Cross-Cultural Considerations in NLP (C3NLP)*, pages 114–130, Dubrovnik, Croatia. Association for Computational Linguistics.

Yong Cao, Li Zhou, Seolhwa Lee, Laura Cabello, Min Chen, and Daniel Hershcovich. 2023. Assessing cross-cultural alignment between chatgpt and human societies: An empirical study.

Aida Mostafazadeh Davani, Mark Diaz, Dylan Baker, and Vinodkumar Prabhakaran. 2023. Disentangling disagreements on offensiveness: A cross-cultural study. In *The 61st Annual Meeting of the Association for Computational Linguistics*.

Emily Denton, Mark Díaz, Ian Kivlichan, Vinodkumar Prabhakaran, and Rachel Rosen. 2021. Whose ground truth? accounting for individual and collective identities underlying dataset annotation. *arXiv preprint arXiv:2112.04554*.

Sunipa Dev, Jaya Goyal, Dinesh Tewari, Shachi Dave, and Vinodkumar Prabhakaran. 2023. Building socio-culturally inclusive stereotype resources with community engagement.

Akshita Jha, Aida Mostafazadeh Davani, Chandan K Reddy, Shachi Dave, Vinodkumar Prabhakaran, and Sunipa Dev. 2023. SeeGULL: A stereotype benchmark with broad geo-cultural coverage leveraging generative models. In *Proceedings of the 61st Annual Meeting of the Association for Computational Linguistics (Volume 1: Long Papers)*, pages 9851–9870, Toronto, Canada. Association for Computational Linguistics.

Vinodkumar Prabhakaran, Rida Qadri, and Ben Hutchinson. 2022. Cultural incongruencies in artificial intelligence.

Rida Qadri, Renee Shelby, Cynthia L Bennett, and Emily Denton. 2023. Ai's regimes of representation: A community-centered study of text-to-image models in south asia. In *Proceedings of the 2023 ACM Conference on Fairness, Accountability, and Transparency*, pages 506–517.

Meaning Representations for Natural Languages: Design, Models and Applications

*Julia Bonn, †Jeffrey Flanigan, ▷Jan Hajič,
‡Ishan Jindal, ◁Yunyao Li, ◇Nianwen Xue
*julia.bonn@colorado.edu, †jmflanig@ucsc.edu, ▷hajic@ufal.mff.cuni.cz,
‡ishan.jindal@ibm.com, ◁yunyaoli@gmail.com, ◇xuen@brandeis.edu

Abstract

This tutorial reviews the design of common meaning representations, SoTA models for predicting meaning representations, and the applications of meaning representations in a wide range of downstream NLP tasks and real-world applications. Reporting by a diverse team of NLP researchers from academia and industry with extensive experience in designing, building and using meaning representations, our tutorial has three components: (1) an introduction to common meaning representations, including basic concepts and design challenges; (2) a review of SoTA methods on building models for meaning representations; and (3) an overview of applications of meaning representations in downstream NLP tasks and real-world applications. We propose a full-day, cutting-edge tutorial for all stakeholders in the AI community, including NLP researchers, domain-specific practitioners, and students.

1. Introduction

This tutorial aims to introduce the NLP community to an emerging research area that has the potential to create linguistic resources and build computational models that provide critical components for interpretable and controllable NLP systems. While large language models have shown remarkable ability to generate fluent and mostly coherent text, the blackbox nature of these models makes it difficult to know where to tweak these models to fix errors or at least anticipate errors if they cannot easily be fixed. For instance, LLMs are known to hallucinate and generate factually incorrect answers when prompted as there is no mechanism in these models to constrain them to only provide factually correct answers. Addressing this issue requires that first of all the models have access to a body of verifiable facts, and then when generating answers to prompts or queries, do not alter them materially to make the answers factually incorrect. Interpretability and controllability in NLP systems are critical in high-stake application scenarios such as the health domain, where AI systems are used as medical assistants.

In the past few decades, there has been a steady accumulation of semantically annotated resources that are increasingly richer in representation. As these resources become available, steady progress has been made in developing computational models that can automatically parse unstructured text into these semantic representations with increasing accuracy. These models have reached a level of accuracy that makes them useful in practical applications. For example, these models have been used in information extraction, where entities and relations are extracted from unstructured text. It is now conceivable that these models can be used to extract verifiable facts at scale to build controllable and interpretable systems that can produce factual correct answers. These rich semantic representations are also needed in human-robot interaction (HRI) systems to facilitate on-the-fly grounding so that the robot can establish connections with its surroundings and interact with them in a meaningful way. These meaning representations are easily translated into logical representations to support logical reasoning that LLMs often struggle with, or they can be used to develop NLP systems for low-resource languages where there is insufficient data to train LLMs, but the richness in semantic representation can to some extent make up for the lack of quantity. This tutorial will provide an overview of these semantic representations, the computational models that are trained on them, as well as the practical applications built with these representations. We will also delve into future directions for this line of research and examine how these meaning representations might be used to build interpretable and controllable applications, used in human-robot interaction scenarios, and low-resource settings.

2. Target audience

This tutorial welcomes all stakeholders in the NLP community, including NLP researchers, domain-specific practitioners, and students. Our tutorial presumes no prior knowledge on the core concepts of meaning representation. However, a basic understanding of NLP, machine learning (especially, deep learning) concepts may be helpful. We intend to introduce the necessary concepts related to meaning representation during the introductory section of the tutorial.

In this tutorial, attendees will

- Develop fluency in core concepts of common meaning representations, state-of-the-art mod-

LREC-COLING 2024 Tutorials, pages 13–18
20-25 May, 2024.

els for producing these meaning representations, and potential use cases.

- Gain insights into the practical benefits and challenges around leveraging meaning representations for downstream applications.
- Discuss and reflect on open questions related to meaning representations.

3. Outline

3.1. Background

In this tutorial, we primarily discuss one thread of meaning representations that encompasses the Proposition Bank (PropBank) (Palmer et al., 2005), Abstract Meaning Representations (AMR) (Banarescu et al., 2013) as well as Uniform Meaning Representations (UMR) (Gysel et al., 2021), a recent extension to AMR, but will situate our discussion with a comparison with related meaning representations. We will discuss the representations themselves, as well as the latest semantic role labeling (SRL) and AMR parsing techniques using these representations, and overview applications of these meaning representations to practical natural language applications.

The proposed tutorial is organized as follows:

I. Introduction (15 minutes). This section provides a high-level overview of the evolution of common meaning representation, discussing key concepts, unique challenges, and examples of applications.

II. Common Meaning Representations (150 minutes) This section provides an in-depth review of three common meaning representation – PropBank, Abstract Meaning Representation, and Uniform Meaning Representation. It also provides a brief overview of other common meaning representations and a comparison between these meaning representations. Concretely, we will organize this section as follows:

- **PropBank**
  - An intuitive introduction of Propbank-style semantic roles
  - Defining predicate-specific semantic roles in frame files
  - Semantic roles for complicated predicates
  - Relation of propbank-style semantic roles to FrameNet and VerbNet semantic roles
- **Abstract Meaning Representation (AMR)** This section discusses different aspects of AMR, and covers how AMR represents word senses, semantic roles, named entity types, date entity types, and relations.
  - Format and basics
  - Some details and design decisions
  - Multi-sentence AMRs
  - Relation to other formalisms
- **Uniform Meaning Representation (UMR)** This section overviews Uniform Meaning Representations, and discusses how UMR builds on AMR and extends it to cross-lingual settings.
  - Sentence-level representations of UMR: aspect, person, number, and quantification scope
  - Document-level representations: temporal and modal dependencies, coreference
  - Cross-lingual applicability of UMR.
  - UMR-Writer: tool for annotating UMRs
- **Other Related Meaning Representations** This section provides a brief overview of other common meaning representations such as MRS, Tectogammatical Representation used in the Prague Dependency Treebanks (PDT), etc.
  - Discourse Representa1on Structures (annotations in Groening Meaning Bank and Parallel Meaning Bank)
  - Minimal Recursion Semantics
  - Universal Conceptual Cognitive Annotation
  - Prague Semantic Dependencies (Tectogrammatical annotation of syntax and semantics in the PDT-style treebanks)
- **Comparison of Meaning Representations** This section presents a qualitative comparison of the three meaning representations on their commonalities and differences.
  - Alignment to text / compositionality
  - Logical and executable forms
  - Lexicon and ontology differences
  - Task-specific representations
  - Discourse-level representations
- **Building Meaning Representation Datasets** This section discusses the general approaches, challenges, and emerging trend in building data sets for meaning representations.

III. Modeling Meaning Representation (100 minutes) This section discusses computational models for SRL and AMR parsing, from early approaches to current end-to-end SoTA methods.

- Semantic role labeling
- AMR parsing
- AMR generation

IV. Applying Meaning Representation (75 minutes) This section shares applications of the meaning representations for a wide range of tasks from information extraction to question answering. This section also discusses how the differences in these meaning representations impact the choice of which one(s) to use for which downstream tasks.

- Applications of Meaning Representations
- Case Studies

V. Open Questions and Future Directions (15 minutes) The final section concludes the tutorial by raising open research questions about the representation, modeling, and application of meaning representations in NLP and how they could complement LLMs.

4. Diversity considerations

Representing languages of the world. We devote considerable time to discuss the meaning representation for low-resource languages, which tend to have distinct linguistic properties that have previously received little attention. This contributes to greater fairness in the field.

Diversity of the team. This tutorial is to be given by a team of researchers from six different institutions across academia and industry, both junior instructors (including 1 assistant professor, 1 advanced PhD student, and 1 junior industry researcher) and researchers with extensive experience in academic and corporate research settings. The team includes creators, modelers, and users of common meaning representations. The team also has a good gender balance (two female and four male instructors).

5. Reading list

[LAW'2013] Laura Banarescu, Claire Bonial, Shu Cai, Madalina Georgescu, Kira Griffitt, Ulf Hermjakob, Kevin Knight, Philipp Koehn, Martha Palmer, and Nathan Schneider. 2013. Abstract Meaning Representation for sembanking. In Proceedings of the 7th Linguistic Annotation Workshop and Interoperability with Discourse, pages 178–186, Sofia, Bulgaria. Association for Computational Linguistic

[NAACL'2022] Li Zhang, Ishan Jindal, and Yunyao Li. "Label definitions improve semantic role labeling." In Proceedings of the 2022 Conference of the North American Chapter of the Association for Computational Linguistics: Human Language Technologies, pp. 5613-5620. 2022.

[LREC'2022] Ishan Jindal, Alexandre Rademaker, Michał Ulewicz, Ha Linh, Huyen Nguyen, Khoi-Nguyen Tran, Huaiyu Zhu, and Yunyao Li. "Universal proposition bank 2.0." In Proceedings of the Thirteenth Language Resources and Evaluation Conference, pp. 1700-1711. 2022.

[KI'2021] Jens E. L. Van Gysel, Meagan Vigus, Jayeol Chun, Kenneth Lai, Sarah Moeller, Jiarui Yao, Tim O'Gorman, Andrew Cowell, William Croft, Chu-Ren Huang, Jan Hajič, James H. Martin, Stephan Oepen, Martha Palmer, James Pustejovsky, Rosa Vallejos, and Nianwen Xue. "Designing a uniform meaning representation for natural language processing." KI-Künstliche Intelligenz 35, no. 3-4 (2021): 343-360.

[NAACL'2018] Fei Liu, Jeffrey Flanigan, Sam Thomson, Norman Sadeh, and Noah A. Smith. 2015. "Toward Abstractive Summarization Using Semantic Representations." In Proceedings of the 2015 Conference of the North American Chapter of the Association for Computational Linguistics: Human Language Technologies, pages 1077–1086, Denver, Colorado.

[NAACL'2016] Flanigan, Jeffrey, Chris Dyer, Noah A. Smith, and Jaime G. Carbonell. "Generation from abstract meaning representation using tree transducers." In Proceedings of the 2016 conference of the north american chapter of the association for computational linguistics: Human language technologies, pp. 731-739. 2016.

[NAACL'2015] Wang, Chuan, Nianwen Xue, and Sameer Pradhan. "A transition-based algorithm for AMR parsing." In Proceedings of the 2015 Conference of the North American Chapter of the Association for Computational Linguistics: Human Language Technologies, pp. 366-375. 2015.

[ACL'2014] Flanigan, Jeffrey, Sam Thomson, Jaime G. Carbonell, Chris Dyer, and Noah A. Smith. "A discriminative graph-based parser for the abstract meaning representation." In Proceedings of the 52nd Annual Meeting of the Association for Computational Linguistics (Volume 1: Long Papers), pp. 1426-1436. 2014.

6. Presenters

Julia Bonn is an advanced Ph.D. student in Linguistics and Cognitive Science at the University of Colorado, Boulder. During her last 14 years as a Senior Research Assistant at CLEAR, she has been a long-term contributor to PropBank and the PropBank Roleset Lexicon, Verbnet, AMR, and UMR. She is also the developer of SpatialAMR, an extension to AMR annotation for fine-grained, multimodal annotation of spatially rich corpora. Her research interests center on bringing multimodality and pragmatics into cross-lingual meaning representations, and development of lexical resources for these applications with a special focus on how such resources can be designed to better serve polysynthetic languages.

Jan Hajič is the director of the large research infrastructure for Language Resources, Digital Humanities and Arts LINDAT/CLARIAH-CZ, which is part of the EU's CLARIN, DARIAH and EHRI networks. He is also the vice-director of the Institute of Formal and Applied Linguistics at Charles University, Prague, Czech Republic. His interests span the morphology and part-of-speech tagging of inflective languages, machine translation, deep language understanding, and the application of statistical machine learning in NLP. His work experience includes both industrial research (IBM Research Yorktown Heights, NY, USA, in 1991-1993) and academia (Charles University in Prague, Czech Republic and Johns Hopkins University, Baltimore, MD, USA, 1999-2000, adjunct position at University of Colorado, USA, 2017-2025). He has published more than 200 conference and journal papers, a book and book chapters, encyclopedia and handbook entries. He regularly teaches both regular courses as well as tutorials and lectures at various international training schools. He has been the PI or Co-PI of numerous international as well as large national grants and projects (EU and NSF). He is the chair of the Executive Board of META-NET, European research network in language technology, and is a member of several other international boards and committees.

Jeffrey Flanigan is an Assistant Professor in the Department of Computer Science and Engineering at the University of California Santa Cruz. His research includes semantic parsing and generation, question answering, and the use of semantic representations in downstream applications such as summarization and machine translation. Previously he has given a tutorial in AMR at NAACL 2015, and a tutorial on Meaning Representations at EMNLP 2022. He served as a senior area chair for CoNNL in 2022.

Ishan Jindal is a Staff Research Scientist with IBM Research - Almaden. He got his PhD degree in Electrical Engineering from Wayne State University, Michigan. His research interest lies at the intersection of Machine Learning (Deep Learning) and Natural Language Processing (NLP), with a particular focus on multilingual shallow semantic parsing and model analysis for enterprise use cases and their applications in various NLP downstream applications. His work has been published at top-tier conferences, including ICASSP, EMNLP, NAACL, ICDM, ISIT, Big Data, and LREC. He has served as an area chair PC member in many conferences (e.g., ACL, EMNLP, NAACL, EACL, and AAAI) and journals (e.g., TNNLS and TACL).

Yunyao Li is the Director of Machine Learning, Adobe Experience Platform. She was the Head of Machine Learning at the Apple Knowledge Platform and a Distinguished Research Staff Member and Senior Research Manager with IBM Research. She is particularly known for her work in scalable NLP, enterprise search, and database usability. She was an IBM Master Inventor. Her technical contributions have been recognized by prestigious awards on a regular basis, such as IBM Corporate Technical Award (2022), IBM Outstanding Research Achievement Awards (2021, 2020, 2019), ISWC Best Demo Award (2020), and YWCA's Tribute to Women Award (2019), among others. She is a member of inaugural New Voices Program of the American National Academies and represented US young scientists at World Laureates Forum Young Scientists Forum in 2019. Regularly organizes conferences, workshops, and panels at top AI conferences and served on prestigious program committees, editorial board and review panels. She is an ACM Distinguished Member and an elected member of the North American Chapter of the Association for Computational Linguistics (NAACL) Executive Board (2023-2024).

Nianwen Xue is a Professor and chair in the Computer Science Department and the Language & Linguistics Program at Brandeis University. His core research interests include developing linguistic corpora annotated with syntactic, semantic, and discourse structures, as well as machine learning approaches to syntactic, semantic, and discourse parsing. He is an action editor for Computational Linguistics. and currently serves on the editorial boards of Language Resources and Evaluation (LRE). He also served as the editor-in-chief of the ACM Transactions on Asian and Low-Resource Language Information Processing (TALLIP) from 2016 to 2019, and and has frequently served as area chairs for ACL, EMNLP, and COLING. He is the program co-chair of the 2024 Joint International Conference on Computational Linguistics, Language Resources, and Evaluation.

7. Ethics Statement

Infusing meaning representations into NLP models are shown to be effective in injecting knowledge into such models. As such, meaning representations allow deep understanding of languages and identify more nuanced instances of ethics concerns (e.g. biases). Furthermore, meaning representations allow the building of fully interpretable yet effective models. We hope that this tutorial helps the audience develop a deeper appreciation for such topics and equips them with powerful tools to mitigate recent concerns that have arisen with NLP models with regard to explainability and bias.

8. Bibliographical References

Omri Abend and Ari Rappoport. 2013. Universal conceptual cognitive annotation (ucca). In *Proceedings of the 51st Annual Meeting of the As-*

sociation for Computational Linguistics (Volume 1: Long Papers), pages 228–238.

Arvind Agarwal, Laura Chiticariu, Poornima Chozhiyath Raman, Marina Danilevsky, Diman Ghazi, Ankush Gupta, Shanmukha C. Guttula, Yannis Katsis, Rajasekar Krishnamurthy, Yunyao Li, Shubham Mudgal, Vitobha Munigala, Nicholas Phan, Dhaval Sonawane, Sneha Srinivasan, Sudarshan R. Thitte, Mitesh Vasa, Ramiya Venkatachalam, Vinitha Yaski, and Huaiyu Zhu. 2021. Development of an enterprise-grade contract understanding system. In *Proceedings of the 2021 Conference of the North American Chapter of the Association for Computational Linguistics: Human Language Technologies: Industry Papers, NAACL-HLT 2021, Online, June 6-11, 2021*, pages 222–229. Association for Computational Linguistics.

Collin F Baker, Charles J Fillmore, and John B Lowe. 1998. The berkeley framenet project. In *36th Annual Meeting of the Association for Computational Linguistics and 17th International Conference on Computational Linguistics, Volume 1*, pages 86–90.

Laura Banarescu, Claire Bonial, Shu Cai, Madalina Georgescu, Kira Griffitt, Ulf Hermjakob, Kevin Knight, Philipp Koehn, Martha Palmer, and Nathan Schneider. 2013. Abstract Meaning Representation for sembanking. In *Proceedings of the 7th Linguistic Annotation Workshop and Interoperability with Discourse*, pages 178–186, Sofia, Bulgaria. Association for Computational Linguistics.

Jasmijn Bastings, Ivan Titov, W. Aziz, Diego Marcheggiani, and Khalil Sima'an. 2017. Graph convolutional encoders for syntax-aware neural machine translation. In *EMNLP*.

Johan Bos, Valerio Basile, Kilian Evang, Noortje Venhuizen, and Johannes Bjerva. 2017a. The groningen meaning bank. In Nancy Ide and James Pustejovsky, editors, *Handbook of Linguistic Annotation*, volume 2, pages 463–496. Springer.

Johan Bos, Valerio Basile, Kilian Evang, Noortje J Venhuizen, and Johannes Bjerva. 2017b. The groningen meaning bank. In *Handbook of linguistic annotation*, pages 463–496. Springer.

Deng Cai and Wai Lam. 2019. Core semantic first: A top-down approach for amr parsing. *arXiv preprint arXiv:1909.04303*.

Deng Cai and Wai Lam. 2020. Amr parsing via graph-sequence iterative inference. *arXiv preprint arXiv:2004.05572*.

Ann Copestake, Dan Flickinger, Carl Pollard, and Ivan A Sag. 2005. Minimal recursion semantics: An introduction. *Research on language and computation*, 3(2):281–332.

David Dowty. 1991. Thematic proto-roles and argument selection. *language*, 67(3):547–619.

Hao Fei, Fei Li, Bobo Li, and Donghong Ji. 2021a. Encoder-decoder based unified semantic role labeling with label-aware syntax. In *Proc. AAAI Conf. Artif. Intell.*, pages 1479–1488.

Hao Fei, Meishan Zhang, Bobo Li, and Donghong Ji. 2021b. End-to-end semantic role labeling with neural transition-based model. In *Proc. AAAI Conf. Artif. Intell.*, pages 566–575.

Veena G, Deepa Gupta, Akshay Anil, and Akhil M S. 2019. An ontology driven question answering system for legal documents. *2019 2nd International Conference on Intelligent Computing, Instrumentation and Control Technologies (ICICCT)*, 1:947–951.

Sahil Garg, Aram Galstyan, Ulf Hermjakob, and Daniel Marcu. 2016. Extracting biomolecular interactions using semantic parsing of biomedical text. In *Thirtieth AAAI Conference on Artificial Intelligence*.

Shaoru Guo, Yong Guan, Ru Li, Xiaoli Li, and Hongye Tan. 2020. Incorporating syntax and frame semantics in neural network for machine reading comprehension. In *COLING*.

Jens E. L. Van Gysel, Meagan Vigus, Jayeol Chun, Kenneth Lai, Sarah Moeller, Jiarui Yao, Timothy J. O'Gorman, Andrew Cowell, W. Bruce Croft, Chu Ren Huang, Jan Hajic, James H. Martin, Stephan Oepen, Martha Palmer, James Pustejovsky, Rosa Vallejos, and Nianwen Xue. 2021. Designing a uniform meaning representation for natural language processing. *Künstliche Intelligenz*, pages 1–18.

Hans Kamp and Uwe Reyle. 2013. *From discourse to logic: Introduction to modeltheoretic semantics of natural language, formal logic and discourse representation theory*, volume 42. Springer Science & Business Media.

Hoang Thanh Lam, Gabriele Picco, Yufang Hou, Young-Suk Lee, Lam M. Nguyen, Dzung T. Phan, Vanessa López, and Ramón Fernandez Astudillo. 2021. Ensembling graph predictions for AMR parsing. *CoRR*, abs/2110.09131.

Young-Suk Lee, Ramon Fernandez Astudillo, Tahira Naseem, Revanth Gangi Reddy, Radu Florian, and Salim Roukos. 2020. Pushing the limits of amr parsing with self-learning. *arXiv preprint arXiv:2010.10673*.

Kexin Liao, Logan Lebanoff, and Fei Liu. 2018. Abstract meaning representation for multi-document summarization. *arXiv preprint arXiv:1806.05655*.

Ling Liu, Ishan Jindal, and Yunyao Li. 2022. Is semantic-aware bert more linguistically aware? a case study on natural language inference. In *Annual Conference of the North American Chapter of the Association for Computational Linguistics*.

Ana Marasović and Anette Frank. 2018. Srl4orl: Improving opinion role labeling using multi-task learning with semantic role labeling. In *NAACL*.

Arindam Mitra and Chitta Baral. 2016. Addressing a question answering challenge by combining statistical methods with inductive rule learning and reasoning. In *Proceedings of the AAAI Conference on Artificial Intelligence*, volume 30(1).

Long HB Nguyen, Viet H Pham, and Dien Dinh. 2021. Improving neural machine translation with amr semantic graphs. *Mathematical Problems in Engineering*, 2021.

Stephan Oepen, Marco Kuhlmann, Yusuke Miyao, Daniel Zeman, Silvie Cinková, Dan Flickinger, Jan Hajic, and Zdenka Uresova. 2015. Semeval 2015 task 18: Broad-coverage semantic dependency parsing. In *Proceedings of the 9th International Workshop on Semantic Evaluation (SemEval 2015)*, pages 915–926.

Martha Palmer, Daniel Gildea, and Paul Kingsbury. 2005. The proposition bank: An annotated corpus of semantic roles. *Computational linguistics*, 31(1):71–106.

Karin Kipper Schuler. 2005. *VerbNet: A broad-coverage, comprehensive verb lexicon*. University of Pennsylvania.

Peng Shi and Jimmy Lin. 2019. Simple bert models for relation extraction and semantic role labeling. *arXiv preprint arXiv:1904.05255*.

Jacob Solawetz and Stefan Larson. 2021. Lsoie: A large-scale dataset for supervised open information extraction. In *EACL*.

Dongqin Xu, Junhui Li, Muhua Zhu, Min Zhang, and Guodong Zhou. 2020. Improving amr parsing with sequence-to-sequence pre-training. *arXiv preprint arXiv:2010.01771*.

Nianwen Xue and Martha Palmer. 2004. Calibrating features for semantic role labeling. In *EMNLP*, pages 88–94.

Hongming Zhang, Haoyu Wang, and Dan Roth. 2020a. Unsupervised label-aware event trigger and argument classification. *ArXiv*, abs/2012.15243.

Hongming Zhang, Haoyu Wang, and Dan Roth. 2021. Zero-shot label-aware event trigger and argument classification. In *FINDINGS*.

Li Zhang, Ishan Jindal, and Yunyao Li. 2022. Label definitions improve semantic role labeling. In *Proceedings of the 2022 Conference of the North American Chapter of the Association for Computational Linguistics: Human Language Technologies*, pages 5613–5620.

Meishan Zhang, Peilin Liang, and Guohong Fu. 2019. Enhancing opinion role labeling with semantic-aware word representations from semantic role labeling. In *NAACL*.

Zhuosheng Zhang, Yuwei Wu, Zhao Hai, Z. Li, Shuailiang Zhang, Xi Zhou, and Xiang Zhou. 2020b. Semantics-aware bert for language understanding. *ArXiv*, abs/1909.02209.

Jiawei Zhou, Tahira Naseem, Ramón Fernandez Astudillo, and Radu Florian. 2021. Amr parsing with action-pointer transformer. *arXiv preprint arXiv:2104.14674*.

Navigating the Modern Evaluation Landscape: Considerations in Benchmarks and Frameworks for Large Language Models (LLMs)

Leshem Choshen[*†], **Ariel Gera**[†], **Yotam Perlitz**[†],
Michal Shmueli-Scheuer[†], **Gabriel Stanovsky**[◇]
[*]MIT, [†]IBM Research, [◇]The Hebrew University of Jerusalem

Abstract

General-Purpose language models have changed the world of natural language processing, if not the world itself. The evaluation of such versatile models, while supposedly similar to evaluation of generation models before them, in fact presents a host of new evaluation challenges and opportunities. This tutorial welcomes people from diverse backgrounds and assumes little familiarity with metrics, datasets, prompts and benchmarks. It will lay the foundations and explain the basics and their importance, while touching on the major points and breakthroughs of the recent era of evaluation. We will contrast new to old approaches, from evaluating on multi-task benchmarks rather than on dedicated datasets to efficiency constraints, and from testing stability and prompts on in-context learning to using the models themselves as evaluation metrics. Finally, we will present a host of open research questions in the field of robsut, efficient, and reliable evaluation.

Keywords: Language models, Benchmarks, efficient evaluation, language model as metrics,

1. Tutorial Description - Introduction

1.1. Background and Goals

Evaluation benchmarks have been a cornerstone of machine learning progress for years now. However, the introduction of pretrained models has profoundly altered the way benchmarks are used. Instead of focused questions, benchmarks now require assessing a vast and general set of abilities, for which diverse samples are collected (Liang et al., 2022; Gao et al., 2021). This is a first of many changes that are transforming the field of model evaluation, and that entail increasingly complex evaluation endeavours, compared to traditional single-task evaluation efforts.

On the other hand, the new era offers advantages in evaluation, requiring less data for training and better, flexible metrics. Evaluation is no longer done through fine-tuning, i.e. training on a train set for every task to be evaluated, but relies entirely on zero-shot or in-context learning. In that manner, instead of supplying training, the benchmark is a test set only. Another advantage of current models is that they can serve to evaluate other models, following the assumption that error detection is easier than generation. This approach offers a way to test answers in areas where it was hardly possible before.

With all of those changes, also comes great compute. Evaluating on a broad range of datasets, with more models, and with long and complex tasks, all brought growing compute needs, sometimes more costly than the model pretraining (Biderman et al., 2023).

This tutorial aims to introduce the still relevant concepts of evaluation (e.g., evaluation goals or N-gram based reference metrics) and contrast those with the new and changing needs of the general models we employ today. Such needs include leveraging another language model as an evaluator, a language model based metric, taking inference costs into account, evaluating each model on a diverse set of tasks, evaluating on diverse prompts, and more.

A complementary goal of the tutorial is to provide a structured and organized view of LLMs' benchmarking. Such a view is largely missing in the academic literature, where each paper typically addresses a specific problem in isolation, normally in an ad-hoc manner. This view is also missing from the practical solutions presented by the industry, where different decisions are taken without a proper explanation which might cause some vague or incomplete understanding by the community. We present a complete pipeline of LLMs benchmarking, and discuss decisions that need to be considered throughout the pipeline. We will also share our experience and lessons learned from evaluating LLMs. Finally, the tutorial will discuss future challenges of LLMs benchmarking.

1.2. Tutorial type

This is a *cutting-edge* tutorial that aims at bridging the gaps in this emerging field. The need for timely discussions of LLM benchmarking is ever more pressing in light of the rapid advancement in the field that has caused great shifts in benchmarking such as new evaluation paradigms (e.g., ICL), and ever growing benchmarks aiming to validate unprecedented amounts of new abilities. Specifically,

LREC-COLING 2024 Tutorials, pages 19–25
20-25 May, 2024.

this tutorial differs from recent performance benchmarking tutorials (Coleman et al., 2019) that mainly deal with evaluations of training and inference performance for hardware, software, and services as opposed to our focus on quality. Others like (Boyd-Graber et al., 2022) focus on human evaluation and explainability of LLMs or NLG metrics (Khapra and Sai, 2021) which covers a small section of overall benchmarking considerations.

2. Target Audience

While the tutorial will present the current state of the art and cutting-edge research, it should accommodate entry-level audience. The tutorial assumes little to no knowledge about evaluation, merely expecting some understanding of what Language Models are currently capable of and why they are useful. Thus, the tutorial is the best fit for people who have worked on a specific aspect of evaluation, but are less familiar with the big picture, researchers who are new to evaluation, and researchers who are less familiar with new challenges specific to large language models, such as benchmarking across many datasets, evaluating in open-domain tasks and prompting.

3. Outline

Part 1: Introduction (35 min)
Part 1.1: Introduction to Benchmarking

- What are the goals of model evaluation?
- Benchmarking building blocks- task, dataset, and metric

Part 1.2: Introduction to LLM Benchmarking

- Models: what do we evaluate?
- What are the main challenges? or, why it is not trivial?
- Common and important tasks
- Measurements - automatic metrics and human evaluation
- Benchmarking paradigms - fine-tuning, zero shot learner, few shot leaner
- Other important hyperparameters, instructions, prompts matter
- Reviewing general benchmarks
- Reviewing specific downstream tasks
- How do objectives and considerations (what, when, and whom) affect benchmarking decisions?

Part 2: Framework for Benchmarking (10 min)

- What are the requirements from the framework?
- Open source frameworks (e.g., HELM, OpenAI Evals, LM-evaluation-harness)
- Business frameworks

Part 3: Metrics (45 min)

- Classic N-gram based metrics
- Language Model based metrics
- Reference-less Metrics
- Language models as evaluators
- Fine-grained and specialized metrics
- Challenge sets, perturbation and data-based metrics

Part 4: Prompts (45 min)

- The importance of prompts
  - Who writes the prompts? What goals do they serve?
- Overview of evaluation protocol for prompts
  - Typically, a single prompt is used to evaluate across models
- Prompt banks
- Different desiderata for different use-cases
  - LLM developers
  - Developers for targeted downstream applications
  - Developers of open-ended user-facing ap:plciations

Part 5: Efficient Benchmark Design (45 min)

- Benchmarks Objectives
- Benchmarks Compute (survey)
- Benchmark decisions, or, common ways to reduce compute (survey)
- What makes a good benchmark (validity, reliability)
- Best practices for compute reduction in LLM benchmarks

Part 6: Manual Evaluation Efforts (30 min)

- Is human evaluation being abandoned?
- The alignment paradigm
- LLM-Human feedback loops

4. Diversity Considerations

The tutorial promotes a variety of topics related to diversity and fairness including efficient benchmarking to enable fair evaluation for low-resource groups, and reducing energy consumption. In addition, some of the topics are directly related to increasing transparency around model evaluation.

The presenters are diverse in terms of gender, age, background, location and affiliation.

5. Reading List

1. Surveys on evaluation of LLMs (Chang et al., 2023; Ziyu et al., 2023; Gehrmann et al., 2023)
2. Pre-training paradigms (Min et al., 2023)
3. Current benchmarks: HELM (Liang et al., 2022), big-bench (Srivastava et al., 2022), LM-evaluation-harness (Gao et al., 2021)
4. Prompts: creating paraphrases (Lester et al., 2021; Gonen et al., 2022; Honovich et al., 2022), robustness to paraphrases (Gu et al., 2022; Sun et al., 2023; Mizrahi et al., 2024)
5. Metrics: survey (Sai et al., 2022), models as evaluators (Zheng et al., 2023)
6. Efficient-benchmarking: (Perlitz et al., 2023a; Vivek et al., 2023; Liang et al., 2022),
7. Manual Evaluation: survey (Bojic et al., 2023), reproducibility (Belz et al., 2023)

6. Presenters

Leshem Choshen

leshem.choshen@mail.huji.ac.il

Leshem Choshen is a postdoctoral researcher at MIT/IBM, aiming to collaboratively pretrain through model recycling (Don-Yehiya et al., 2022b; Yadav et al., 2023), efficient evaluation (Choshen et al., 2022b; Perlitz et al., 2023a), and manageable pretraining research (e.g., co-organizing the babyLM shared task (Warstadt et al., 2023)). Before leading a small research group at IBM, he received the postdoctoral Rothschild and Fulbright fellowships as well as IAAI and Blavatnik best Ph.D. awards. With broad NLP and ML interests, he also worked on Reinforcement Learning, and Understanding of how neural networks learn (Choshen et al., 2022a; Din et al., 2023), with a specific interest in evaluation (Choshen and Abend, 2019; Choshen et al., 2020), evaluation of evaluation (Choshen and Abend, 2018b,a), reference-less metrics (Choshen and Abend, 2018c; Honovich et al., 2021), quality estimation (Don-Yehiya et al., 2022a) and related topics. In parallel, he participated in Project Debater, creating a machine that could hold a formal debate, ending in a Nature cover and live debate (Slonim et al., 2021).

Ariel Gera

ariel.gera1@ibm.com

Ariel is a research scientist at IBM Research AI, with diverse interests in both NLG and text classification. Ariel is currently pursuing research on utilizing the outputs of different model layers (Gera et al., 2023) and on efficient and reliable evaluation for NLG tasks. Following his research on argumentation (Bilu et al., 2019) as part of Project Debater (Slonim et al., 2021), he has worked on numerous threads related to training models with limited supervision. These include studies of active learning (Ein-Dor et al., 2020; Perlitz et al., 2023c), few-shot (Shnarch et al., 2022a) and zero-shot (Gera et al., 2022), as well as development of the Label Sleuth platform for building text classifiers with a human in the loop (Shnarch et al., 2022b). Ariel has an MSc in Cognitive Science from the Hebrew University, for psychological studies of emotion perception.

Yotam Perlitz

yotam.perlitz@ibm.com

Yotam Perlitz is an AI Research scientist at IBM Research AI, advocating for more transparent and efficient LLM benchmarks (Perlitz et al., 2023a; Bandel et al., 2024), factually correct Data-to-text generation (Perlitz et al., 2023b, 2022) and data-efficient LLM training (Gera et al., 2022; Perlitz et al., 2023c). Previously, Yotam had investigated coarse to fine methods for objects detection (Dana et al., 2021) as well as exotic transmission phenomena through various phases of matter (Perlitz and Michaeli, 2018) as part of his M.Sc at the Weizmann institute of Science.

Michal Shmueli-Scheuer

shmueli@il.ibm.com

Michal is a principal researcher in the Language and Retrieval research group in IBM Research AI. Her area of expertise is in the fields of NLG and NLP including data to text, conversational bots, summarization of scientific documents, and affective computing. Michal is leading the work of LLMs Evaluation in IBM. She has published in leading NLP and AI conferences and journals, including ACL, EMNLP, NAACL, AAAI, and IUI. She regularly reviews for top NLP and AI conferences. She was an organizer of the 1st and 2nd Scientific Document Processing (SDP) workshops at 2020 (EMNLP) and 2021 (COLING), and co-organized shared tasks for Scientific document summarization in those workshops. Michal received her PhD from the University of California, Irvine in 2009.

Gabriel Stanovsky

gabriel.stanovsky@mail.huji.ac.il

Gabriel Stanovsky is a senior lecturer (assistant professor) in the school of computer science and engineering at the Hebrew University of Jerusalem, and a research scientist at the Allen Institute for AI (AI2). He did his postdoctoral research at the University of Washington and AI2 in Seattle, working with Prof. Luke Zettlemoyer and Prof. Noah Smith, and his PhD with Prof. Ido Dagan at Bar-Ilan University. He is interested in developing natural language processing models which deal with real-world texts and help answer multi-disciplinary research questions, in archaeology, law, medicine, and more. His work has received awards at top-tier venues, including ACL, NAACL, and CoNLL, and recognition in popular journals such as Science and New Scientist, and The New York Times.

7. Ethics Statement

During the tutorial, we will emphasize the importance of being aware of and addressing biases in benchmarks and frameworks. We will advocate for transparency in benchmark creation and evaluation methodologies. In addition, we will acknowledge the environmental impact of large-scale models by discussing efficient benchmarking approaches. Finally, we will highlight the importance of community engagement and collaboration for the benefit of diverse perspectives and the benefit of science.

References

Elron Bandel, Yotam Perlitz, Elad Venezian, Roni Friedman-Melamed, Ofir Arviv, Matan Orbach, Shachar Don-Yehyia, Dafna Sheinwald, Ariel Gera, Leshem Choshen, et al. 2024. Unitxt: Flexible, shareable and reusable data preparation and evaluation for generative ai. *arXiv preprint arXiv:2401.14019*.

Anya Belz, Craig Thomson, Ehud Reiter, and Simon Mille. 2023. Non-repeatable experiments and non-reproducible results: The reproducibility crisis in human evaluation in NLP. In *Findings of the Association for Computational Linguistics: ACL 2023*, pages 3676–3687, Toronto, Canada. Association for Computational Linguistics.

Stella Biderman, USVSN Sai Prashanth, Lintang Sutawika, Hailey Schoelkopf, Quentin Anthony, Shivanshu Purohit, and Edward Raf. 2023. Emergent and predictable memorization in large language models. *arXiv preprint arXiv:2304.11158*.

Yonatan Bilu, Ariel Gera, Daniel Hershcovich, Benjamin Sznajder, Dan Lahav, Guy Moshkowich, Anael Malet, Assaf Gavron, and Noam Slonim. 2019. Argument invention from first principles. In *Proceedings of the 57th Annual Meeting of the Association for Computational Linguistics*, pages 1013–1026, Florence, Italy. Association for Computational Linguistics.

Iva Bojic, Jessica Chen, Si Yuan Chang, Qi Chwen Ong, Shafiq Joty, and Josip Car. 2023. Hierarchical evaluation framework: Best practices for human evaluation. In *Proceedings of the 3rd Workshop on Human Evaluation of NLP Systems (HumEval)*.

Jordan Boyd-Graber, Samuel Carton, Shi Feng, Q Vera Liao, Tania Lombrozo, Alison Smith-Renner, and Chenhao Tan. 2022. Human-centered evaluation of explanations. In *Proceedings of the 2022 Conference of the North American Chapter of the Association for Computational Linguistics: Human Language Technologies: Tutorial Abstracts*, pages 26–32.

Yupeng Chang, Xu Wang, Jindong Wang, Yuan Wu, Kaijie Zhu, Hao Chen, Linyi Yang, Xiaoyuan Yi, Cunxiang Wang, Yidong Wang, et al. 2023. A survey on evaluation of large language models. *arXiv preprint arXiv:2307.03109*.

Leshem Choshen and Omri Abend. 2018a. Automatic metric validation for grammatical error correction. In *Proceedings of the 56th Annual Meeting of the Association for Computational Linguistics (Volume 1: Long Papers)*, pages 1372–1382, Melbourne, Australia. Association for Computational Linguistics.

Leshem Choshen and Omri Abend. 2018b. Inherent biases in reference-based evaluation for grammatical error correction. In *Proceedings of the 56th Annual Meeting of the Association for Computational Linguistics (Volume 1: Long Papers)*, pages 632–642, Melbourne, Australia. Association for Computational Linguistics.

Leshem Choshen and Omri Abend. 2018c. Reference-less measure of faithfulness for grammatical error correction. In *Proceedings of the 2018 Conference of the North American Chapter of the Association for Computational Linguistics: Human Language Technologies, Volume 2 (Short Papers)*, pages 124–129, New Orleans, Louisiana. Association for Computational Linguistics.

Leshem Choshen and Omri Abend. 2019. Automatically extracting challenge sets for non-local phenomena in neural machine translation. In

Proceedings of the 23rd Conference on Computational Natural Language Learning (CoNLL), pages 291–303, Hong Kong, China. Association for Computational Linguistics.

Leshem Choshen, Guy Hacohen, Daphna Weinshall, and Omri Abend. 2022a. The grammar-learning trajectories of neural language models. In *Proceedings of the 60th Annual Meeting of the Association for Computational Linguistics (Volume 1: Long Papers)*, pages 8281–8297, Dublin, Ireland. Association for Computational Linguistics.

Leshem Choshen, Dmitry Nikolaev, Yevgeni Berzak, and Omri Abend. 2020. Classifying syntactic errors in learner language. In *Proceedings of the 24th Conference on Computational Natural Language Learning*, pages 97–107, Online. Association for Computational Linguistics.

Leshem Choshen, Elad Venezian, Shachar Don-Yehia, Noam Slonim, and Yoav Katz. 2022b. Where to start? analyzing the potential value of intermediate models. *arXiv preprint arXiv:2211.00107*.

Cody Coleman, Wen mei Hwu, Gennady Pekhimenko Vijay Janapa Reddi, Carole-Jean Wu, and Jinjun Xiong. 2019. mlperf-bench: Benchmarking deep learning systems. Tutorial,IEEE International Symposium on Performance Analysis of Systems and Software.

Alexandra Dana, Maor Shutman, Yotam Perlitz, Ran Vitek, Tomer Peleg, and Roy J Jevnisek. 2021. You better look twice: a new perspective for designing accurate detectors with reduced computations.

Alexander Yom Din, Taelin Karidi, Leshem Choshen, and Mor Geva. 2023. Jump to conclusions: Short-cutting transformers with linear transformations. *ArXiv*, abs/2303.09435.

Shachar Don-Yehiya, Leshem Choshen, and Omri Abend. 2022a. PreQuEL: Quality estimation of machine translation outputs in advance. In *Proceedings of the 2022 Conference on Empirical Methods in Natural Language Processing*, pages 11170–11183, Abu Dhabi, United Arab Emirates. Association for Computational Linguistics.

Shachar Don-Yehiya, Elad Venezian, Colin Raffel, Noam Slonim, Yoav Katz, and Leshem Choshen. 2022b. Cold fusion: Collaborative descent for distributed multitask finetuning. *ArXiv*, abs/2212.01378.

Liat Ein-Dor, Alon Halfon, Ariel Gera, Eyal Shnarch, Lena Dankin, Leshem Choshen, Marina Danilevsky, Ranit Aharonov, Yoav Katz, and Noam Slonim. 2020. Active learning for bert: An empirical study. In *EMNLP*.

Leo Gao, Jonathan Tow, Stella Biderman, Sid Black, Anthony DiPofi, Charles Foster, Laurence Golding, Jeffrey Hsu, Kyle McDonell, Niklas Muennighoff, Jason Phang, Laria Reynolds, Eric Tang, Anish Thite, Ben Wang, Kevin Wang, and Andy Zou. 2021. A framework for few-shot language model evaluation.

Sebastian Gehrmann, Elizabeth Clark, and Thibault Sellam. 2023. Repairing the cracked foundation: A survey of obstacles in evaluation practices for generated text. *Journal of Artificial Intelligence Research*, 77:103–166.

Ariel Gera, Roni Friedman, Ofir Arviv, Chulaka Gunasekara, Benjamin Sznajder, Noam Slonim, and Eyal Shnarch. 2023. The benefits of bad advice: Autocontrastive decoding across model layers. In *Proceedings of the 61st Annual Meeting of the Association for Computational Linguistics (Volume 1: Long Papers)*, pages 10406–10420, Toronto, Canada. Association for Computational Linguistics.

Ariel Gera, Alon Halfon, Eyal Shnarch, Yotam Perlitz, Liat Ein-Dor, and Noam Slonim. 2022. Zero-shot text classification with self-training. In *Proceedings of the 2022 Conference on Empirical Methods in Natural Language Processing*, pages 1107–1119, Abu Dhabi, United Arab Emirates. Association for Computational Linguistics.

Hila Gonen, Srini Iyer, Terra Blevins, Noah A Smith, and Luke Zettlemoyer. 2022. Demystifying prompts in language models via perplexity estimation. *arXiv preprint arXiv:2212.04037*.

Jiasheng Gu, Hanzi Xu, Liangyu Nie, and Wenpeng Yin. 2022. Robustness of learning from task instructions. *arXiv preprint arXiv:2212.03813*.

Or Honovich, Leshem Choshen, Roee Aharoni, Ella Neeman, Idan Szpektor, and Omri Abend. 2021. q^2: Evaluating factual consistency in knowledge-grounded dialogues via question generation and question answering. In *Proceedings of the 2021 Conference on Empirical Methods in Natural Language Processing*, pages 7856–7870, Online and Punta Cana, Dominican Republic. Association for Computational Linguistics.

Or Honovich, Thomas Scialom, Omer Levy, and Timo Schick. 2022. Unnatural instructions: Tuning language models with (almost) no human labor. *arXiv preprint arXiv:2212.09689*.

Mitesh M Khapra and Ananya B Sai. 2021. A tutorial on evaluation metrics used in natural language generation. In *Proceedings of the 2021 Conference of the North American Chapter of the Association for Computational Linguistics: Human Language Technologies: Tutorials*, pages 15–19.

Brian Lester, Rami Al-Rfou, and Noah Constant. 2021. The power of scale for parameter-efficient prompt tuning. *arXiv preprint arXiv:2104.08691*.

Percy Liang, Rishi Bommasani, Tony Lee, Dimitris Tsipras, Dilara Soylu, Michihiro Yasunaga, Yian Zhang, Deepak Narayanan, Yuhuai Wu, Ananya Kumar, et al. 2022. Holistic evaluation of language models. *arXiv preprint arXiv:2211.09110*.

Bonan Min, Hayley Ross, Elior Sulem, Amir Pouran Ben Veyseh, Thien Huu Nguyen, Oscar Sainz, Eneko Agirre, Ilana Heintz, and Dan Roth. 2023. Recent advances in natural language processing via large pre-trained language models: A survey. *ACM Computing Surveys*, 56(2):1–40.

Moran Mizrahi, Guy Kaplan, Dan Malkin, Rotem Dror, Dafna Shahaf, and Gabriel Stanovsky. 2024. State of what art? a call for multi-prompt llm evaluation.

Yotam Perlitz, Elron Bandel, Ariel Gera, Ofir Arviv, Liat Ein-Dor, Eyal Shnarch, Noam Slonim, Michal Shmueli-Scheuer, and Leshem Choshen. 2023a. Efficient benchmarking (of language models). *ArXiv*, abs/2308.11696.

Yotam Perlitz, Liat Ein-Dor, Dafna Sheinwald, Noam Slonim, and Michal Shmueli-Scheuer. 2023b. Diversity enhanced table-to-text generation via type control.

Yotam Perlitz, Ariel Gera, Michal Shmueli-Scheuer, Dafna Sheinwald, Noam Slonim, and Liat Ein-Dor. 2023c. Active learning for natural language generation.

Yotam Perlitz and Karen Michaeli. 2018. Helical liquid in carbon nanotubes wrapped with DNA molecules. *Physical Review B*, 98(19).

Yotam Perlitz, Dafna Sheinwald, Noam Slonim, and Michal Shmueli-Scheuer. 2022. nbiig: A neural bi insights generation system for table reporting.

Ananya B Sai, Akash Kumar Mohankumar, and Mitesh M Khapra. 2022. A survey of evaluation metrics used for nlg systems. *ACM Computing Surveys (CSUR)*, 55(2):1–39.

Eyal Shnarch, Ariel Gera, Alon Halfon, Lena Dankin, Leshem Choshen, Ranit Aharonov, and Noam Slonim. 2022a. Cluster & tune: Boost cold start performance in text classification. In *Proceedings of the 60th Annual Meeting of the Association for Computational Linguistics (Volume 1: Long Papers)*, pages 7639–7653, Dublin, Ireland. Association for Computational Linguistics.

Eyal Shnarch, Alon Halfon, Ariel Gera, Marina Danilevsky, Yannis Katsis, Leshem Choshen, Martin Santillan Cooper, Dina Epelboim, Zheng Zhang, and Dakuo Wang. 2022b. Label sleuth: From unlabeled text to a classifier in a few hours. In *Proceedings of the 2022 Conference on Empirical Methods in Natural Language Processing: System Demonstrations*, pages 159–168, Abu Dhabi, UAE. Association for Computational Linguistics.

Noam Slonim, Yonatan Bilu, Carlos Alzate, Roy Bar-Haim, Ben Bogin, Francesca Bonin, Leshem Choshen, Edo Cohen-Karlik, Lena Dankin, Lilach Edelstein, Liat Ein-Dor, Roni Friedman-Melamed, Assaf Gavron, Ariel Gera, Martin Gleize, Shai Gretz, Dan Gutfreund, Alon Halfon, Daniel Hershcovich, Ron Hoory, Yufang Hou, Shay Hummel, Michal Jacovi, Charles Jochim, Yoav Kantor, Yoav Katz, David Konopnicki, Zvi Kons, Lili Kotlerman, Dalia Krieger, Dan Lahav, Tamar Lavee, Ran Levy, Naftali Liberman, Yosi Mass, Amir Menczel, Shachar Mirkin, Guy Moshkowich, Shila Ofek-Koifman, Matan Orbach, Ella Rabinovich, Ruty Rinott, Slava Shechtman, Dafna Sheinwald, Eyal Shnarch, Ilya Shnayderman, Aya Soffer, Artem Spector, Benjamin Sznajder, Assaf Toledo, Orith Toledo-Ronen, Elad Venezian, and Ranit Aharonov. 2021. An autonomous debating system. *Nature*, 591:379 – 384.

Aarohi Srivastava, Abhinav Rastogi, Abhishek Rao, Abu Awal Md Shoeb, Abubakar Abid, Adam Fisch, Adam R Brown, Adam Santoro, Aditya Gupta, Adrià Garriga-Alonso, et al. 2022. Beyond the imitation game: Quantifying and extrapolating the capabilities of language models. *arXiv preprint arXiv:2206.04615*.

Jiuding Sun, Chantal Shaib, and Byron C Wallace. 2023. Evaluating the zero-shot robustness of instruction-tuned language models. *arXiv preprint arXiv:2306.11270*.

Rajan Vivek, Kawin Ethayarajh, Diyi Yang, and Douwe Kiela. 2023. Anchor points: Benchmarking models with much fewer examples. *ArXiv*, abs/2309.08638.

Alex Warstadt, Leshem Choshen, Aaron Mueller, Ethan Wilcox, Williams Adina, Chengxu Zhuang, Linzen Tal, and Ryan Cotrerell. 2023. Findings of the BabyLM Challenge: Sample-efficient pretraining on developmentally plausible corpora. In

Proceedings of the BabyLM Challenge. Association for Computational Linguistics (ACL).

Prateek Yadav, Derek Tam, Leshem Choshen, Colin Raffel, and Mohit Bansal. 2023. Resolving interference when merging models. *ArXiv*, abs/2306.01708.

Lianmin Zheng, Wei-Lin Chiang, Ying Sheng, Siyuan Zhuang, Zhanghao Wu, Yonghao Zhuang, Zi Lin, Zhuohan Li, Dacheng Li, Eric Xing, et al. 2023. Judging LLM-as-a-judge with mt-bench and chatbot arena. *arXiv preprint arXiv:2306.05685*.

Zhuang Ziyu, Chen Qiguang, Ma Longxuan, Li Mingda, Han Yi, Qian Yushan, Bai Haopeng, Zhang Weinan, and Ting Liu. 2023. Through the lens of core competency: Survey on evaluation of large language models. In *Proceedings of the 22nd Chinese National Conference on Computational Linguistics (Volume 2: Frontier Forum)*, pages 88–109.

Mining, Assessing, and Improving Arguments in NLP and the Social Sciences

Gabriella Lapesa*, Eva Maria Vecchi†, Serena Villata‡, Henning Wachsmuth**

*GESIS Leibniz Institute for the Social Sciences and Heinrich-Heine University Düsseldorf,
†University of Stuttgart, Institute for Natural Language Processing
‡Université Côte d'Azur Inria CNRS I3S
**Leibniz University Hannover, Institute of Artificial Intelligence
*gabriella.lapesa@gesis.org, †eva-maria.vecchi@ims.uni-stuttgart.de,
‡villata@i3S.unice.fr, **h.wachsmuth@ai.uni-hannover.de

Abstract

Computational argumentation is an interdisciplinary research field, connecting Natural Language Processing (NLP) to other disciplines such as the social sciences. The focus of recent research has concentrated on *argument quality assessment*: what makes an argument good or bad? We present a tutorial with a strong interdisciplinary and interactive nature structured along three main coordinates: (1) the notions of argument quality (AQ) across disciplines (how do we recognize good and bad arguments?), with a particular focus on the interface between Argument Mining (AM) and Deliberation Theory; (2) the modeling of subjectivity (who argues to whom; what are their beliefs?); and (3) the generation of improved arguments (what makes an argument better?). The tutorial will also touch upon a series of topics that are particularly relevant for the LREC-COLING audience (the issue of resource quality for the assessment of AQ; the interdisciplinary application of AM and AQ in a text-as-data approach to political science), in line with the developments in NLP (LLMs for AQ assessment), and relevant for the societal applications of AQ assessment (bias and debiasing). We will involve the participants in two annotation studies on the assessment and the improvement of quality. The full materials of this tutorial can be found at `https://sites.google.com/view/argmintutorial-2024/home-page`.

Keywords: argument mining, quality assessment, annotation, data quality

1. Introduction

Computational argumentation is a field encompassing varying tasks on the automated analysis and synthesis of natural language arguments. Until recently, research in Natural Language Processing (NLP) mostly dealt with *Argument Mining* (AM), that is, the identification of argumentative claims that convey a stance towards some controversial issue, along with evidence given as reasons for the claims. AM has been studied for various genres (Mochales and Moens, 2011; Habernal and Gurevych, 2017; Dusmanu et al., 2017a) and argument models (Toulmin, 1958; Walton et al., 2008; Freeman, 2011).

Whether we conceptualize the function of argumentation as "reason giving" or "persuasion" (refer to Lawrence and Reed (2019) for a discussion of this dichotomy) the question of what makes an argument good (or better than another argument) has been at the core of research in argument mining (Wachsmuth et al., 2017; Lauscher et al., 2020; Marro et al., 2022). A first edition of this tutorial has been taught by the same authors of this tutorial at EACL 2023 (Lapesa et al., 2023). In the following, we present the main tutorial coordinates, shared with the previous edition (Section 1.1). This LREC-COLING 2024 edition, beyond the obvious update of the literature, will feature new topics that we devised to fit the conference audience, to account for the fast pace of research in NLP, particularly in the context of large language models, and to broaden the interdisciplinary scope of the tutorial (Section 1.2).

1.1. Tutorial coordinates

In this tutorial, we start from the body of research on AM. Unlike earlier NLP tutorials on argumentation (Budzynska and Reed, 2019; Bar-Haim et al., 2021), however, our focus is a task that recently got into the center of attention: *argument quality assessment*, that is, to rate or to compare how good arguments are with respect to one or more defined quality dimensions.

The NLP Perspective: Assessing Argument Quality Let us start with the concrete example of argument quality annotations in Figure 1, taken from Lauscher et al. (2020). The topic is "freedom of speech", and the stance is "against" (i.e., the government has the right to censorship). Quality is assessed here in four dimensions: *cogency* (is the conclusion adequately supported with acceptable, relevant, and sufficient premises?), *effectiveness* (how persuasive is the argument?), *reasonableness* (is the argument good in the context of the debate in which it is framed?), and *overall quality*.

The example illustrates the challenges which

LREC-COLING 2024 Tutorials, pages 26–32

Title: *Should 'blogging' be a capital crime? Iran is considering it...*
Stance: *A government has the right to censor speech (...)*

Text: *My government doesn't give me freedom of speech, so I have to argue for this side. Freedom of speech is bad because ... um ... then Our Leader's beliefs could be challenged. No one wants that. I mean, if everyone would just say and believe what Our Leader says to, we wouldn't need those firing squads altogether! Everyone wins.*

	Cogency	Effectiveness	Reasonableness	Overall
Annotator 1	4	1	1	2
Annotator 2	4	5	3	4
Annotator 3	2	2	2	2

Figure 1: Argument quality assessment from Lauscher et al. (2020): Example argument, annotated for four dimensions by three annotators, with partial agreement.

we take as coordinates of this tutorial. The first challenge is the identification and definition of appropriate *dimensions* for quality assessment: for example, in this case, the effectiveness label conflates several aspects. The second challenge in quality assessment is *subjectivity*. In our example, the three annotators (linguistics experts) clearly disagree in their assessment. Lauscher et al. (2020) report that a crucial factor of disagreement of Annotators 1 and 2 was their perception of the ironic tone behind the text. Interestingly, for both of them, the text has a medium-high degree of cogency (so it is logically pretty "healthy"). A further challenge would be to improve the quality of this argument: How would we make this argument more effective? Do we need more irony, less irony, or a stronger statement of the stance?

To inform participants about argument quality, the tutorial will systematically review existing research on argument quality based on the literature (Wachsmuth et al., 2017), outlining the subjectiveness of quality dimensions as a key problem. In an interactive annotation session, participants will explore and discuss the assessment of quality on real-life arguments. They will be encouraged to take a critical standpoint to the annotation guidelines, learning in a concrete scenario how difficult it is to establish a trade-off between expressivity of the annotation schema and feasibility of the task.

The Social Science Perspective: Assessing Deliberative Quality To demonstrate the impact of argument quality in practice, the tutorial will bridge research in NLP with the social sciences, looking at deliberative democracy in particular. Deliberative democracy is an approach to democratic processes which does not focus on the output of decision-making, but on the discourse exchange that precedes it (Bächtiger and Parkinson, 2019). Crucially, deliberative theory scholars have been asking the same question as computational argumentation: What makes a contribution to a discussion good? This has led to the development of a *discourse quality index* to assess the quality of a discourse contribution (Steenbergen et al., 2003; Gerber et al., 2016).

Modeling Subjectivity Next, we will deal with subjectivity, modeling the parties involved in debates along with their values and beliefs. The connections of argument quality and deliberative quality highlight the subjective nature of argumentation, one of the three main coordinates of this tutorial. Subjectivity has been the trigger of an "affective turn" in both deliberative theory and computational argumentation. In the former, this has implied a switch from a purely rational perspective on deliberation to one which incorporates emotions, personal narratives, humor (Hoggett and Thompson, 2002; Black, 2020; Esau, 2018; Esau and Friess, 2022). In the latter, the affective turn has brought personal argumentation at center stage, highlighting the role played by human values (Kiesel et al., 2022), moral discourse (Alshomary et al., 2022), and narratives (Falk and Lapesa, 2022). In the tutorial, we aim to encourage participants to reflect on the two-fold role that subjectivity plays in quality assessment: subjective factors in quality assessment (e.g., interpretation of humor, as in the example above), and subjective factors in the production of an argument (e.g., all the "personal argumentation" ingredients listed before).

Improving Arguments The subjectivity topic will lead to another interactive session where the goal is to improve the quality of arguments. Limitations will be discussed as well as first research on quality-related argument generation (Gurcke et al., 2021; Skitalinskaya et al., 2023), before the tutorial concludes with an outlook on future perspectives.

1.2. Further topics

Data Quality What are the requirement for a high-quality resource to model AQ assessment? Is annotator disagreement necessarily a cue to bad quality? What is the role of human baselines in AQ assessment? Which sample should the annotated data be representative of? Which challenges are posed by crowdsourcing as an annotation method? We will wrap up every session with a dedicated slot for reflection on available resources and desiderata.

Bias and Debiasing Tightly related to the notion of data quality is the one of bias in AM datasets (Spliethöver and Wachsmuth, 2020) and debiasing methods for AM (Holtermann et al., 2022)

LLMs and AQ Assessment The fast developments and performance boosts offered by LLMs represent an incredible opportunity. What are the challenges and the potential risks of LLMs for AQ assessment?

Text-as-Data Approaches to political science AM and text-as-data approaches to political science research find a natural overlap in the tasks of claim, stance, evidence detection. Moving a step forward, what is the relation between AQ and widely investigated phenomena in political science, such as electoral success or polarization?

2. Target Audience

The tutorial targets both participants who are new to the field of computational argumentation and those who need a comprehensive overview of techniques and applications. As the tutorial is interdisciplinary by design, it is also of interest to participants from a social sciences background who hope to integrate their knowledge within NLP. Finally, we expect the tutorial to attract attention from people interested in NLP techniques that currently impact the social and political world, in general. Basic knowledge of linguistics and computational linguistics is required.

3. Outline

Part I (60 min.) Mining Arguments

- Overview of computational argumentation
- Argument mining: Humans vs. computers
- Achieved results and open challenges
- Data quality: resources overview & reflection on desiderata

Part II (60 min.) The NLP Perspective: Assessing Argument Quality

- What makes an argument "good"?
- Logical, rhetorical, and dialectical dimensions of argument quality
- Subjectiveness as the key challenge for annotation and modeling
- Discussion of the notions of argument quality: Are they sufficient? Are they all necessary?
- Data quality: resources overview & reflection on desiderata

Part III (60 min.) Interactive Session 1

- Annotation: Assessment of sample arguments
- Consolidation: To what extent participants agree? Where not, and why?
- Discussion: What are alternative strategies to subjective quality annotation?

Part IV (60 min.) The Social Sciences Perspective

- Direct democracy, deliberative theories, and e-deliberation
- Deliberative quality: Features and annotation
- Integration of deliberative features in computational architectures
- Application: Argument quality for social good
- Application: Argument Mining in political science text-as-data research.
- Data quality: resources overview & reflection on desiderata

Part V (60 min.) Modeling Subjectivity

- Authors, audiences, and third parties
- Human values, moral foundations, narratives
- Issues with subjectivity: exploiting annotators' disagreements
- Bias and debiasing
- Data quality: resources overview & reflection on desiderata

Part VI (60 min.) Interactive Session 2

- Annotation: Rewriting of sample arguments
- Consolidation: What was improved and how?
- Discussion: What can be improved, what not?

Part VII (60 min.) Conclusion: open challenges and lessons learned

- Generation Methods to improve argument quality
- Challenges: multilinguality, multimodality
- LLMs for AQ assessment
- Conclusions and next steps for the field

4. Diversity Considerations

We believe that exposing the students to the deliberative perspective of argumentation will be fruitful and enriching, as it might not be known to the typical *CL audience. It is our goal that participants leave our tutorial having learned the value of taking multiple disciplinary perspectives into account, even in a rather technical (logic- and NLP-oriented) subject such as computational argumentation. Besides, our focus on subjectivity and personal argumentation as positive features (and not bugs) brings individuals and their differences at center stage, contributing to inclusivity in the field.

5. Reading List

Survey Papers (Cabrio and Villata, 2018; Lawrence and Reed, 2019; Vecchi et al., 2021; Lauscher et al., 2022; Wang et al., 2023)
Mining Arguments (Habernal and Gurevych, 2017; Daxenberger et al., 2017; Dusmanu et al., 2017b; Schaefer and Stede, 2020)
Assessing Argument Quality (Wachsmuth et al., 2017; Lauscher et al., 2020; Marro et al., 2022; Ziegenbein et al., 2023)
Assessing Deliberative Quality (Steenbergen et al., 2003; Gerber et al., 2016)
Improving Arguments (Hua and Wang, 2018; Gurcke et al., 2021; Syed et al., 2023; Skitalinskaya and Wachsmuth, 2023; Skitalinskaya et al., 2023)
Challenges (Durmus et al., 2019; Toledo-Ronen et al., 2020; Spliethöver and Wachsmuth, 2020)

6. Presenters

Gabriella Lapesa is a team lead for Data Science Methods in the Department for Computational Social Sciences at the Leibniz Institute for Social Sciences (GESIS Köln) and a junior professor of Responsible Data Science and Machine Learning at the Heinrich-Heine University of Düsseldorf. She also leads the research group E-DELIB (*Powering-up E-DELIBeration: towards AI-supported moderation*) at the University of Stuttgart. Her research targets the intersection between NLP and the Social Sciences, with a general focus focus on the development of NLP methods to support social science research and real-world applications (i.e., moderation in deliberative discussions). She co-chaired the 9th Argument Mining workshop (2022) and co-taught a course and a tutorial on interdisciplinary Argument Mining, respectively ESSLLI 2022 (with E.M. Vecchi) and EACL 2023 (with the other authors of this proposal).

Eva Maria Vecchi holds a Ph.D. degree in cognitive and neurosciences. She is a postdoctoral researcher at the Institute for Natural Language Processing at IMS Stuttgart, working on the E-DELIB project. Her focus is on the interdisciplinary effort between NLP techniques for argument mining (AM) and theories in the social sciences with the goal of a more collaborative, productive, and ethical endeavor for e-Deliberation. She has taught courses and tutorials on AM and other topics, e.g., ESSLLI 2022 (with G. Lapesa) and EACL 2023 (with the authors of this proposal). Her current research aims at a better understanding of the role bias has in computational argumentation and e-Deliberation, particularly the impact it has on the models, implementation, and social aspects of computational argumentation.

Serena Villata is a research director in computer science at CNRS, and she pursues her research at the I3S laboratory in Sophia Antipolis (France). Her research area is computational argumentation, with a focus on legal and medical texts, political debates and social network harmful content (abusive language, disinformation). Her work conjugates argument-based reasoning frameworks with natural language arguments extracted from text. She is the author of over 150 scientific publications on the topic. She holds a Chair of the Interdisciplinary Institute for AI 3IA Côte d'Azur on "Artificial Argumentation for Humans". Serena has co-chaired the 7th Workshop on Argument Mining at COLING 2020. She has also given tutorials on Argument Mining at ESSLLI 2017[1] and IJCAI 2016[2].

[1] https://www.irit.fr/esslli2017/courses/39.html

[2] https://ijcai-16.org/index.php/welcome/view/accepted_tutorials/

Henning Wachsmuth is the head of the Natural Language Processing Group at Leibniz University Hannover. He is an internationally leading researcher on computational argumentation with about 70 publications on the topic, many at major NLP and AI venues. Other interests include social bias mitigation, computational reframing, and explainable NLP. Henning has co-chaired the 6th Workshop on Argument Mining at ACL 2019, and has given tutorials on argumentation at ASIRF 2018 (Cole and Achilles, 2019), EuroCSS 2018,[3] KI 2019 (Benzmüller and Stuckenschmidt, 2019), and KI 2020 (Schmid et al., 2020). He is an initiator of the CLEF shared task series Touché on argument retrieval (Bondarenko et al., 2022), and co-chaired SemEval tasks on argument reasoning comprehension (Habernal et al., 2018), propaganda technique detection (Da San Martino et al., 2020), and identifying human values in arguments (Kiesel et al., 2023).

7. Ethics statement

The breadth of computational argumentation research, from previous focus on mining to more recent interest in assessment and improvement, encompasses huge benefit to various fields,e.g., NLP and Computational Social Sciences; however, we acknowledge the responsibility of the research to remain sensitive to the ethical concerns that are both generally shared in these fields as well as unique to automated assessment and improvement of arguments. Privacy concerns arise regarding the mining and analysis of private or sensitive data, such as social media posts, emails, or personal correspondence, without informed consent or when the data is not properly anonymized.

Argument quality assessment may be used in sensitive applications, e.g., argumentative writing support, legal or ethical decision-making processes, or guidance on political opinion formation, in which factual errors, bias concerns, and unfair evaluations are particularly problematic, as they may easily lead to or perpetrate wrong or shifted beliefs. Implementing measures to assess and improve arguments, particularly when incorporating subjectivity and human values, may open the door to the manipulation of arguments, such as strategically crafting arguments to achieve desired outcomes. In the contexts of social sciences, political campaigns, and social media, this is of considerable concern as it can lead to the spread of misinformation and unethical persuasion tactics at both a local and global level.

[3] http://symposium.computationalsocialscience.eu/2018/

8. Bibliographical References

Milad Alshomary, Roxanne El Baff, Timon Gurcke, and Henning Wachsmuth. 2022. The moral debater: A study on the computational generation of morally framed arguments. In *Proceedings of the 60th Annual Meeting of the Association for Computational Linguistics (Volume 1: Long Papers)*, pages 8782–8797, Dublin, Ireland. Association for Computational Linguistics.

Andre Bächtiger and John Parkinson. 2019. *Towards a New Deliberative Quality*. Oxford University Press, Cambridge, MA, USA.

Roy Bar-Haim, Liat Ein-Dor, Matan Orbach, Elad Venezian, and Noam Slonim. 2021. Advances in debating technologies: Building AI that can debate humans. In *Proceedings of the 59th Annual Meeting of the Association for Computational Linguistics and the 11th International Joint Conference on Natural Language Processing: Tutorial Abstracts*, pages 1–5, Online. Association for Computational Linguistics.

Christoph Benzmüller and Heiner Stuckenschmidt, editors. 2019. *KI 2019: Advances in Artificial Intelligence - 42nd German Conference on AI, Kassel, Germany, September 23-26, 2019, Proceedings*, volume 11793 of *Lecture Notes in Computer Science*. Springer.

Laura Black. 2020. Framing democracy and conflict through storytelling in deliberative groups. *Regular Issue*, 9(1).

Alexander Bondarenko, Maik Fröbe, Johannes Kiesel, Shahbaz Syed, Timon Gurcke, Meriem Beloucif, Alexander Panchenko, Chris Biemann, Benno Stein, Henning Wachsmuth, Martin Potthast, and Matthias Hagen. 2022. Overview of touché 2022: ArgumentÂ retrieval. In *Experimental IR Meets Multilinguality, Multimodality, and Interaction*, pages 311–336, Cham. Springer International Publishing.

Katarzyna Budzynska and Chris Reed. 2019. Advances in argument mining. In *Proceedings of the 57th Annual Meeting of the Association for Computational Linguistics: Tutorial Abstracts*, pages 39–42, Florence, Italy. Association for Computational Linguistics.

Elena Cabrio and S. Villata. 2018. Five years of argument mining: a data-driven analysis. In *Proceedings of the Twenty-Seventh International Joint Conference on Artificial Intelligence, IJCAI 2018*, pages 5427–5433.

Amelia W. Cole and Linda Achilles. 2019. Autumn school for information retrieval and foraging 2018. *SIGIR Forum*, 52(2):87?91.

Giovanni Da San Martino, Alberto Barrón-Cedeño, Henning Wachsmuth, Rostislav Petrov, and Preslav Nakov. 2020. SemEval-2020 task 11: Detection of propaganda techniques in news articles. In *14th International Workshop on Semantic Evaluation (SemEval 2020)*, pages 1377–1414, Barcelona (online). Association for Computational Linguistics.

Johannes Daxenberger, Steffen Eger, Ivan Habernal, Christian Stab, and Iryna Gurevych. 2017. What is the essence of a claim? cross-domain claim identification. In *Proceedings of the 2017 Conference on Empirical Methods in Natural Language Processing*, pages 2055–2066, Copenhagen, Denmark. Association for Computational Linguistics.

Esin Durmus, Faisal Ladhak, and Claire Cardie. 2019. The role of pragmatic and discourse context in determining argument impact. In *Proceedings of the 2019 Conference on Empirical Methods in Natural Language Processing and the 9th International Joint Conference on Natural Language Processing (EMNLP-IJCNLP)*, pages 5668–5678, Hong Kong, China. Association for Computational Linguistics.

Mihai Dusmanu, Elena Cabrio, and Serena Villata. 2017a. Argument mining on Twitter: Arguments, facts and sources. In *Proceedings of the 2017 Conference on Empirical Methods in Natural Language Processing*, pages 2317–2322, Copenhagen, Denmark. Association for Computational Linguistics.

Mihai Dusmanu, Elena Cabrio, and Serena Villata. 2017b. Argument mining on twitter: Arguments, facts and sources. In *Proceedings of the 2017 Conference on Empirical Methods in Natural Language Processing*, pages 2317–2322.

Katharina Esau. 2018. Capturing citizens' values: On the role of narratives and emotions in digital participation. *Analyse & Kritik*, 40(1):55–72.

Katharina Esau and Daniel Friess. 2022. What creates listening online? exploring reciprocity in online political discussions with relational content analysis. *Journal of Deliberative Democracy*, 18(1):1–16.

Neele Falk and Gabriella Lapesa. 2022. Reports of personal experiences and stories in argumentation: datasets and analysis. In *Proceedings of the 60th Annual Meeting of the Association for Computational Linguistics (Volume 1: Long*

Papers), pages 5530–5553, Dublin, Ireland. Association for Computational Linguistics.

James B. Freeman. 2011. *Argument Structure: Representation and Theory*. Springer.

Marlené Gerber, André Bächtiger, Susumu Shikano, Simon Reber, and Samuel Rohr. 2016. Deliberative abilities and influence in a transnational deliberative poll (europolis). *British Journal of Political Science*, 48(4):1093–1118.

Timon Gurcke, Milad Alshomary, and Henning Wachsmuth. 2021. Assessing the sufficiency of arguments through conclusion generation. In *Proceedings of the 8th Workshop on Argument Mining*, pages 67–77, Punta Cana, Dominican Republic. Association for Computational Linguistics.

Ivan Habernal and Iryna Gurevych. 2017. Argumentation mining in user-generated web discourse. *Computational Linguistics*, 43(1).

Ivan Habernal, Henning Wachsmuth, Iryna Gurevych, and Benno Stein. 2018. SemEval 2018 Task 12: The Argument Reasoning Comprehension Task. In *12th International Workshop on Semantic Evaluation (SemEval 2018)*. Association for Computational Linguistics.

Paul Hoggett and Simon Thompson. 2002. Toward a democracy of the emotions. *Constellations*, 9(1):106–126.

Carolin Holtermann, Anne Lauscher, and Simone Ponzetto. 2022. Fair and argumentative language modeling for computational argumentation. In *Proceedings of the 60th Annual Meeting of the Association for Computational Linguistics (Volume 1: Long Papers)*, pages 7841–7861, Dublin, Ireland. Association for Computational Linguistics.

Xinyu Hua and Lu Wang. 2018. Neural argument generation augmented with externally retrieved evidence. In *Proceedings of the 56th Annual Meeting of the Association for Computational Linguistics (Volume 1: Long Papers)*, pages 219–230, Melbourne, Australia. Association for Computational Linguistics.

Johannes Kiesel, Milad Alshomary, Nicolas Handke, Xiaoni Cai, Henning Wachsmuth, and Benno Stein. 2022. Identifying the human values behind arguments. In *Proceedings of the 60th Annual Meeting of the Association for Computational Linguistics (Volume 1: Long Papers)*, pages 4459–4471, Dublin, Ireland. Association for Computational Linguistics.

Johannes Kiesel, Milad Alshomary, Nailia Mirzakhmedova, Maximilian Heinrich, Nicolas Handke, Henning Wachsmuth, and Benno Stein. 2023. SemEval-2023 task 4: ValueEval: Identification of human values behind arguments. In *Proceedings of the 17th International Workshop on Semantic Evaluation (SemEval-2023)*, pages 2287–2303, Toronto, Canada. Association for Computational Linguistics.

Gabriella Lapesa, Eva Maria Vecchi, Serena Villata, and Henning Wachsmuth. 2023. Mining, assessing, and improving arguments in NLP and the social sciences. In *Proceedings of the 17th Conference of the European Chapter of the Association for Computational Linguistics: Tutorial Abstracts*, pages 1–6, Dubrovnik, Croatia. Association for Computational Linguistics.

Anne Lauscher, Lily Ng, Courtney Napoles, and Joel Tetreault. 2020. Rhetoric, logic, and dialectic: Advancing theory-based argument quality assessment in natural language processing. In *Proceedings of the 28th International Conference on Computational Linguistics*, pages 4563–4574, Barcelona, Spain (Online). International Committee on Computational Linguistics.

Anne Lauscher, Henning Wachsmuth, Iryna Gurevych, and Goran Glavaš. 2022. Scientia Potentia Est—On the Role of Knowledge in Computational Argumentation. *Transactions of the Association for Computational Linguistics*, 10:1392–1422.

John Lawrence and Chris Reed. 2019. Argument mining: A survey. *Computational Linguistics*, 45(4):765–818.

Santiago Marro, Elena Cabrio, and Serena Villata. 2022. Graph embeddings for argumentation quality assessment. In *Findings of EMNLP*.

Raquel Mochales and Marie-Francine Moens. 2011. Argumentation mining. *Artificial Intelligence and Law*, 19(1):1–22.

Robin Schaefer and Manfred Stede. 2020. Annotation and detection of arguments in tweets. In *Proceedings of the 7th Workshop on Argument Mining*, pages 53–58, Online. Association for Computational Linguistics.

Ute Schmid, Franziska Klügl, , and Diedrich Wolter, editors. 2020. *KI 2020: Advances in Artificial Intelligence: 43rd German Conference on AI, Bamberg, Germany, September 21–25, 2020, Proceedings*. Springer-Verlag, Berlin, Heidelberg.

Gabriella Skitalinskaya, Maximilian Spliethöver, and Henning Wachsmuth. 2023. Claim optimization in computational argumentation. In *Pro-*

ceedings of the 16th International Natural Language Generation Conference, pages 134–152, Prague, Czechia. Association for Computational Linguistics.

Gabriella Skitalinskaya and Henning Wachsmuth. 2023. To revise or not to revise: Learning to detect improvable claims for argumentative writing support. In *Proceedings of the 61st Annual Meeting of the Association for Computational Linguistics (Volume 1: Long Papers)*, pages 15799–15816, Toronto, Canada. Association for Computational Linguistics.

Maximilian Spliethöver and Henning Wachsmuth. 2020. Argument from old man's view: Assessing social bias in argumentation. In *Proceedings of the 7th Workshop on Argument Mining*, pages 76–87, Online. Association for Computational Linguistics.

Marco R. Steenbergen, Andre Baechtiger, Markus Spörndli, and Jürg Steiner. 2003. Measuring political deliberation: A discourse quality index. *Comparative European Politics*, 1:21–48.

Shahbaz Syed, Timon Ziegenbein, Philipp Heinisch, Henning Wachsmuth, and Martin Potthast. 2023. Frame-oriented summarization of argumentative discussions. In *Proceedings of the 24th Meeting of the Special Interest Group on Discourse and Dialogue*, pages 114–129, Prague, Czechia. Association for Computational Linguistics.

Orith Toledo-Ronen, Matan Orbach, Yonatan Bilu, Artem Spector, and Noam Slonim. 2020. Multilingual argument mining: Datasets and analysis. In *Findings of the Association for Computational Linguistics: EMNLP 2020*, pages 303–317, Online. Association for Computational Linguistics.

Stephen E. Toulmin. 1958. *The Uses of Argument*. Cambridge University Press.

Eva Maria Vecchi, Neele Falk, Iman Jundi, and Gabriella Lapesa. 2021. Towards argument mining for social good: A survey. In *Proceedings of the 59th Annual Meeting of the Association for Computational Linguistics and the 11th International Joint Conference on Natural Language Processing (Volume 1: Long Papers)*, pages 1338–1352.

Henning Wachsmuth, Nona Naderi, Yufang Hou, Yonatan Bilu, Vinodkumar Prabhakaran, Tim Alberdingk Thijm, Graeme Hirst, and Benno Stein. 2017. Computational argumentation quality assessment in natural language. In *Proceedings of the 15th Conference of the European Chapter of the Association for Computational Linguistics: Volume 1, Long Papers*, pages 176–187, Valencia, Spain. Association for Computational Linguistics.

Douglas Walton, Christopher Reed, and Fabrizio Macagno. 2008. *Argumentation Schemes*. Cambridge University Press.

Xiaoou Wang, Elena Cabrio, and Serena Villata. 2023. Argument and counter-argument generation: A critical survey. In *Natural Language Processing and Information Systems*, pages 500–510, Cham. Springer Nature Switzerland.

Timon Ziegenbein, Shahbaz Syed, Felix Lange, Martin Potthast, and Henning Wachsmuth. 2023. Modeling appropriate language in argumentation. In *Proceedings of the 61st Annual Meeting of the Association for Computational Linguistics (Volume 1: Long Papers)*, pages 4344–4363, Toronto, Canada. Association for Computational Linguistics.

Knowledge Editing for Large Language Models

Ningyu Zhang, Yunzhi Yao, Shumin Deng
Zhejiang University, National University of Singapore
zhangningyu@zju.edu.cn, yyztodd@zju.edu.cn, shumin@nus.edu.sg

Abstract

Even with their remarkable capabilities, Large Language Models (LLMs) like ChatGPT are not without challenges, particularly in maintaining factual accuracy and logical consistency. A primary concern is the ability to efficiently update these LLMs to rectify inaccuracies without undergoing comprehensive retraining or continuous training processes, which can be resource-intensive and time-consuming. The ability to edit LLMs presents a promising solution, allowing for modifications in specific areas of interest while preserving the model's overall performance across various tasks. This tutorial is designed to familiarize NLP researchers with the latest advancements and emerging techniques in editing LLMs. Our goal is to offer a thorough and up-to-date review of state-of-the-art methodologies, complemented by practical tools, and to highlight new avenues for research within the community. All referenced resources are available at `https://github.com/zjunlp/KnowledgeEditingPapers`.

Keywords: Knowledge Editing, Large Language Model

1. Introduction

Large Language Models (LLMs) have demonstrated impressive potential in generating text that closely resembles human writing, as evidenced by numerous studies. However, despite their advanced capabilities, models such as ChatGPT can sometimes struggle to maintain factual accuracy or logical coherence. There's also the risk of them generating content that could be considered harmful or offensive, compounded by their inability to recognize events occurring after their last training update. Addressing these issues without resorting to comprehensive retraining or ongoing training processes—both of which require substantial resources and time—presents a significant challenge. In response, the concept of **knowledge editing for LLMs** has emerged as a promising solution. This approach offers an efficient means to adjust the model's behavior in targeted areas without detrimentally affecting its performance across other tasks.

In this tutorial, our goal is to familiarize researchers with the latest advancements and emerging strategies in the realm of knowledge editing for LLMs. We aim to provide a systematic and comprehensive overview of state-of-the-art methods, enriched with practical tools, and to explore new avenues of research for our audience. The session will begin with an introduction to the tasks associated with knowledge editing for LLMs, alongside relevant evaluation metrics and benchmark datasets. We will then progress to discussing a range of knowledge editing methodologies, with a particular emphasis on those that maintain the original parameters of LLMs. These methods typically adjust the model's responses in specific instances by integrating an auxiliary network that works in tandem with the unmodified core model. The discussion will shift towards techniques that directly modify the parameters of LLMs, targeting the adjustment of model parameters linked to undesirable outputs. Throughout the tutorial, we aim to share insights from various research communities involved in knowledge editing, introduce open-source tools such as EasyEdit[1], and delve into both the challenges and opportunities presented by knowledge editing for LLMs. This session seeks to provide valuable knowledge to the community, underlining potential issues and uncovering prospects in the field of knowledge editing. The detailed schedule and content structure of the tutorial are outlined in the referenced schedule Table 1.

Our tutorial is grounded in the exploration of principles that guide the encapsulation of knowledge within pre-trained language models, drawing upon a range of pivotal studies such as those by Geva et al. (2021); Haviv et al. (2023); Hao et al. (2021); Hernandez et al. (2023b); Yao et al. (2023a); Cao et al. (2023b). These works provide foundational insights into how language models store and process information. The practice of knowledge editing, which includes the manipulation of a model's external knowledge, shares commonalities with knowledge augmentation techniques. This is because updating a model's stored knowledge essentially involves infusing it with new, relevant information. Additionally, we view knowledge editing as a nuanced form of lifelong learning (Biesialska et al., 2020) and unlearning (Wu et al., 2022; Tarun et al., 2021), where models are designed to dynamically incorporate and adjust new knowledge, while also shedding outdated or incorrect data. This approach is crucial for enhancing the model's relevance and accuracy over time. Moreover, by enabling models to discard harmful or toxic

[1] `https://github.com/zjunlp/EasyEdit`

LREC-COLING 2024 Tutorials, pages 33–41
20-25 May, 2024.

information, knowledge editing presents a viable strategy for addressing the security and privacy challenges that accompany the use of Large Language Models (Geva et al., 2022). In our tutorial, we will explore these dimensions in depth, offering insights into how knowledge editing contributes to the ongoing evolution of language models. We will also suggest possible future directions for research in this area. Attendees will find all related materials and slides available at https://github.com/zjunlp/KnowledgeEditingPapers, ensuring they have access to a comprehensive set of resources to further their understanding and application of knowledge editing techniques.

2. Target Audience

This tutorial is designed to appeal to a broad spectrum of participants, including academics like researchers and students, as well as industry professionals engaged in the fields of Natural Language Processing (NLP) and Artificial Intelligence (AI). It is structured to be accessible and informative for anyone with a basic understanding of NLP and AI principles. Furthermore, participants with a foundational knowledge of neural networks will find the content particularly advantageous. For those already familiar with LLMs and techniques for parameter-efficient tuning, this tutorial will significantly enrich their learning experience, providing deeper insights and practical applications in these areas.

3. Outline

The tutorial mainly consists of the following parts, as shown in Table 1.

1. **Introduction** (15 minutes)
   - Background
   - Why knowledge editing for LLMs?
2. **Preliminaries** (15 minutes)
   - Pre-trained language models
   - Definition of knowledge editing for LLMs
   - Metrics and benchmark datasets
3. **Knowledge Editing for LLMs**
   - Knowledge editing methods of preserving LLMs' parameters (40 minutes)

   Coffee Break (30 minutes)

   - Knowledge editing methods of modifying LLMs' Parameters (40 minutes)
4. **Extensions** (40 minutes)
   - Knowledge editing for multilingual, multimodal LLMs
   - Knowledge fairness, bias and security issues
5. **Open-sourced Tools** (30 minutes)
6. **Discussion on Main Issues & Opportunities** (30 minutes)

4. Suggested Duration

Half day (4 hours, including 30-minute break)

5. History

The presenters have organized the following tutorials:

- AACL 2023[2]: Editing Large Language Models (3-hour tutorial)
- IJCAI 2023[3]: Open-Environment Knowledge Graph Construction and Reasoning: Challenges, Approaches, and Opportunities (3-hour tutorial)
- AACL 2022[4]: Efficient and Robust Knowledge Graph Construction (3-hour tutorial)
- The 18th Reasoning Web Summer School[5]: Cross-Modal Knowledge Discovery, Inference, and Challenges (3-hour tutorial)

6. Diversity Considerations

The presenting team comprises individuals from two academic institutions, featuring a diverse mix of roles such as professors, a research fellow, and a Ph.D. candidate. Among the four speakers, one is a woman, highlighting the team's commitment to inclusivity and diversity in academic representation.

7. Estimated Number of Participants

LLMs are increasingly being applied across a wide array of tasks. Given the need for frequent post-training adjustments to correct errors and mitigate

[2]Resources will be available at https://github.com/zjunlp/KnowledgeEditingPapers.

[3]https://openkg-tutorial.github.io/.

[4]https://github.com/NLP-Tutorials/AACL-IJCNLP2022-KGC-Tutorial.

[5]https://2022.declarativeai.net/events/reasoning-web/rw-lectures.

Presentation Topic	Presenter	Time
Introduction	Ningyu Zhang	15min
Preliminaries	Ningyu Zhang	15min
Methods for Preserve LLMs' Parameters	Yunzhi Yao	40min
Coffee break	-	30min
Methods for Modify LLMs' Parameters	Yunzhi Yao	40min
Extensions	Shumin Deng	40min
Open-sourced Tools	Yunzhi Yao	30min
Discussion on Main Issues & Opportunities	Ningyu Zhang	30min

Table 1: Tutorial Schedule

undesirable behaviors in many of these applications, there is a rising interest in methods for efficient and immediate model modifications. Consequently, we expect this tutorial to attract an audience of more than 100 attendees, reflecting the growing focus on adaptable and flexible approaches to enhancing LLM performance.

8. Ethical Considerations

Knowledge editing involves techniques designed to modify the behavior of pre-trained models. It's crucial, however, to acknowledge the potential risks: if misapplied, knowledge editing could cause models to produce harmful or inappropriate content. Thus, prioritizing safe and responsible practices in the application of knowledge editing is imperative. Ethical guidelines should steer the use of these techniques, accompanied by robust safeguards to deter misuse and prevent the generation of damaging outcomes.

9. Reading list

- "A Comprehensive Study of Knowledge Editing for Large Language Models", (Zhang et al., 2024)
- "Editing Large Language Models: Problems, Methods, and Opportunities", (Yao et al., 2023b)
- "Detoxifying Large Language Models via Knowledge Editing", (Wang et al., 2024a)
- "Editing Conceptual Knowledge for Large Language Models", (Wang et al., 2024b)
- "Evaluating the Ripple Effects of Knowledge Editing in Language Models", (Cohen et al., 2023a)
- "Can We Edit Multimodal Large Language Models?", (Cheng et al., 2023a)
- "Unveiling the Pitfalls of Knowledge Editing for Large Language Models", (Li et al., 2023)
- "Editing Personality for LLMs", (Mao et al., 2023)
- "Editing Language Model-based Knowledge Graph Embeddings", (Cheng et al., 2023b)
- "Memory-Based Model Editing at Scale", (Mitchell et al., 2022c)
- "Calibrating Factual Knowledge in Pretrained Language Models", (Dong et al., 2022)
- "Transformer-Patcher: One Mistake worth One Neuron", (Huang et al., 2023)
- "Can We Edit Factual Knowledge by In-Context Learning?", (Zheng et al., 2023)
- "Editing Factual Knowledge in Language Models", (Cao et al., 2021)
- "Fast Model Editing at Scale", (Mitchell et al., 2022a)
- "Knowledge Neurons in Pretrained Transformers", (Dai et al., 2022a)
- "Locating and Editing Factual Associations in GPT", (Meng et al., 2022a)
- "Mass-Editing Memory in a Transformer", (Meng et al., 2023)
- "MQUAKE: Assessing Knowledge Editing in-Language Models via Multi-Hop Questions", (Zhong et al., 2023)
- "Can LMs Learn New Entities from Descriptions? Challenges in Propagating Injected Knowledge", (Gupta et al., 2023)
- "Detecting Edit Failures In Large Language Models: An Improved Specificity Benchmark", (Hoelscher-Obermaier et al., 2023)
- "Editing Commonsense Knowledge in GPT", (Gupta et al., 2023)

10. Presenters

Ningyu Zhang is an associate professor/doctoral supervisor at Zhejiang University, leading the group about KG and NLP technologies. He has supervised to construct a information extraction toolkit named DeepKE[6] (2.8K+ stars on Github). His research interest include knowledge graph and natural language processing. He has published many papers in top international academic conferences and journals such as Natural Machine Intelligence, Nature Communications, NeurIPS, ICLR, AAAI, IJCAI, WWW, KDD, SIGIR, ACL, ENNLP, NAACL, and IEEE/ACM Transactions on Audio Speech and Language. He has served as Area Chair for ACL/EMNLP 2023, ARR Action Editor, Senior Program Committee member for IJCAI 2023, Program Committee member for EMNLP, NAACL, NeurIPS, ICLR, ICML, WWW, SIGIR, KDD, AAAI, and reviewer for TKDE, TKDD.

Email: zhangningyu@zju.edu.cn

Homepage: `https://person.zju.edu.cn/en/ningyu`

Yunzhi Yao is a Ph.D candidate at at School of Computer Science and Technology, Zhejiang University. His research interests focus on Editing Large Language Models and Knowledge-enhanced Natural Language Processing. He has been research intern at Microsoft Research Asia supervised by Shaohan Huang, and research intern at Alibaba Group. He has published many papers in ACL, EMNLP, NAACL, SIGIR. For tutorial experience, he has given talks at AI-TIME to deliver his recent works. Moreover, he is the first author of the paper "**Editing Large Language Models: Problems, Methods, and Opportunities**" and one of the developers of the knowledge editing framework EasyEdit, which is related to this tutorial.

Email: yyztodd@zju.edu.cn

Homepage: `https://scholar.google.ch/citations?user=nAagIwEAAAAJ`

Shumin Deng is a research fellow at Department of Computer Science, School of Computing (SoC), National University of Singapore. She have obtained her Ph.D. degree at School of Computer Science and Technology, Zhejiang University. Her research interests focus on Natural Language Processing, Knowledge Graph, Information Extraction, Neuro-Symbolic Reasoning and LLM Reasoning. She has been awarded 2022 Outstanding Graduate of Zhejiang Province, China; 2020 Outstanding Intern in Academic Cooperation of Alibaba Group. She is a member of ACL, and a member of the Youth Working Committee of the Chinese Information Processing Society of China. She has serves as a Research Session (Information Extraction) Chair for EMNLP 2022, and a Publication Chair for CoNLL 2023. She has been a Journal Reviewer for many high-quality journals, such as TPAMI, TASLP, TALLIP, WWWJ, ESWA, KBS and so on; and serves as a Program Committee member for NeurIPS, ICLR, ACL, EMNLP, EACL, AACL, WWW, AAAI, IJCAI, CIKM and so on. She has constructed a billion-scale Open Business Knowledge Graph (OpenBG), and released a leaderboard[7] which has attracted thousands of teams and researchers.

Email: shumin@nus.edu.sg

Homepage: `https://231sm.github.io/`

11. Bibliographical References

Ahmed Alajrami and Nikolaos Aletras. 2022. How does the pre-training objective affect what large language models learn about linguistic properties? In *Proceedings of the 60th Annual Meeting of the Association for Computational Linguistics (Volume 2: Short Papers), ACL 2022, Dublin, Ireland, May 22-27, 2022*, pages 131–147. Association for Computational Linguistics.

Badr AlKhamissi, Millicent Li, Asli Celikyilmaz, Mona T. Diab, and Marjan Ghazvininejad. 2022. A review on language models as knowledge bases. *CoRR*, abs/2204.06031.

Rohan Anil, Andrew M Dai, Orhan Firat, Melvin Johnson, Dmitry Lepikhin, Alexandre Passos, Siamak Shakeri, Emanuel Taropa, Paige Bailey, Zhifeng Chen, et al. 2023. Palm 2 technical report. *arXiv preprint arXiv:2305.10403*.

Iz Beltagy, Arman Cohan, Robert L. Logan IV, Sewon Min, and Sameer Singh. 2022. Zero- and few-shot NLP with pretrained language models. In *Proceedings of the 60th Annual Meeting of the Association for Computational Linguistics, ACL 2022 - Tutorial Abstracts, Dublin, Ireland, May 22-27, 2022*, pages 32–37. Association for Computational Linguistics.

Emily M. Bender, Timnit Gebru, Angelina McMillan-Major, and Shmargaret Shmitchell. 2021. On the dangers of stochastic parrots: Can language models be too big? *Proceedings of the 2021 ACM Conference on Fairness, Accountability, and Transparency*.

Magdalena Biesialska, Katarzyna Biesialska, and Marta R. Costa-jussà. 2020. Continual lifelong learning in natural language processing: A survey. In *COLING*, pages 6523–6541. International Committee on Computational Linguistics.

[6] `https://github.com/zjunlp/DeepKE.`

[7] `https://tianchi.aliyun.com/dataset/dataDetail?dataId=122271&lang=en-us.`

Tom B. Brown, Benjamin Mann, Nick Ryder, Melanie Subbiah, Jared Kaplan, Prafulla Dhariwal, Arvind Neelakantan, Pranav Shyam, Girish Sastry, Amanda Askell, Sandhini Agarwal, Ariel Herbert-Voss, Gretchen Krueger, Tom Henighan, Rewon Child, Aditya Ramesh, Daniel M. Ziegler, Jeffrey Wu, Clemens Winter, Christopher Hesse, Mark Chen, Eric Sigler, Mateusz Litwin, Scott Gray, Benjamin Chess, Jack Clark, Christopher Berner, Sam McCandlish, Alec Radford, Ilya Sutskever, and Dario Amodei. 2020. Language models are few-shot learners. In *NeurIPS*.

Boxi Cao, Hongyu Lin, Xianpei Han, and Le Sun. 2023a. The life cycle of knowledge in big language models: A survey. *CoRR*, abs/2303.07616.

Boxi Cao, Qiaoyu Tang, Hongyu Lin, Xianpei Han, Jiawei Chen, Tianshu Wang, and Le Sun. 2023b. Retentive or forgetful? diving into the knowledge memorizing mechanism of language models. *arXiv preprint arXiv:2305.09144*.

Nicola De Cao, Wilker Aziz, and Ivan Titov. 2021. Editing factual knowledge in language models. In *Proceedings of the 2021 Conference on Empirical Methods in Natural Language Processing, EMNLP 2021, Virtual Event / Punta Cana, Dominican Republic, 7-11 November, 2021*, pages 6491–6506. Association for Computational Linguistics.

Nicholas Carlini, Florian Tramèr, Eric Wallace, Matthew Jagielski, Ariel Herbert-Voss, Katherine Lee, Adam Roberts, Tom B. Brown, Dawn Xiaodong Song, Úlfar Erlingsson, Alina Oprea, and Colin Raffel. 2020. Extracting training data from large language models. In *USENIX Security Symposium*.

Xiang Chen, Ningyu Zhang, Xin Xie, Shumin Deng, Yunzhi Yao, Chuanqi Tan, Fei Huang, Luo Si, and Huajun Chen. 2022. Knowprompt: Knowledge-aware prompt-tuning with synergistic optimization for relation extraction. In *WWW '22: The ACM Web Conference 2022, Virtual Event, Lyon, France, April 25 - 29, 2022*, pages 2778–2788. ACM.

Yuheng Chen, Pengfei Cao, Yubo Chen, Kang Liu, and Jun Zhao. 2023. Journey to the center of the knowledge neurons: Discoveries of language-independent knowledge neurons and degenerate knowledge neurons.

Siyuan Cheng, Bozhong Tian, Qingbin Liu, Xi Chen, Yongheng Wang, Huajun Chen, and Ningyu Zhang. 2023a. Can we edit multimodal large language models? *arXiv preprint arXiv:2310.08475*.

Siyuan Cheng, Ningyu Zhang, Bozhong Tian, Zelin Dai, Feiyu Xiong, Wei Guo, and Huajun Chen. 2023b. Editing language model-based knowledge graph embeddings. *CoRR*, abs/2301.10405.

Roi Cohen, Eden Biran, Ori Yoran, Amir Globerson, and Mor Geva. 2023a. Evaluating the ripple effects of knowledge editing in language models. *CoRR*, abs/2307.12976.

Roi Cohen, Eden Biran, Ori Yoran, Amir Globerson, and Mor Geva. 2023b. Evaluating the ripple effects of knowledge editing in language models. *arXiv preprint arXiv:2307.12976*.

Roi Cohen, Eden Biran, Ori Yoran, Amir Globerson, and Mor Geva. 2023c. Evaluating the ripple effects of knowledge editing in language models. *ArXiv*, abs/2307.12976.

Damai Dai, Li Dong, Yaru Hao, Zhifang Sui, Baobao Chang, and Furu Wei. 2022a. Knowledge neurons in pretrained transformers. In *Proceedings of the 60th Annual Meeting of the Association for Computational Linguistics (Volume 1: Long Papers), ACL 2022, Dublin, Ireland, May 22-27, 2022*, pages 8493–8502. Association for Computational Linguistics.

Damai Dai, Yutao Sun, Li Dong, Yaru Hao, Zhifang Sui, and Furu Wei. 2022b. Why can GPT learn in-context? language models secretly perform gradient descent as meta-optimizers. *CoRR*, abs/2212.10559.

Joe Davison, Joshua Feldman, and Alexander M. Rush. 2019. Commonsense knowledge mining from pretrained models. In *Proceedings of the 2019 Conference on Empirical Methods in Natural Language Processing and the 9th International Joint Conference on Natural Language Processing, EMNLP-IJCNLP 2019, Hong Kong, China, November 3-7, 2019*, pages 1173–1178. Association for Computational Linguistics.

Shumin Deng, Chengming Wang, Zhoubo Li, Ningyu Zhang, Zelin Dai, Hehong Chen, Feiyu Xiong, Ming Yan, Qiang Chen, Mosha Chen, Jiaoyan Chen, Jeff Z. Pan, Bryan Hooi, and Huajun Chen. 2023. Construction and applications of billion-scale pre-trained multimodal business knowledge graph. In *ICDE*. IEEE.

Bhuwan Dhingra, Jeremy R. Cole, Julian Martin Eisenschlos, Daniel Gillick, Jacob Eisenstein, and William W. Cohen. 2022. Time-aware language models as temporal knowledge bases. *Trans. Assoc. Comput. Linguistics*, 10:257–273.

Qingxiu Dong, Damai Dai, Yifan Song, Jingjing Xu, Zhifang Sui, and Lei Li. 2022. Calibrating factual knowledge in pretrained language models. In *Findings of the Association for Computational Linguistics: EMNLP 2022, Abu Dhabi, United Arab Emirates, December 7-11, 2022*, pages 5937–5947. Association for Computational Linguistics.

Mor Geva, Avi Caciularu, Kevin Ro Wang, and Yoav Goldberg. 2022. Transformer feed-forward layers build predictions by promoting concepts in the vocabulary space. In *Proceedings of the 2022 Conference on Empirical Methods in Natural Language Processing, EMNLP 2022, Abu Dhabi, United Arab Emirates, December 7-11, 2022*, pages 30–45. Association for Computational Linguistics.

Mor Geva, Roei Schuster, Jonathan Berant, and Omer Levy. 2021. Transformer feed-forward layers are key-value memories. In *Proceedings of the 2021 Conference on Empirical Methods in Natural Language Processing, EMNLP 2021, Virtual Event / Punta Cana, Dominican Republic, 7-11 November, 2021*, pages 5484–5495. Association for Computational Linguistics.

Anshita Gupta, Debanjan Mondal, Akshay Krishna Sheshadri, Wenlong Zhao, Xiang Lorraine Li, Sarah Wiegreffe, and Niket Tandon. 2023. Editing commonsense knowledge in GPT. *CoRR*, abs/2305.14956.

Y. Hao, Li Dong, Furu Wei, and Ke Xu. 2021. Self-attention attribution: Interpreting information interactions inside transformer. In *Proc. of AAAI*.

Peter Hase, Mohit Bansal, Been Kim, and Asma Ghandeharioun. 2023. Does localization inform editing? surprising differences in causality-based localization vs. knowledge editing in language models. *ArXiv*, abs/2301.04213.

Adi Haviv, Ido Cohen, Jacob Gidron, Roei Schuster, Yoav Goldberg, and Mor Geva. 2023. Understanding transformer memorization recall through idioms. In *Proceedings of the 17th Conference of the European Chapter of the Association for Computational Linguistics*, pages 248–264, Dubrovnik, Croatia. Association for Computational Linguistics.

Evan Hernandez, Belinda Z. Li, and Jacob Andreas. 2023a. Inspecting and editing knowledge representations in language models.

Evan Hernandez, Belinda Z. Li, and Jacob Andreas. 2023b. Measuring and manipulating knowledge representations in language models. *CoRR*, abs/2304.00740.

Jason Hoelscher-Obermaier, Julia Persson, Esben Kran, Ioannis Konstas, and Fazl Barez. 2023. Detecting edit failures in large language models: An improved specificity benchmark. *CoRR*, abs/2305.17553.

Ari Holtzman, Peter West, and Luke Zettlemoyer. 2023a. Generative models as a complex systems science: How can we make sense of large language model behavior? *CoRR*, abs/2308.00189.

Ari Holtzman, Peter West, and Luke Zettlemoyer. 2023b. Generative models as a complex systems science: How can we make sense of large language model behavior? *ArXiv*, abs/2308.00189.

Zeyu Huang, Yikang Shen, Xiaofeng Zhang, Jie Zhou, Wenge Rong, and Zhang Xiong. 2023. Transformer-patcher: One mistake worth one neuron. In *The Eleventh International Conference on Learning Representations*.

Jacques Thibodeau. 2022. But is it really in rome? an investigation of the rome model editing technique.

Zhengbao Jiang, Frank F. Xu, Jun Araki, and Graham Neubig. 2020. How can we know what language models know. *Trans. Assoc. Comput. Linguistics*, 8:423–438.

Nikhil Kandpal, H. Deng, Adam Roberts, Eric Wallace, and Colin Raffel. 2022. Large language models struggle to learn long-tail knowledge. In *International Conference on Machine Learning*.

Nikhil Kandpal, Haikang Deng, Adam Roberts, Eric Wallace, and Colin Raffel. 2023. Large language models struggle to learn long-tail knowledge. In *International Conference on Machine Learning, ICML 2023, 23-29 July 2023, Honolulu, Hawaii, USA*, volume 202 of *Proceedings of Machine Learning Research*, pages 15696–15707. PMLR.

Diederik P Kingma and Jimmy Ba. 2014. Adam: A method for stochastic optimization. *arXiv preprint arXiv:1412.6980*.

Patrick Lewis, Ethan Perez, Aleksandra Piktus, Fabio Petroni, Vladimir Karpukhin, Naman Goyal, Heinrich Küttler, Mike Lewis, Wen-tau Yih, Tim Rocktäschel, et al. 2020. Retrieval-augmented generation for knowledge-intensive nlp tasks. *Advances in Neural Information Processing Systems*, 33:9459–9474.

Zhoubo Li, Ningyu Zhang, Yunzhi Yao, Mengru Wang, Xi Chen, and Huajun Chen. 2023. Unveiling the pitfalls of knowledge editing for large language models. *CoRR*, abs/2310.02129.

Yuxi Ma, Chi Zhang, and Song-Chun Zhu. 2023. Brain in a vat: On missing pieces towards artificial general intelligence in large language models. *CoRR*, abs/2307.03762.

Shengyu Mao, Ningyu Zhang, Xiaohan Wang, Mengru Wang, Yunzhi Yao, Yong Jiang, Pengjun Xie, Fei Huang, and Huajun Chen. 2023. Editing personality for llms. *CoRR*, abs/2310.02168.

Kevin Meng, David Bau, Alex Andonian, and Yonatan Belinkov. 2022a. Locating and editing factual associations in GPT. *Advances in Neural Information Processing Systems*, 36.

Kevin Meng, Arnab Sen Sharma, Alex J Andonian, Yonatan Belinkov, and David Bau. 2023. Mass-editing memory in a transformer. In *The Eleventh International Conference on Learning Representations*.

Zaiqiao Meng, Fangyu Liu, Ehsan Shareghi, Yixuan Su, Charlotte Collins, and Nigel Collier. 2022b. Rewire-then-probe: A contrastive recipe for probing biomedical knowledge of pre-trained language models. In *Proceedings of the 60th Annual Meeting of the Association for Computational Linguistics (Volume 1: Long Papers), ACL 2022, Dublin, Ireland, May 22-27, 2022*, pages 4798–4810. Association for Computational Linguistics.

Jack Merullo, Carsten Eickhoff, and Elizabeth-Jane Pavlick. 2023a. Language models implement simple word2vec-style vector arithmetic. *ArXiv*, abs/2305.16130.

Jack Merullo, Carsten Eickhoff, and Ellie Pavlick. 2023b. Language models implement simple word2vec-style vector arithmetic. *CoRR*, abs/2305.16130.

Eric Mitchell, Charles Lin, Antoine Bosselut, Chelsea Finn, and Christopher D. Manning. 2022a. Fast model editing at scale. In *The Tenth International Conference on Learning Representations, ICLR 2022, Virtual Event, April 25-29, 2022*. OpenReview.net.

Eric Mitchell, Charles Lin, Antoine Bosselut, Chelsea Finn, and Christopher D Manning. 2022b. Fast model editing at scale. In *International Conference on Learning Representations*.

Eric Mitchell, Charles Lin, Antoine Bosselut, Christopher D. Manning, and Chelsea Finn. 2022c. Memory-based model editing at scale. In *International Conference on Machine Learning*.

Shikhar Murty, Christopher D. Manning, Scott M. Lundberg, and Marco Túlio Ribeiro. 2022. Fixing model bugs with natural language patches. In *Proceedings of the 2022 Conference on Empirical Methods in Natural Language Processing, EMNLP 2022, Abu Dhabi, United Arab Emirates, December 7-11, 2022*, pages 11600–11613. Association for Computational Linguistics.

Yasumasa Onoe, Michael J. Q. Zhang, Shankar Padmanabhan, Greg Durrett, and Eunsol Choi. 2023. Can lms learn new entities from descriptions? challenges in propagating injected knowledge. *CoRR*, abs/2305.01651.

OpenAI. 2023. GPT-4 technical report. *CoRR*, abs/2303.08774.

Long Ouyang, Jeffrey Wu, Xu Jiang, Diogo Almeida, Carroll L. Wainwright, Pamela Mishkin, Chong Zhang, Sandhini Agarwal, Katarina Slama, Alex Ray, John Schulman, Jacob Hilton, Fraser Kelton, Luke Miller, Maddie Simens, Amanda Askell, Peter Welinder, Paul F. Christiano, Jan Leike, and Ryan Lowe. 2022. Training language models to follow instructions with human feedback. In *NeurIPS*.

Jane Pan, Tianyu Gao, Howard Chen, and Danqi Chen. 2023. What in-context learning" learns" in-context: Disentangling task recognition and task learning. *arXiv preprint arXiv:2305.09731*.

Shuofei Qiao, Yixin Ou, Ningyu Zhang, Xiang Chen, Yunzhi Yao, Shumin Deng, Chuanqi Tan, Fei Huang, and Huajun Chen. 2023. Reasoning with language model prompting: A survey. In *Proceedings of the 61st Annual Meeting of the Association for Computational Linguistics (Volume 1: Long Papers), ACL 2023, Toronto, Canada, July 9-14, 2023*, pages 5368–5393. Association for Computational Linguistics.

Colin Raffel, Noam Shazeer, Adam Roberts, Katherine Lee, Sharan Narang, Michael Matena, Yanqi Zhou, Wei Li, and Peter J. Liu. 2020a. Exploring the limits of transfer learning with a unified text-to-text transformer. *Journal of Machine Learning Research*, 21(140):1–67.

Colin Raffel, Noam Shazeer, Adam Roberts, Katherine Lee, Sharan Narang, Michael Matena, Yanqi Zhou, Wei Li, and Peter J. Liu. 2020b. Exploring the limits of transfer learning with a unified text-to-text transformer. *J. Mach. Learn. Res.*, 21:140:1–140:67.

Victor Sanh, Lysandre Debut, Julien Chaumond, and Thomas Wolf. 2019. Distilbert, a distilled version of BERT: smaller, faster, cheaper and lighter. *CoRR*, abs/1910.01108.

Xinyue Shen, Zeyuan Chen, Michael Backes, and Yang Zhang. 2023. In chatgpt we trust? measuring and characterizing the reliability of chatgpt.

Anton Sinitsin, Vsevolod Plokhotnyuk, Dmitry Pyrkin, Sergei Popov, and Artem Babenko. 2020. Editable neural networks. In *International Conference on Learning Representations*.

Hao Sun, Zhexin Zhang, Jiawen Deng, Jiale Cheng, and Minlie Huang. 2023. Safety assessment of chinese large language models. *CoRR*, abs/2304.10436.

Alon Talmor, Yanai Elazar, Yoav Goldberg, and Jonathan Berant. 2020. olmpics - on what language model pre-training captures. *Trans. Assoc. Comput. Linguistics*, 8:743–758.

Ayush K Tarun, Vikram S Chundawat, Murari Mandal, and Mohan S. Kankanhalli. 2021. Fast yet effective machine unlearning. *IEEE transactions on neural networks and learning systems*, PP.

Bozhong Tian, Siyuan Cheng, Xiaozhuan Liang, Ningyu Zhang, Yi Hu, Kouying Xue, Yanjie Gou, Xi Chen, and Huajun Chen. 2024. Instructedit: Instruction-based knowledge editing for large language models. *arXiv preprint arXiv:2402.16123*.

Kushal Tirumala, Aram H. Markosyan, Luke Zettlemoyer, and Armen Aghajanyan. 2022. Memorization without overfitting: Analyzing the training dynamics of large language models. In *NeurIPS*.

Hugo Touvron, Thibaut Lavril, Gautier Izacard, Xavier Martinet, Marie-Anne Lachaux, Timothée Lacroix, Baptiste Rozière, Naman Goyal, Eric Hambro, Faisal Azhar, Aurélien Rodriguez, Armand Joulin, Edouard Grave, and Guillaume Lample. 2023. Llama: Open and efficient foundation language models. *CoRR*, abs/2302.13971.

Ben Wang and Aran Komatsuzaki. 2021a. GPT-J-6B: A 6 Billion Parameter Autoregressive Language Model. `https://github.com/kingoflolz/mesh-transformer-jax`.

Ben Wang and Aran Komatsuzaki. 2021b. Gpt-j-6b: A 6 billion parameter autoregressive language model.

Mengru Wang, Ningyu Zhang, Ziwen Xu, Zekun Xi, Shumin Deng, Yunzhi Yao, Qishen Zhang, Linyi Yang, Jindong Wang, and Huajun Chen. 2024a. Detoxifying large language models via knowledge editing. *arXiv preprint arXiv:2403.14472*.

Peng Wang, Ningyu Zhang, Xin Xie, Yunzhi Yao, Bozhong Tian, Mengru Wang, Zekun Xi, Siyuan Cheng, Kangwei Liu, Guozhou Zheng, and Huajun Chen. 2023. Easyedit: An easy-to-use knowledge editing framework for large language models. *CoRR*, abs/2308.07269.

Xiaohan Wang, Shengyu Mao, Ningyu Zhang, Shumin Deng, Yunzhi Yao, Yue Shen, Lei Liang, Jinjie Gu, and Huajun Chen. 2024b. Editing conceptual knowledge for large language models. *arXiv preprint arXiv:2403.06259*.

Xiaozhi Wang, Kaiyue Wen, Zhengyan Zhang, Lei Hou, Zhiyuan Liu, and Juanzi Li. 2022. Finding skill neurons in pre-trained transformer-based language models. In *Proceedings of the 2022 Conference on Empirical Methods in Natural Language Processing, EMNLP 2022, Abu Dhabi, United Arab Emirates, December 7-11, 2022*, pages 11132–11152. Association for Computational Linguistics.

Peter West, Chandra Bhagavatula, Jack Hessel, Jena D. Hwang, Liwei Jiang, Ronan Le Bras, Ximing Lu, Sean Welleck, and Yejin Choi. 2022. Symbolic knowledge distillation: from general language models to commonsense models. In *Proceedings of the 2022 Conference of the North American Chapter of the Association for Computational Linguistics: Human Language Technologies, NAACL 2022, Seattle, WA, United States, July 10-15, 2022*, pages 4602–4625. Association for Computational Linguistics.

Ga Wu, Masoud Hashemi, and Christopher Srinivasa. 2022. Puma: Performance unchanged model augmentation for training data removal. In *AAAI Conference on Artificial Intelligence*.

Weiqi Wu, Chengyue Jiang, Yong Jiang, Pengjun Xie, and Kewei Tu. 2023. Do plms know and understand ontological knowledge? In *Proceedings of the 61st Annual Meeting of the Association for Computational Linguistics (Volume 1: Long Papers), ACL 2023, Toronto, Canada, July 9-14, 2023*, pages 3080–3101. Association for Computational Linguistics.

Yang Xu, Yutai Hou, and Wanxiang Che. 2022. Language anisotropic cross-lingual model editing. *ArXiv*, abs/2205.12677.

Yang Xu, Yutai Hou, Wanxiang Che, and Min Zhang. 2023. Language anisotropic cross-lingual model editing. In *Findings of the Association for Computational Linguistics: ACL 2023, Toronto, Canada, July 9-14, 2023*, pages 5554–5569. Association for Computational Linguistics.

Yunzhi Yao, Shaohan Huang, Ningyu Zhang, Li Dong, Furu Wei, and Huajun Chen. 2022. Kformer: Knowledge injection in transformer feed-forward layers. In *Natural Language Processing and Chinese Computing*.

Yunzhi Yao, Peng Wang, Shengyu Mao, Chuanqi Tan, Fei Huang, Huajun Chen, and Ningyu Zhang. 2023a. Knowledge rumination for pre-trained language models. *CoRR*, abs/2305.08732.

Yunzhi Yao, Peng Wang, Bozhong Tian, Siyuan Cheng, Zhoubo Li, Shumin Deng, Huajun Chen, and Ningyu Zhang. 2023b. Editing large language models: Problems, methods, and opportunities. *CoRR*, abs/2305.13172.

Chenyu Zhang, Benjamin Van Durme, Zhuowan Li, and Elias Stengel-Eskin. 2022a. Visual commonsense in pretrained unimodal and multimodal models. In *Proceedings of the 2022 Conference of the North American Chapter of the Association for Computational Linguistics: Human Language Technologies, NAACL 2022, Seattle, WA, United States, July 10-15, 2022*, pages 5321–5335. Association for Computational Linguistics.

Ningyu Zhang, Yunzhi Yao, Bozhong Tian, Peng Wang, Shumin Deng, Mengru Wang, Zekun Xi, Shengyu Mao, Jintian Zhang, Yuansheng Ni, Siyuan Cheng, Ziwen Xu, Xin Xu, Jia-Chen Gu, Yong Jiang, Pengjun Xie, Fei Huang, Lei Liang, Zhiqiang Zhang, Xiaowei Zhu, Jun Zhou, and Huajun Chen. 2024. A comprehensive study of knowledge editing for large language models. *CoRR*, abs/2401.01286.

Ningyu Zhang, Jintian Zhang, Xiaohan Wang, Honghao Gui, Kangwei Liu, Yinuo Jiang, Xiang Chen, Shengyu Mao, Shuofei Qiao, Yuqi Zhu, Zhen Bi, Jing Chen, Xiaozhuan Liang, Yixin Ou, Runnan Fang, Zekun Xi, Xin Xu, Lei Li, Peng Wang, Mengru Wang, Yunzhi Yao, Bozhong Tian, Yin Fang, Guozhou Zheng, and Huajun Chen. 2023. Knowlm: An open-sourced knowledgeable large langugae model framework.

Xikun Zhang, Antoine Bosselut, Michihiro Yasunaga, Hongyu Ren, Percy Liang, Christopher D Manning, and Jure Leskovec. 2022b. GreaseLM: Graph REASoning enhanced language models. In *International Conference on Learning Representations*.

Zhengyan Zhang, Xu Han, Zhiyuan Liu, Xin Jiang, Maosong Sun, and Qun Liu. 2019. ERNIE: enhanced language representation with informative entities. In *Proceedings of the 57th Conference of the Association for Computational Linguistics, ACL 2019, Florence, Italy, July 28- August 2, 2019, Volume 1: Long Papers*, pages 1441–1451. Association for Computational Linguistics.

Wayne Xin Zhao, Kun Zhou, Junyi Li, Tianyi Tang, Xiaolei Wang, Yupeng Hou, Yingqian Min, Beichen Zhang, Junjie Zhang, Zican Dong, Yifan Du, Chen Yang, Yushuo Chen, Zhipeng Chen, Jinhao Jiang, Ruiyang Ren, Yifan Li, Xinyu Tang, Zikang Liu, Peiyu Liu, Jian-Yun Nie, and Ji-Rong Wen. 2023. A survey of large language models. *CoRR*, abs/2303.18223.

Ce Zheng, Lei Li, Qingxiu Dong, Yixuan Fan, Zhiyong Wu, Jingjing Xu, and Baobao Chang. 2023. Can we edit factual knowledge by in-context learning? *ArXiv*.

Zexuan Zhong, Zhengxuan Wu, Christopher D. Manning, Christopher Potts, and Danqi Chen. 2023. Mquake: Assessing knowledge editing in language models via multi-hop questions. *CoRR*, abs/2305.14795.

Xuhui Zhou, Yue Zhang, Leyang Cui, and Dandan Huang. 2020. Evaluating commonsense in pre-trained language models. In *The Thirty-Fourth AAAI Conference on Artificial Intelligence, AAAI 2020, The Thirty-Second Innovative Applications of Artificial Intelligence Conference, IAAI 2020, The Tenth AAAI Symposium on Educational Advances in Artificial Intelligence, EAAI 2020, New York, NY, USA, February 7-12, 2020*, pages 9733–9740. AAAI Press.

Chen Zhu, Ankit Singh Rawat, Manzil Zaheer, Srinadh Bhojanapalli, Daliang Li, Felix X. Yu, and Sanjiv Kumar. 2020. Modifying memories in transformer models. *ArXiv*, abs/2012.00363.

The DBpedia Databus Tutorial: Increase the Visibility and Usability of Your Data

Milan Dojchinovski
DBpedia Association
Leipzig, Germany
Czech Technical University in Prague
Prague, Czech Republic
dojcinovski.milan@gmail.com

Abstract

This tutorial introduces DBpedia Databus (`https://databus.dbpedia.org`), a FAIR data publishing platform, to address challenges faced by data producers and consumers. It covers data organization, publishing, and consumption on the DBpedia Databus, with an exclusive focus on Linguistic Knowledge Graphs. The tutorial offers practical insights for knowledge graph stakeholders, aiding data integration and accessibility in the Linked Open Data community. Designed for a diverse audience, it fosters hands-on learning to familiarize participants with the DBpedia Databus technology.

Keywords: DBpedia, DBpedia Databus, Knowledge Graphs, LOD

1. Introduction

DBpedia (`https://www.dbpedia.org`) is a crowd-sourced community effort which has been initiated in 2007 with the ultimate goal to extract structured knowledge from various Wikimedia projects. This structured information resembles an open knowledge graph, the DBpedia Knowledge Graph, which is publicly available for use for everyone on the Web. Along DBpedia, large number of other knowledge graphs have been published following the Linked Data principles as part of the Linked Open Data cloud initiative. Up until now, the LOD cloud (`https://lod-cloud.net/`) consists of over 1,314 knowledge graphs which are publicly available under an open license. Despite of this increase, several issues have arisen. First, users find difficulties in finding relevant data due to a lack of effective search mechanisms. Second, due to the uncontrolled way of publishing the metadata, the publishers introduce various diverse metadata schema which is not aligned and very often not in line with the best practices. And third, the process for integration of new knowledge graphs and the link sets in the LOD cloud is poorly governed and outdated. All these issues have a significant negative impact on the LOD cloud ecosystem where the knowledge consumers have to invest huge amounts of effort when consuming data, while knowledge graph providers struggle with the data publishing mechanisms.

In this tutorial, we address the above-mentioned problems using the DBpedia Databus technology (`https://databus.dbpedia.org`), a FAIR data publishing platform. In the tutorial, first, the participants will gain basic information on the DBpedia Knowledge Graph and the DBpedia community. Then, a main focus of the tutorial will be put on the DBpedia's Databus publishing platform. In practical examples we will illustrate the potential and the benefit of using DBpedia Databus. The participants will learn:

- what is the **DBpedia Databus**,
- how the **data is organized** on the DBpedia Databus,
- how to benefit from the **Databus collections** concept,
- how to **publish data** on the DBpedia Databus,
- how to **consume data** from the DBpedia Databus,
- how to **create knowledge graphs** using the Databus and
- how to deploy a **local instance** the DBpedia Databus platform.

The tutorial will be organized as a highly interactive event. The presenters together with the participants will work together and learn how publish data on the Databus, how to organize the data on the databus and how to then consume the published data.

The domain focus of the tutorial are *Lingustic Knowledge Graphs*. The tutorial will exclusively address Linguistic Knowledge Graphs and the participants will be invited to publish linguistic datasets on the Databus.

Few weeks before the execution of the tutorial, the organizers will provide instructions to the potential participants with guides and tips which will help them benefit the most from the tutorial. In particular,

LREC-COLING 2024 Tutorials, pages 42–44
20-25 May, 2024.

the organizers will invite participants to 'bring' their data as hosted on some public server (e.g. Zenodo) and on-site, during the event the participants will learn how to publish and register their data on the Databus.

2. Target Audience

The tutorial primarily targets knowledge graph publishers and knowledge graph consumers. We welcome stakeholders who work with open data (e.g. in the context of the LOD cloud) as well as those that maintain proprietary (commercial) knowledge graphs and would like to learn how to use the Databus technology in private settings.

In addition, the tutorial also targets existing and potential new users of DBpedia, developers that wish to learn how to replicate DBpedia Databus platform, providers interested in exploiting the DBpedia KG, data providers interested in integrating data assets with the DBpedia KG and data scientists (e.g. linguists). The tutorial is also dedicated for people from the public and private sector who are interested in implementing knowledge graph technologies, and in particular, DBpedia.

We expect about 50 on-site participants and similar number for online participants with background in linguistics, knowledge graphs, linked data and semantic web in general, knowledge engineering and knowledge extraction.

3. Outline

We will organize the DBpedia Databus tutorial with a 20% lecture-style sessions and 80% hand-on exercises. The tutorial is planned as 4h long event.

- **Intro:** Meet and greet, introduction to the tutorial (5 min)
- **Session 1:** Overview of the DBpedia technology, by Milan Dojchinovski (10 min)
- **Session 2:** The DBpedia Databus in a Nutshell, by Jan Forberg (25 min)
- **Session 3:** Your data on the Databus, by Kirill Yankov (70 min)
- **coffee break** (30 min)
- **Session 4:** Oragnizing and consuming data from the Databus, by Kirill Yankov (60 min)
- **Session 5:** Deploying own DBpedia Databus, by Jan Forberg (30 min)
- **Outro:** Q&A and wrap-up (10 min)

Note: we are flexible with the schedule and will adjust and adapt it dynamically based on the participants requirements and interests.

4. Diversity Considerations

The DBpedia Databus tutorial addresses the diversity aspects as described below.

Improved Diversity and Increased Fairness DBpedia Databus plays a crucial role in advancing diversity and fairness within the field of language technologies. By providing an extensive and openly accessible repository of knowledge, it can empower researchers to conduct more inclusive and equitable analyses. Researchers can draw from the diverse set of datasets hosted on DBpedia Databus, ensuring a more comprehensive representation of global knowledge diversity. Moreover, DBpedia Databus promotes fairness by offering a standardized and transparent approach to data handling, mitigating biases in data selection and representation. The tutorial will delve into best practices for promoting fairness in knowledge graphs research, highlighting the ethical considerations and safeguards for working with diverse datasets, ultimately contributing to the development of more equitable methodologies within the field.

Underrepresented Groups of Participants DBpedia Databus holds particular relevance for underrepresented groups of potential participants in language technologies. For instance, linguists and researchers focusing on underrepresented languages and language communities will find immense value in our tutorial. DBpedia Databus can support research on languages and dialects that have been historically marginalized, offering a platform to amplify their linguistic nuances and significance. The platform's geographic inclusivity also means that it provides an opportunity to study languages from regions that have been underrepresented in the computational linguistics community. This tutorial will provide insights and practical guidance on utilizing DBpedia Databus for these specific contexts, ensuring that the linguistic diversity and richness of underrepresented groups are recognized and studied.

Presenters from Underrepresented Groups One of the tutorial presenters have diverse and underrepresented background, further enriching the learning experience. Milan Dojchinovski brings expertise in linguistic research within underrepresented Macedonian language community.

5. Reading List

Following resources can help the participants to better understand the contents of the tutorial and its background.

- *The New DBpedia Release Cycle: Increasing Agility and Efficiency in Knowledge Extraction Workflows* (Hofer et al., 2020) Hofer et al. SEMANTICS, 2020.

- *DBpedia – A Large-scale, Multilingual Knowledge Base Extracted from Wikipedia* (Lehmann et al., 2015) Lehmann et. al. 2015.
- *DBpedia - A crystallization point for the Web of Data* (Bizer et al., 2009) Bizer et al. Journal of Web Semantics, 2009.
- (Sep 13, 2023) *DBpedia tutorial co-located with the Language, Data and Knowledge conference 2023 (LDK)*[1].
- (May 2, 2022) *DBpedia tutorial co-located with the Knowledge Graph Conference (KGC) 2022*[2].
- (Apr 25, 2022) *DBpedia Tutorial at The Web Conference (WWW) 2022*[3].

6. Presenters and Organizers

Milan Dojchinovski Milan holds a Research Associate position at the Institute for Applied Informatics (InfAI) and an Assistant Professor position at the CTU in Prague. He has 10+ years experience in the computer industry in Germany, Czech Republic and Slovenia. His research interests are in Semantic Web, NLP and Knowledge Graph technologies. Since 2013 Milan is an active member of the DBpedia community project. He holds a PhD in Information Science from the Czech Technical University in Prague in the context of Linked Data, Knowledge Extraction and Web Services technologies. Milan is the main lead of the DBpedia tutorial series.
Kirill Yankov Kirill is a back-end developer at the KILT Competence Center at the Institute for Applied Informatics. Since 2021 he has been involved in DBpedia developments and contributed to the development of the DBpedia Databus. Kirill has been part of the core organization team of the series of DBpedia tutorials organized since 2021.
Jan Forberg Jan is a full stack developer at the KILT Competence Center at the Institute for Applied Informatics. Since 2016 he has been involved in DBpedia and contributed to the development of the DBpedia Databus, Dockerized DBpedia and DBpedia Lookup. Jan has been part of the core organization team of the online series of DBpedia tutorials organized since 2020.
Julia Holze Julia is head of the Organizational Development of the DBpedia Association. She holds a M.A. degree in Media & Communication Science. She will be responsible for the community outreach, support the organization of this tutorial and spread news to the DBpedia Community.
Sebastian Hellmann Sebastian is the executive director and board member of the non-profit DBpedia Association. He is a senior member of the "Agile Knowledge Engineering and Semantic Web" AKSW research center, focusing on semantic technology research. He is the head of the "KILT" Competence Center at InfAI. Sebastian is also a contributor to various open-source projects and communities such as DBpedia, NLP2RDF, DL-Learner and OWLG, and has been involved in numerous EU research projects. Sebastian will monitor and guide the tutorial preparations.

7. Ethics Statement

The tutorial is designed with a strong commitment to ethical standards to ensure that participants are equipped with knowledge and practices that will not introduce ethical issues or problems. We will emphasize ethical considerations in all aspects of the tutorial, from data selection and publishing to respectful engagement with diverse datasets. Our goal is to provide a safe and inclusive learning environment where participants can explore the intricacies of DBpedia Databus without compromising ethical standards. We are dedicated to upholding the highest ethical principles throughout the tutorial to foster a culture of responsible and ethical research.

8. Bibliographical References

Christian Bizer, Jens Lehmann, Georgi Kobilarov, Sören Auer, Christian Becker, Richard Cyganiak, and Sebastian Hellmann. 2009. Dbpedia-a crystallization point for the web of data. *Journal of web semantics*, 7(3):154–165.

Marvin Hofer, Sebastian Hellmann, Milan Dojchinovski, and Johannes Frey. 2020. The new dbpedia release cycle: Increasing agility and efficiency in knowledge extraction workflows. In *16th International Conference on Semantic Systems, SEMANTiCS 2020, Amsterdam, The Netherlands, September 7–10, 2020, Proceedings 16*, pages 1–18. Springer International Publishing.

Jens Lehmann, Robert Isele, Max Jakob, Anja Jentzsch, Dimitris Kontokostas, Pablo N Mendes, Sebastian Hellmann, Mohamed Morsey, Patrick Van Kleef, Sören Auer, et al. 2015. Dbpedia–a large-scale, multilingual knowledge base extracted from wikipedia. *Semantic web*, 6(2):167–195.

[1] https://www.dbpedia.org/events/dbpedia-tutorial-at-ldk-2023/

[2] https://www.dbpedia.org/events/dbpedia-tutorial-2-0-kg-conference/

[3] https://www.dbpedia.org/events/tut-at-the-web-conf/

NLP for Chemistry – Introduction and Recent Advances

Camilo Thorne **Saber Akhondi**
Elsevier, Data Science, Life Sciences
c.thorne.1@elsevier.com s.akhondi@elsevier.com

Abstract

In this half-day tutorial we will be giving an introductory overview to a number of recent applications of natural language processing to a relatively underrepresented application domain: chemistry. Specifically, we will see how neural language models (transformers) can be applied (oftentimes with near-human performance) to chemical text mining, reaction extraction, or more importantly computational chemistry (forward and backward synthesis of chemical compounds). At the same time, a number of gold standards for experimentation have been made available to the research –academic and otherwise– community. Theoretical results will be, whenever possible, supported by system demonstrations in the form of Jupyter notebooks. This tutorial targets an audience interested in bioinformatics and biomedical applications, but pre-supposes no advanced knowledge of either.

Keywords: Chemical text mining, information extraction, transformer models, chemical entity formats

Introduction

Overview Chemistry was for long a *terra incognita* for natural language processing (NLP). While strong overlap with computational and statistical physics (in e.g., so-called computational chemistry) gave rise to the application of many statistical models, methods derived from NLP have only reached wide acceptance in the past twenty years (Sun et al., 2011; Akhondi et al., 2015). The aim of this tutorial is to provide a basic introduction to this emerging field, and overview some of its latest advances. Given its breath, we will focus on four fundamental use cases.

Outline This tutorial will be organized as follows:

- **Block 1**. Basic chemical notions and techniques.
  50 minutes, followed by a 10 minute break.
- **Block 2**. Text mining in the chemistry domain.
  50 minutes, followed by a 10 minute break.
- **Block 3**. Distributional models for (computational) chemistry.
  50 minutes, followed by a 10 minute break.
- **Block 4**. Large language models, multimodality, applications.
  50 minutes.

For an overview of the material to be discussed in each block, please see below. The tutorial assumes no prior knowledge, with the exception to exposure to Python and natural language processing. Knowledge of chemistry is beneficial but not required.

Basic chemical notions and techniques In chemistry, the primary objects of interest are chemical compounds and reactions. A *compound* is a complex structure composed of *atoms* and *bonds*. Compounds are in turn the building blocks of *reactions*, which are relations or events wherein multiple compounds, a.k.a. *reactants*, are combined to synthesise novel compounds a.k.a *products*.

While a number of manually curated public (e.g., PubChem or SureChemBL) and commercial (e.g. Reaxys© or SciFinder©) chemical databases exist, most of the information about compounds and reactions is reported first in chemical publications, such as chemical patents and chemical journals. Their volume being so big, NLP applications have become critical in the curation and enrichment of these databases (Sun et al., 2011). A number of basic NLP tasks need to be solved for this to be possible (Sun et al., 2011; Leaman et al., 2016). **(a)** Texts need to be segmented and, crucially, tokenized. **(b)** Chemical entities need to be extracted, and normalized or disambiguated against entity identifiers in chemical databases. **(c)** Relations need to be identified. This has motivated research in this area, as well as the emergence of chemical NLP benchmarks to train machine learning models, such as e.g. the CHEMDNER (Krallinger et al., 2015) chemical named entity recognition corpus.

One particular challenge here is the syntax of vocabulary of chemical text, specially, names. While the key representation of a molecule (Sun et al., 2011) is graphical (atoms being the vertexes, and bonds the edges), a number of alternative naming conventions and textual (linear) serialization formats exist (see Figure 2), such as: **(a)** Trivial names –these are standard names for compounds. **(b)** IUPAC names –these are semi-formal names built with special characters. **(c)** SMILES strings –these are linear representations of the graph obtained by topologically ordering a spanning tree of the graph. This traditionally made tokenization a hard task, as traditional methods would break IUPAC names or SMILES (Akkasi et al., 2016). Also,

LREC-COLING 2024 Tutorials, pages 45–49
20-25 May, 2024.

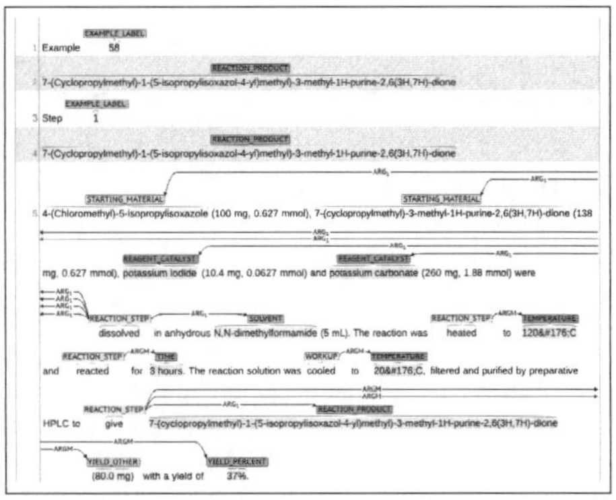

Figure 1: US patent snippet with reaction annotations (entities and events), in BRAT format (He et al., 2021).

even with formal representations, some degree of ambiguity seems unavoidable, stressing the need chemical name normalization at all levels (Akhondi et al., 2015).

Text mining in the chemistry domain An important contribution to this field in recent years has been the ChEMU series of shared chemical test mining tasks, organized within the CLEF 2020, 2021 and 2022 conference. In these shared tasks a novel set of chemical NLP gold sets, each constituted of 1,500 snippets of reaction texts (multi-paragraph passages describing reactions) derived from English chemical patents were made available for the research community, the main being: **(a)** A chemical named entity recognition (NER) set, with entities differentiated by the role they play in reactions (He et al., 2021). **(b)** A event extraction (EE) set, where individual reactions are annotated as events (He et al., 2021). **(c)** An anaphora resolution set, that resolves anaphors across reaction texts (Fang et al., 2021). Figure 1 illustrates the first two levels of annotations on a sample snippet. Results from the shared tasks showed that a wide variety of techniques, including symbolic, heuristic-based text processing, can achieve good results. At the same time, models derived from the BERT family of neural language models can achieve SOTA results on a par or higher than inter-annotator agreement. See Table 1 for the first two benchmarks.

Alongside this, there has also been progress on related tasks such as chemical indexing (Sun et al., 2011; Akhondi et al., 2019; Leaman et al., 2016), where the goal is to identify the most relevant chemical entities for indexing and search.

Distributional models for (computational) chemistry Multiple analogies between chemical compounds and natural or formal languages can be drawn, in particular that, like a sentence, a molecule can be understood as a (recursive) composition of atomic units or "words": base compounds and atoms. Linearized representations of chemical molecules such as SMILES strings make this analogy even more apparent (see Figure 2). SMILES strings can be tokenized (see Figure 2), and embeddings and similar deep-learning molecular representations can thus be successfully learnt via neural language models (Tshitoyan et al., 2019). Such representations can be as expressive (sometimes even more expressive) than traditional cheminformatics representations based on manually engineered chemical and physical features of molecules.

Model	NER (F1)	EE (F1)
NextMove	89.1	89.7
PubMedBERT	94.7	92.0
MelaxTech	95.7	95.3
LG-AI	97.5	92.3

Table 1: Results on the ChEMU NER and EE benchmarks (He et al., 2021; Jang et al., 2022). The latter three are based on BERT resp. encoder-only transformer models. NextMove's methods are on the other hard, based on more classical methods such as dependency parsing, grammars and transducers.

Model	Acc1	Acc2	Acc3
Dual-TF	55.3	66.7	73.0
Graph2SMILES	52.9	66.5	70.0
Chemformer	53.6	61.1	61.7
T5Chem	46.5	64.4	70.5

Table 2: SOTA (mid-2023) on USPTO-50k (Irwin et al., 2022; Sun et al., 2021; Tetko et al., 2020; Lu and Zhang, 2022a). Notice that two out of four models are text-to-text transformers (encoder-decoders).

In particular, chemical transformations such as single-step retro-synthesis –predicting the reactant(s)– or its dual, forward synthesis –predicting the product(s)– can be modelled as sequence-to-sequence problems, viz., translations between the SMILES strings to the left and right of the chemical equation symbol » (see Figure 3). It can thus be solved using text-to-text transformer models from the Bart or T5 families (**?**Irwin et al., 2022; Lu and Zhang, 2022a). This is evident in Table 2, that shows the current SOTA on the main single-step chemical synthesis benchmark, the USPTO-50k gold set. This is a manually curated set of 50,000 reactions extracted from US chemistry patents. All models are deep learning models, with the first two based on the analysis of the source graphical, 2-dimensional representations of molecules, and the latter two, on neural language models and reaction SMILES.

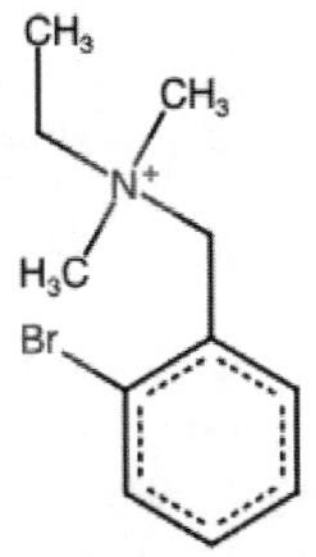

SMILES	`CC[N+](C)(C)Cc1ccccc1Br`
tokens	`CC[N+]( C[N+](C [N+](C) (C)( C)(C )(C) (C)C C)Cc )Cc1 Cc1c c1cc 1ccc cccc cccc ccc1 cc1Br`

Figure 2: SMILES representation and tokenization of "Bretylium" (a.k.a. "N-(2-Brombenzyl)-N,N-dimethylethanaminium" in IUPAC notation) into 16 4-chargramms.

`C.O=O.O=O » O=C=O.O.O`

Figure 3: The combustion of methane represented in (reaction) SMILES. Dots, viz, the character ., are used as separators for the reactants, listed to the left hand side of the reaction symbol », and the products, listed to the right.

In fact, neural word embeddings, learnt from chemical corpora, seem nowadays powerful enough (Thorne and Akhondi, 2020) to learn representations of entities that correlate with molecular-based representations (see Figure 4).

Large language models, multimodality, applications The current surge in large language models (LLMs), viz., decoder-only generative transformer models with billions of parameters and trained over corpora comprising billions of words, has also reached the chemical domain. Researchers have demonstrated (Bran et al., 2023; **?**) that general-purpose models like Open-AI's GPT-3 and GPT-4, or scholarly LLMs such as Galactica (Taylor et al., 2022) can be used as chemistry and computational chemistry assistants, even if chemistry-specific models (such as e.g. SMILES-GPT (Adilov, 2021)) still underperform. Figure 5 shows that they can be used to suggest, e.g., reactions and (even if not necessarily always factually correct) synthesis procedures, potentially helping drafting novel plans.

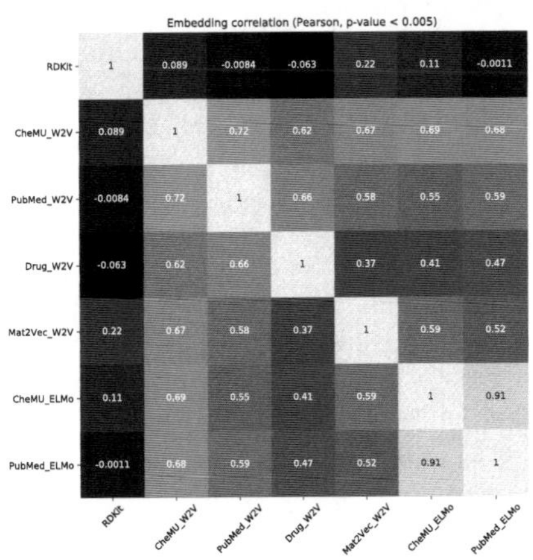

Figure 4: Correlations between chemical (word) embeddings (Thorne and Akhondi, 2020).

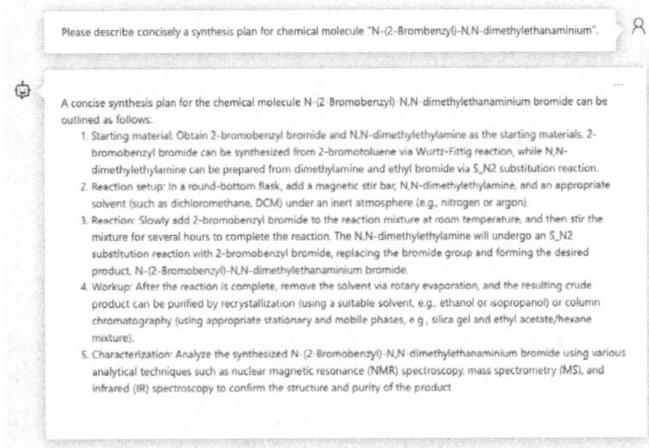

Figure 5: Asking GPT-4 (8,192-token input context version) to concisely describe a synthesis plan (sequence of reactions and reaction steps) for "N-(2-Brombenzyl)-N,N-dimethylethanaminium". We sampled with temperature $t \geq 0.7$, likelihood $p \geq 0.95$ and a 800-token stop citerion.

Another emerging field of chemical NLP research is work on multi-modality. As seen earlier, it is possible to learn neural language models on chemical texts and linearized representations of compounds and reactions, and apply them to text mining and computational chemistry tasks. However, not all chemical information is conveyed textually. A significant part is conveyed in images, structured in tables, etc. Hence the need to learn wider, more expressive representation spaces that e.g. enrich current spaces with physiochemical features and other dimensions (Soares et al., 2023; Lu and Zhang, 2022b).

Reading List and Tools

In this section we highlight the key literature pointers the audience should be aware of for a better understanding of this tutorial. We also point at some basic software tools. Readers are invited to click on the hyper-links.

Key papers While all papers cited earlier are useful, we suggest to start with (Sun et al., 2011), which covers well the problems in chemical text mining, as well as approaches that precede deep learning. Is also important to understand chemical representation formats. Regarding text mining, we suggest (He et al., 2021) and (Lu and Zhang, 2022a) for distributional models. Lastly, (Bran et al., 2023) for recent applications (large language models).

Key software tools The main open source software tool used in the cheminformatics community is perhaps RDkit, a Python library that we will be using in our demos and Jupyter notebooks. For a more extensive overview of all software tools (including tools written in languages other than Python), please check this GitHub repository. It also contains links to predictive models beyond NLP. These tools are sometimes essential for (pre)processing chemical data.

Key models Regarding word embeddings, we suggest to check out the ChELMo embeddings, pre-trained on chemical patents (even if not transformer-based) Regarding text mining models, many are closed-source. We will provide some Elsevier deep learning -based demonstration models as part of this tutorial. An open source –if dated and written in Java– starting point is ChemSpot (based on conditional random fields and manual features,). Regarding distributional models over SMILES, we recommend T5Chem.

Key chemical NLP benchmarks While the papers cited mention multiple benchmarks, we suggest to focus on the following four: **(a)** The chemical NER BioSemantics corpus. **(b)** The chemical NER CHEMDNER corpus. **(c)** The ChEMU benchmarks. **(d)** Lastly, the USPTO-50k collection of chemical reactions, the most important public benchmark for computational chemistry.

Presenters

Camilo Thorne (personal website; Google Scholar) is currently Principal Data Scientist at Elsevier. His work focuses on applying current NLP SOTA (large language models and other transformer-based NLP techniques) to the life sciences domain, and in particular to chemistry. His background spans both industry and academia. Prior to Elsevier he worked as postdoctoral fellow in biomedical NLP at the universities of Mannheim and Stuttgart, Germany, and as computational linguist at IBM, Italy. He holds a PhD in computer science from the Free University of Bozen-Bolzano, where he studied controlled natural languages and semantic web formalisms. Last, but not least, he holds extensive teaching and public speaking experience in his fields of interest.

Saber Akhondi (Google Scholar) is currently Senior Director/Head of Data Science at Elsevier He heads a group of 10+ data scientists, where he applies NLP and machine learning techniques to extract information useful for large commercial and research communities in the life sciences. He has extensive experience in the area of chemical text mining, with multiple high impact publications, and multiple international project coordination activities (ChEMU, BioSemantics). Saber Akhondi holds a PhD from Erasmus University Rotterdam, where he developed novel methods for the detection, normalization and indexing of chemical entities.

Diversity Considerations

This topic contributes to topic diversity by introducing an underrepresented application domain of natural language processing (and machine learning): computational chemistry. It will be of particular interest to researchers in the biomedical and bioinformatics domain, and more generally, to researchers of cross-disciplinary life sciences and data science backgrounds.

Other Information

Presenters This tutorial will be given by two persons, who will alternate each other for the different blocks.

Course infrastructure The presenters will try to illustrate practically the methods described with Jupyter notebooks whenever possible. Slides, notebooks and announcements will be distributed and managed through a public GitHub repository (or a public website) and Google Colab, accessible to all participants. For the tutorial, we request only a room sufficiently large for all registered attendants, with good internet connection and a projector.

Ethics Statement

Methods will be demonstrated using datasets and platforms that are freely accessible for research purposes.

Bibliographical References

Sanjar Adilov. 2021. Generative pre-training from molecules. *ChemRxiv*.

Saber A. Akhondi, Sorel Muresan, Antony J. Williams, and Jan A. Kors. 2015. Ambiguity of non-systematic chemical identifiers within and between small-molecule databases. *J. Cheminformatics*, 7:54:1–54:10.

Saber A. Akhondi, Hinnerk Rey, Markus Schwörer, Michael Maier, John P. Toomey, Heike Nau, Gabriele Ilchmann, Mark Sheehan, Matthias Irmer, Claudia Bobach, Marius A. Doornenbal, Michelle Gregory, and Jan A. Kors. 2019.

Automatic identification of relevant chemical compounds from patents. *Database J. Biol. Databases Curation*, page baz001.

Abbas Akkasi, Ekrem Varoglu, and Nazife Dimililer. 2016. Chemtok: A new rule based tokenizer for chemical named entity recognition. *BioMed Research International*.

Andres M Bran, Sam Cox, Oliver Schilter, Carlo Baldassari, Andrew D White, and Philippe Schwaller. 2023. Chemcrow: Augmenting large-language models with chemistry tools. *CoRR*.

Biaoyan Fang, Christian Druckenbrodt, Saber A. Akhondi, Jiayuan He, Timothy Baldwin, and Karin Verspoor. 2021. Chemu-ref: A corpus for modeling anaphora resolution in the chemical domain. In *Proceedings of the 16th Conference of the European Chapter of the Association for Computational Linguistics: Main Volume, EACL 2021, Online, April 19 - 23, 2021*, pages 1362–1375. Association for Computational Linguistics.

Jiayuan He, Dat Quoc Nguyen, Saber A. Akhondi, Christian Druckenbrodt, Camilo Thorne, Ralph Hoessel, Zubair Afzal, Zenan Zhai, Biaoyan Fang, Hiyori Yoshikawa, Ameer Albahem, Lawrence Cavedon, Trevor Cohn, Timothy Baldwin, and Karin Verspoor. 2021. Chemu 2020: Natural language processing methods are effective for information extraction from chemical patents. *Frontiers Res. Metrics Anal.*, 6:654438.

Ross Irwin, Spyridon Dimitriadis, Jiazhen He, and Esben Jannik Bjerrum. 2022. Chemformer: a pre-trained transformer for computational chemistry. *Machine Learning: Science and Technology*, 3(1):015022.

Youngrok Jang, Hosung Song, Junho Lee, Gyeonghun Kim, Yireun Kim, Stanley Jungkyu Choi, Honglak Lee, and Kyunghoon Bae. 2022. Context aware named entity recognition and relation extraction with domain-specific language model. In *Proceedings of the Working Notes of CLEF 2022 - Conference and Labs of the Evaluation Forum, Bologna, Italy, September 5th - to - 8th, 2022*, volume 3180 of *CEUR Workshop Proceedings*, pages 782–796. CEUR-WS.org.

Martin Krallinger, Florian Leitner, Obdulia Rabal, Miguel Vazquez, Julen Oyarzabal, and Alfonso Valencia. 2015. CHEMDNER: the drugs and chemical names extraction challenge. *J. Cheminformatics*, 7(S-1):S1.

Robert Leaman, Chih-Hsuan Wei, Cherry Zou, and Zhiyong Lu. 2016. Mining chemical patents with an ensemble of open systems. *Database J. Biol. Databases Curation*.

Jieyu Lu and Yingkai Zhang. 2022a. Unified deep learning model for multitask reaction predictions with explanation. *Journal of Chemical Information and Modeling*.

Jieyu Lu and Yingkai Zhang. 2022b. Unified deep learning model for multitask reaction predictions with explanation. *J. Chem. Inf. Model.*, 62(6):1376–1387.

Eduardo Soares, Emilio Vital Brazil, Karen Fiorela Aquino Gutierrez, Renato Cerqueira, Dan Sanders, Kristin Schmidt, and Dmitry Zubarev. 2023. Beyond chemical language: A multimodal approach to enhance molecular property prediction. *CoRR*.

Bingjun Sun, Prasenjit Mitra, C. Lee Giles, and Karl T. Mueller. 2011. Identifying, indexing, and ranking chemical formulae and chemical names in digital documents. *ACM Trans. Inf. Syst.*, 29(2).

Ruoxi Sun, Hanjun Dai, Li Li, Steven Kearnes, and Bo Dai. 2021. Towards understanding retrosynthesis by energy-based models. In *Advances in Neural Information Processing Systems 34: Annual Conference on Neural Information Processing Systems 2021, NeurIPS 2021, December 6-14, 2021, virtual*, pages 10186–10194.

Ross Taylor, Marcin Kardas, Guillem Cucurull, Thomas Scialom, Anthony Hartshorn, Elvis Saravia, Andrew Poulton, Viktor Kerkez, and Robert Stojnic. 2022. Galactica: A large language model for science. *CoRR*.

Igor V. Tetko, Pavel Karpov, Ruud van Deursen, and Guillaume Godin. 2020. Augmented transformer achieves 97% and 85% for top5 prediction of direct and classical retro-synthesis. *CoRR*.

Camilo Thorne and Saber A. Akhondi. 2020. Word embeddings for chemical patent natural language processing. *CoRR*.

Vahe Tshitoyan, John Dagdelen, Leigh Weston, Alexander Dunn, Ziqin Rong, Olga Kononova, Kristin A. Persson, Gerbrand Ceder, and Anubhav Jain. 2019. Unsupervised word embeddings capture latent knowledge from materials science literature. *Nat.*, 571(7763):95–98.

Formal Semantic Controls over Language Models

Danilo S. Carvalho[1,2], **Yingji Zhang**[1]†, **Andre Freitas**[1,2,3]
Department of Computer Science[1], National Biomarker Centre, CRUK-MI[2] - University of Manchester
Idiap Research Institute[3]
United Kingdom, Switzerland
<firstname.lastname>@[postgrad.†]manchester.ac.uk

Abstract

Text embeddings provide a concise representation of the semantics of sentences and larger spans of text, rather than individual words, capturing a wide range of linguistic features. They have found increasing application to a variety of NLP tasks, including machine translation and natural language inference. While most recent breakthroughs in task performance are being achieved by large scale distributional models, there is a growing disconnection between their knowledge representation and traditional semantics, which hinders efforts to capture such knowledge in human interpretable form or explain model inference behaviour. In this tutorial, we examine from basics to the cutting edge research on the analysis and control of text representations, aiming to shorten the gap between deep latent semantics and formal symbolics. This includes the considerations on knowledge formalisation, the linguistic information that can be extracted and measured from distributional models, and intervention techniques that enable explainable reasoning and controllable text generation, covering methods from pooling to LLM-based.

1. Introduction

Despite the recent language models' increasing feats of state-of-the-art performance in a large variety of NLP tasks, there is a growing disconnection between their knowledge representation and traditional semantics, which hinders efforts to capture such knowledge in human interpretable form or explain model inference behaviour. To address this disconnection, numerous approaches have been proposed to approximate deep latent representations to symbolic models grounded on formal linguistics and well-defined mathematical properties. Those approaches are mostly developed over sentence and paragraph models, not only due to computational capacity and cost considerations, but also due to their semantic and structural independence as linguistic units (Allerton, 1969), allowing the representation of relationships between words. Such relationships are a necessary element to improve performance on certain tasks, such as information retrieval and machine translation. Thus targeting them strikes a balance between performance scaling and traceability of the captured knowledge.

Research on this topic has steadily advanced together with the general text embedding efforts (Pragst et al., 2020; Liao, 2021), but has gained increased attention in recent years, due to interpretability, control and safety limitations of state-of-the art, very large language models (LLMs). Thus, a key research question is how to harmonise the flexibility and task delivery provided by large distributional models to the ability to trace its knowledge and behaviour in terms of well-defined formal properties. Sentence and paragraph representation models allow experimentation with a focused scope, bringing a diverse set of contributions with fast turnaround. Some of those contributions are then applied to the larger models (Li et al., 2020), which leads to a positive cycle of improvement. Furthermore, solutions involving explainability and safeguarding of conversational models inevitably touch the matter of compositionality in natural language, which is an important aspect of text representation research.

However, the diversity of contributions in this subject also brings fragmentation of the community awareness to common issues, which causes considerable replication of efforts, terminology inconsistencies and overall missed oportunities. An important step to alleviate such issues would be compiling and structuring the main advances and knowledge gained within this subject, and present them in a summarised form to a broad NLP / distributional semantics public.

With this tutorial, we propose to introduce the field of neuro-symbolic methods in text representation to a broader NLP audience and to promote constructive discussion among researchers in this topic. This will be achieved by presenting an overview of the evolution on symbolic-aware latent representations, focused on sentence embeddings, starting from their pure distributional origins as an extension of word embedding methods (Kiros et al., 2015) and covering their evolving approaches, including tensor pooling, contrastive learning and autoencoders, up to the most recent incorporation of LLMs. We give special attention to the issues of explainability and control, which are of crescent relevance to the NLP community as a whole.

LREC-COLING 2024 Tutorials, pages 50–55
20-25 May, 2024.

2. Target Audience

This tutorial is targeted at both academics and practitioners who would like to have a better understanding of the interface between formal linguistics and how they manifest within transformer-based models, and the opportunities and challenges brought by extracting and manipulating symbolic properties in latent spaces. The topics are to be presented in a concise and informative way, not diving into minute technical details of the discussed approaches.

Attendees should have a basic understanding of text embeddings, the transformer architecture and a firm undertanding of basic NLP/CL terminology, such as syntax, semantics, part-of-speech and semantic role labeling. A basic understanding of the mathematical foundation on different loss/objective functions and set theory will certainly improve the tutorial experience, but are not required.

3. Outline

The tutorial is organised to follow a *conceptual* and *chronological* order, prioritising the understanding of concepts and then their application. It is divided in the following chapters:

The evolutionary arch from word embeddings to LLMs vs. formal linguistics

We present the motivation and intuition behind the construction of sentence/paragraph embedding models. Starting from their first popularisation as an extension of word embedding models (Kiros et al., 2015) and their applications to the employment of transformer-based architectures (Reimers and Gurevych, 2019; Sanh et al., 2019; Wang et al., 2020; Ni et al., 2022). We explore the characteristics, improvements and shortcomings of the main approaches, contrasting the evolution of distributional semantics with the staticity of formal linguistics, along with the relevant datasets, metrics and benchmarks. This chapter provides a foundation for understanding the topic.

Contrastive learning and conceptual modeling

Considering the most basic goal of obtaining a sentence representation that can be compared to others for measuring semantic similarity, i.e., whether two sentences have similar meaning, it is not suprising that contrastive learning is among the most popular approaches for this end (Tan et al., 2022a; Cheng et al., 2023; Wang et al., 2022; Wu et al., 2022). Contrastive learning works by presenting a set of similar (positive) and dissimilar (negative) examples w.r.t. to a given sample, so that the model learns to place similar ones closer to each other and push apart the dissimilar ones in its latent space.

Another relevant way of learning sentence representations is by leveraging structured knowledge bases of declarative sentences such as definitions, e.g., dictionaries. The intuition in this case being that similar concepts are defined with similar sentences (Hill et al., 2016; Tsukagoshi et al., 2021). Studies on this problem led to the formulation of a NLP task called *definition modeling* dedicated to learning embeddings from definition sentences (Noraset et al., 2017).

This chapter explores the major concepts and relevant works on contrastive learning for sentence representation and conceptual modeling, covering their main achievements and how they are used currently.

Interpretability and formal linguistics

Explainable and interpretable representations are the ones that can be decomposed into factors that are traceable to human understandable concepts. For example, a sentence representation consisting in only two features: the length of the sentence (number of words) and if the sentence is a question or not, is an interpretable one, as both features are easily understood by humans.

Distributed latent embeddings are typically *not interpretable*, which means that inference results obtained from their application are obscure to humans. This limits their application possibilities and brings safety / bias concerns. For this reason, significant attention is being directed towards the creation of explainable representations, specially regarding models dedicated to sensitive tasks or facing the public. Formal syntactic and semantic concepts, such as subject/object and agent/action, provide a strong grounding for the interpretation of latent features if they can be represented in such models.

This chapter deals with different interpretability concerns and approaches, covering the three levels of transparency in explainable AI: algorithmic transparency, decomposability and simulatability, from a text embedding perspective.

Disentanglement and separability

One of the ways to improve explainability is by disentanglement or separation of representations. Disentanglement consists in the separation of traceable factors by binding them to different dimensions (or set of). For example, having the number (singular/plural) of a subject, or time (past/present/future) of a verb strongly tied to a single or limited set of dimensions of the representation. Separability refers to spatially distinguishable clusters in the latent space. For example, having all sentences with "television" as subject being in a enclosed region in the latent space. Having had significant success in the Computer Vision field, different disentanglement and separability approaches are recently being explored in NLP, notably in sentence representation models (Hu et al., 2017; Chen et al., 2019; Mercatali and Freitas, 2021; Carvalho et al., 2022b).

This chapter explores important concepts regarding the disentanglement/separability of sentence embeddings and how they help achieving explainability.

Control mechanisms for text generation and inference over latent spaces

Most of the current breakthroughs in NLP are related to generative language models, which brought unprecedent levels of attention to such methods both within the NLP community and by the general public. The speed in which this technology has been adopted in a variety of real-world scenarios, from computer programming to medicine, also helped to raise concerns regarding safety, social biases and explainability of the text generated by these systems. Those concerns ultimately translate in the necessity of better control mechanisms over generative models, which are discussed in this chapter, specifically for the case of sentence generation with emphasis on intervention routes through the models' latent spaces, including disentanglement of generative factors (Hu et al., 2017; Mercatali and Freitas, 2021) and linguistic-aware loss functions (Chen et al., 2019).

The role of compositionality in improving representations

One key aspect of condensing sentence information is capturing the relationships between words and how their combination brings forth new meaning: the compositional aspect of language. Compositionality has a pivotal role in the improvement of text representations as the ability to deconstruct relationships such as ellipsis (Wijnholds and Sadrzadeh, 2019) and adjectival modifiers (Carvalho et al., 2022a) can be used to express them in terms of latent space transformations, which provide a mean of linguistic grounded explainability and control.

This chapter discusses central concepts on compositionality, as well as the findings of seminal and recent studies on this subject and their implications.

Employing Autoencoders for efficiency and control

In recent years, Autoencoder architectures became the foundation of a cascade of important contributions to text representation research. They enable the combination of pre-trained encoder and decoder models to learn highly optimised text embeddings (Li et al., 2020), without the need of re-training complex encoders/decoders. Such optimised embeddings can then be analysed and interventions can be applied directly to the Autoencoder latent space (Carvalho et al., 2022b).

In this chapter we explore the benefits and limitations of Autoencoder architectures for sentence embedding and some of their recent developments.

Controlling the semantic properties of large language models

Following the Autoencoder (AE) based developments, we get to the latest incorporation of large language models (LLMs), such as the GPT or LLaMa families, to sentence embedding techniques. While there are still many open research questions regarding the nature of the knowledge embedded in LLM latent spaces, there is a growing consensus on that filtering such knowledge is crucial in enabling their effective and safe use (Meng et al. (2022); Wu et al. (2024); Petroni et al. (2019); Dai et al. (2022), among others), and that it is a certain way of obtaining better text representations (Wijesiriwardene et al., 2024; Zhang et al., 2024). This chapter discusses the main current approaches to achieve semantic control over LLM models, with an emphasis on AE-based studies, but also covering other methods.

Probing sentence latent spaces: geometrical and linguistic properties

Finally, the last chapter discusses techniques for analysis and control of the sentence representations, in particular through intervention to the modeled latent spaces. Namely, different probing methods, and the analysis of geometrical and linguistic properties of the embedding space, such as vector arithmetic, semantic continuity, syntactic and semantic role representation and compositionality. The knowledge gained from all the previous chapters is visited here, so the participants can appreciate the development context of the discussed techniques, as well as their strong and weak points.

Hands-on: Probing Large Language VAEs with LangSpace & LangVAE

In tandem with the discussions on latent space control mechanisms and probing techniques, we demonstrate the applicability and impact of said techniques to current language models hosted in HuggingFace, in a hands-on coding session using our recently developed toolkit. This covers the quick creation and fine tuning of large language

VAEs from stock LLMs, and the probing of created models on predefined tasks using the *LangVAE*[1] and *LangSpace*[2] libraries, respectively.

4. Reading List

Relevant materials to read prior to attending the tutorial include:

- The 2013 review paper: *Representation Learning: A Review and New Perspectives* (Bengio et al., 2013).
- The book *Natural language processing with transformers* (Tunstall et al., 2022)
- The 2020 paper: *Explainable Artificial Intelligence (XAI): Concepts, taxonomies, opportunities and challenges toward responsible AI* (Arrieta et al., 2020).

Further information in the topic can be found in the cited literature and also:

- The book *Representation learning for natural language processing* (Liu et al., 2023).
- Other relevant papers: (Conneau et al., 2018; Kelly et al., 2020; Zhu and de Melo, 2020; Tan et al., 2022b; Opitz and Frank, 2022)

5. Resources

The tutorial resources (slides, code, etc.) will be made available at the web address: `https://danilosc.com/events/tutorial-lrec-2024` and by the ACL anthology portal.

6. Presenters

Danilo S. Carvalho is a Principal Clinical Informatician (Research Associate) at the National Biomarker Centre, Cancer Research UK - Manchester Institute, at the University of Manchester, working on Safe and Explainable Artificial Intelligence (AI) architectures. He has experience in both industry and academia, having presented works at multiple international conferences over the past 10 years, such as EACL and ESANN. His main area of expertise is representation learning for NLP and his research interests include explainable AI and legal and patent text processing.

[1]`https://github.com/neuro-symbolic-ai/LangVAE`

[2]`https://github.com/neuro-symbolic-ai/LangSpace`

Yingji Zhang is a 3rd year PhD student at the University of Manchester. His research interests include natural language inference, controllable natural language generation, and disentangled representation learning.

Andre Freitas is a Senior Lecturer at the Department of Computer Science at the University of Manchester. He leads the Neuro-symbolic AI group at Idiap and at the Department of Computer Science at the University of Manchester. His main research interests are on enabling the development of AI methods to support abstract, explainable and flexible inference. In particular, he investigates how the combination of neural and symbolic data representation paradigms can deliver better inference. Some of his research topics include: explanation generation, natural language inference, explainable question answering, knowledge graphs and open information extraction.

7. Ethics Statement

The analysis and control of text generation models facing end users need to deal with ethics issues regarding biased and potentially unsafe (offensive, incorrect or misleading) outputs. The tutorial also seeks to inform the participants of these issues and the importance of mitigating them with or without the materials discussed.

References

D.J. Allerton. 1969. The sentence as a linguistic unit. *Lingua*, 22:27–46.

Alejandro Barredo Arrieta, Natalia Díaz-Rodríguez, Javier Del Ser, Adrien Bennetot, Siham Tabik, Alberto Barbado, Salvador García, Sergio Gil-López, Daniel Molina, Richard Benjamins, et al. 2020. Explainable artificial intelligence (xai): Concepts, taxonomies, opportunities and challenges toward responsible ai. *Information fusion*, 58:82–115.

Yoshua Bengio, Aaron Courville, and Pascal Vincent. 2013. Representation learning: A review and new perspectives. *IEEE Transactions on Pattern Analysis and Machine Intelligence*, 35(8):1798–1828.

Danilo S Carvalho, Edoardo Manino, Julia Rozanova, Lucas Cordeiro, and André Freitas. 2022a. Montague semantics and modifier consistency measurement in neural language models. *arXiv preprint arXiv:2212.04310*.

Danilo S. Carvalho, Giangiacomo Mercatali, Yingji Zhang, and André Freitas. 2022b. Learning disentangled representations for natural language definitions. In *Findings*.

Mingda Chen, Qingming Tang, Sam Wiseman, and Kevin Gimpel. 2019. A multi-task approach for disentangling syntax and semantics in sentence representations. In *Proceedings of the 2019 Conference of the North American Chapter of the Association for Computational Linguistics: Human Language Technologies, Volume 1 (Long and Short Papers)*, pages 2453–2464.

Qinyuan Cheng, Xiaogui Yang, Tianxiang Sun, Linyang Li, and Xipeng Qiu. 2023. Improving contrastive learning of sentence embeddings from ai feedback. In *Annual Meeting of the Association for Computational Linguistics*.

Alexis Conneau, Germán Kruszewski, Guillaume Lample, Loïc Barrault, and Marco Baroni. 2018. What you can cram into a single $&!#* vector: Probing sentence embeddings for linguistic properties. In *Annual Meeting of the Association for Computational Linguistics*.

Damai Dai, Li Dong, Yaru Hao, Zhifang Sui, Baobao Chang, and Furu Wei. 2022. Knowledge neurons in pretrained transformers. In *Proceedings of the 60th Annual Meeting of the Association for Computational Linguistics (Volume 1: Long Papers)*, pages 8493–8502.

Felix Hill, Kyunghyun Cho, Anna Korhonen, and Yoshua Bengio. 2016. Learning to understand phrases by embedding the dictionary. *Transactions of the Association for Computational Linguistics*, 4:17–30.

Zhiting Hu, Zichao Yang, Xiaodan Liang, Ruslan Salakhutdinov, and Eric P. Xing. 2017. Toward controlled generation of text. In *Proceedings of the 34th International Conference on Machine Learning*, volume 70 of *Proceedings of Machine Learning Research*, pages 1587–1596. PMLR.

Matthew A. Kelly, Yang Xu, Jesús Calvillo, and D. Reitter. 2020. Which sentence embeddings and which layers encode syntactic structure? In *Annual Meeting of the Cognitive Science Society*.

Ryan Kiros, Yukun Zhu, Russ R Salakhutdinov, Richard Zemel, Raquel Urtasun, Antonio Torralba, and Sanja Fidler. 2015. Skip-thought vectors. *Advances in neural information processing systems*, 28.

Chunyuan Li, Xiang Gao, Yuan Li, Baolin Peng, Xiujun Li, Yizhe Zhang, and Jianfeng Gao. 2020. Optimus: Organizing sentences via pre-trained modeling of a latent space. In *Proceedings of the 2020 Conference on Empirical Methods in Natural Language Processing (EMNLP)*, pages 4678–4699.

Danqi Liao. 2021. Sentence embeddings using supervised contrastive learning. *arXiv preprint arXiv:2106.04791*.

Zhiyuan Liu, Yankai Lin, and Maosong Sun. 2023. *Representation learning for natural language processing*. Springer Nature.

Kevin Meng, David Bau, Alex Andonian, and Yonatan Belinkov. 2022. Locating and editing factual associations in gpt. *Advances in Neural Information Processing Systems*, 35:17359–17372.

Giangiacomo Mercatali and André Freitas. 2021. Disentangling generative factors in natural language with discrete variational autoencoders. In *Findings of the Association for Computational Linguistics: EMNLP 2021*, pages 3547–3556.

Jianmo Ni, Gustavo Hernandez Abrego, Noah Constant, Ji Ma, Keith Hall, Daniel Cer, and Yinfei Yang. 2022. Sentence-t5: Scalable sentence encoders from pre-trained text-to-text models. In *Findings of the Association for Computational Linguistics: ACL 2022*, pages 1864–1874.

Thanapon Noraset, Chen Liang, Larry Birnbaum, and Doug Downey. 2017. Definition modeling: Learning to define word embeddings in natural language. In *Thirty-First AAAI Conference on Artificial Intelligence*.

Juri Opitz and Anette Frank. 2022. Sbert studies meaning representations: Decomposing sentence embeddings into explainable semantic features. In *AACL*.

Fabio Petroni, Tim Rocktäschel, Patrick Lewis, Anton Bakhtin, Yuxiang Wu, Alexander H Miller, and Sebastian Riedel. 2019. Language models as knowledge bases? *arXiv preprint arXiv:1909.01066*.

Louisa Pragst, Wolfgang Minker, and Stefan Ultes. 2020. Comparative study of sentence embeddings for contextual paraphrasing. In *International Conference on Language Resources and Evaluation*.

Nils Reimers and Iryna Gurevych. 2019. Sentence-bert: Sentence embeddings using siamese bert-networks. In *Proceedings of the 2019 Conference on Empirical Methods in Natural Language Processing and the 9th International Joint Conference on Natural Language Processing (EMNLP-IJCNLP)*, pages 3982–3992.

Victor Sanh, Lysandre Debut, Julien Chaumond, and Thomas Wolf. 2019. Distilbert, a distilled version of bert: smaller, faster, cheaper and lighter. *arXiv preprint arXiv:1910.01108*.

Haochen Tan, Wei Shao, Han Wu, Ke Yang, and Linqi Song. 2022a. A sentence is worth 128 pseudo tokens: A semantic-aware contrastive learning framework for sentence embeddings. In *Findings of the Association for Computational Linguistics: ACL 2022*, pages 246–256.

Haochen Tan, Wei Shao, Han Wu, Ke Yang, and Linqi Song. 2022b. A sentence is worth 128 pseudo tokens: A semantic-aware contrastive learning framework for sentence embeddings. *ArXiv*, abs/2203.05877.

Hayato Tsukagoshi, Ryohei Sasano, and Koichi Takeda. 2021. Defsent: Sentence embeddings using definition sentences. In *Annual Meeting of the Association for Computational Linguistics*.

Lewis Tunstall, Leandro Von Werra, and Thomas Wolf. 2022. *Natural language processing with transformers*. " O'Reilly Media, Inc.".

Wenhui Wang, Furu Wei, Li Dong, Hangbo Bao, Nan Yang, and Ming Zhou. 2020. Minilm: Deep self-attention distillation for task-agnostic compression of pre-trained transformers. *Advances in Neural Information Processing Systems*, 33:5776–5788.

Yau-Shian Wang, Ashley Wu, and Graham Neubig. 2022. English contrastive learning can learn universal cross-lingual sentence embeddings. *ArXiv*, abs/2211.06127.

Thilini Wijesiriwardene, Ruwan Wickramarachchi, Aishwarya Naresh Reganti, Vinija Jain, Aman Chadha, Amit Sheth, and Amitava Das. 2024. On the relationship between sentence analogy identification and sentence structure encoding in large language models. In *Findings of the Association for Computational Linguistics: EACL 2024*, pages 451–457, St. Julian's, Malta. Association for Computational Linguistics.

Gijs Jasper Wijnholds and Mehrnoosh Sadrzadeh. 2019. Evaluating composition models for verb phrase elliptical sentence embeddings. In *North American Chapter of the Association for Computational Linguistics*.

Xing Wu, Chaochen Gao, Zijia Lin, Jizhong Han, Zhongyuan Wang, and Songlin Hu. 2022. Infocse: Information-aggregated contrastive learning of sentence embeddings. In *Conference on Empirical Methods in Natural Language Processing*.

Zhengxuan Wu, Atticus Geiger, Thomas Icard, Christopher Potts, and Noah Goodman. 2024. Interpretability at scale: Identifying causal mechanisms in alpaca. *Advances in Neural Information Processing Systems*, 36.

Yingji Zhang, Danilo Carvalho, Marco Valentino, Ian Pratt-Hartmann, and Andre Freitas. 2024. Improving semantic control in discrete latent spaces with transformer quantized variational autoencoders. In *Findings of the Association for Computational Linguistics: EACL 2024*, pages 1434–1450, St. Julian's, Malta. Association for Computational Linguistics.

Xunjie Zhu and Gerard de Melo. 2020. Sentence analogies: Linguistic regularities in sentence embeddings. In *International Conference on Computational Linguistics*.

Towards a Human-Computer Collaborative Scientific Paper Lifecycle: A Pilot Study and Hands-On Tutorial

Qingyun Wang[1], **Carl Edwards**[1], **Heng Ji**[1], **Tom Hope**[2,3]

[1] University of Illinois at Urbana-Champaign [2] Allen Institute for Artificial Intelligence (AI2)

[3] The Hebrew University of Jerusalem

{qingyun4,cne2,hengji}@illinois.edu,{tomh}@allenai.org

Abstract

Due to the rapid growth of publications varying in quality, there exists a pressing need to help scientists digest and evaluate relevant papers, thereby facilitating scientific discovery. This creates a number of urgent questions; however, computer-human collaboration in the scientific paper lifecycle is still in the exploratory stage and lacks a unified framework for analyzing the relevant tasks. Additionally, with the recent significant success of large language models (LLMs), they have increasingly played an important role in academic writing. In this **cutting-edge** tutorial, we aim to provide an all-encompassing overview of the paper lifecycle, detailing how machines can augment every stage of the research process for the scientist, including scientific literature understanding, experiment development, manuscript draft writing, and finally draft evaluation. This tutorial is devised for *researchers interested in this rapidly-developing field of NLP-augmented paper writing*. The tutorial will also feature a session of hands-on exercises during which participants can guide machines in generating ideas and automatically composing key paper elements. Furthermore, we will address current challenges, explore future directions, and discuss potential ethical issues. A toolkit designed for human-computer collaboration throughout the paper lifecycle will also be made publically available. The tutorial materials are online at https://sites.google.com/view/coling2024-paper-lifecycle/.

Keywords: Paper Lifecycle Assistant, LLM, Human-Computer Collaboration

1. Introduction

Scientists are experiencing information overload (Landhuis, 2016) due to the rapid growth of scientific literature. From March 13, 2020, to June 2, 2022, during the COVID-19 pandemic, more than a million articles related to the coronavirus were published (Wang et al., 2020a). However, scientists peruse only about 300 papers annually (Van Noorden, 2014). Simply put, when writing new articles, scientists cannot review all related papers. Beyond this, another major obstacle is the quality of the papers. While many research articles, especially preprints, provide new perspectives for researchers, they also duplicate findings, spread misinformation, and show disagreements among themselves (Wang et al., 2021b). This can cause a seemingly paradoxical increase of misinformation in scientific dissemination as the number of papers increases (Casigliani et al., 2020). Finally, field-specific language can be a barrier to scientific communication (Han et al., 2018; Lucy et al., 2023). For example, Glasziou et al. (2020) shows that collaboration and communication for research were extremely limited during the early stage of COVID-19, causing massive waste in research.

To address these pressing issues, researchers are developing AI methods to mitigate distorted scientific dissemination, generate new research directions, and ultimately draft papers. The recent dramatic advances in large language models raise the tantalizing prospect that such a capability is within reach. For example, researchers have tested ChatGPT (OpenAI, 2023) in writing essays (Stokel-Walker, 2022), research papers (Conroy, 2023c), or even grant applications (Park, 2023). According to a Nature postdoc survey (Nordling, 2023), 31% of respondents use AI chatbots in their work. Despite such popularity, fundamental challenges remain for this vision to materialize. Even with the assistance of search engines, LLMs sometimes generate fake references with incorrect metadata or cite papers that do not exist (Conroy, 2023b). Additionally, LLMs tend to generate papers with extensive plagiarism (Anderson et al., 2023) and inaccurate results (Hosseini et al., 2023).

To address those challenges, we will explore the following questions in this tutorial:

- Why do we care about AI-assisted literature review?
- How can humans leverage computers to evaluate the quality of scientific papers?
- How can AI facilitate new scientific ideas?
- How can we address the ethical issue of large language models in the paper lifecycle?

Specifically, we will offer a comprehensive introduction to recent techniques for a series of tasks involved in the paper lifecycle. To begin with, we will divide the paper lifecycle into four parts: the scientific literature review, hypothesis generation and experiments, paper drafting, and paper evaluation. Furthermore, we will engage the audience

LREC-COLING 2024 Tutorials, pages 56–67

in a hands-on Google Colab project to write and evaluate a new paper draft assisted by LLMs. We will also concurrently discuss ethical concerns in the field throughout the tutorial and include a specific section for ethical concerns. Finally, we will discuss the remaining challenges and future directions for the AI-assisted scientific paper lifecycle. We will construct a toolkit and related papers for the AI-assisted scientific paper lifecycle on GitHub.

2. Target Audience

The tutorial will be accessible to all NLP researchers who wish to develop NLP methods for the scientific paper lifecycle. While no specific background knowledge is required, having a basic understanding of pretrained language models, graph neural networks, and other basic deep learning technologies would be helpful. We expect around **50** to **100** participants based on the popularity.

3. Outline – The Paper Lifecycle [210]

3.1. Background and Motivation [15]

We will begin the tutorial with a comprehensive overview of the scientific paper lifecycle by showcasing various applications in accelerating scientific discovery (Gil, 2022; Birhane et al., 2023), including scientific literature review, scientific hypothesis generation, experiment development, paper draft generation, and draft evaluation. Specifically, we will focus on the recent trend of applying LLMs in academic writing, briefly discussing the benefits and potential ethical concerns of this approach.

3.2. Scientific Literature Review [40]

Scientific Knowledge Base Construction [20] We will introduce scientific LLMs, which usually focus on domain-adaptive pre-training (Phan et al., 2021; Scao et al., 2022; Hong et al., 2023). Working with these general model architectures as tools, we will describe why knowledge graphs are still necessary in the LLM era by providing cases where LLMs fail due to a lack of structured knowledge. Then, we will focus on how various scientific information extraction (IE) tasks are formulated (Hou et al., 2019; Cohan et al., 2019; Jain et al., 2020; Cattan et al., 2021; Panapitiya et al., 2021; Shen et al., 2022; Song et al., 2023). Finally, we will discuss how researchers can improve the knowledge base quality and utilize those tools to enhance the paper reading experience (Fok et al., 2023).

Retrieving Relevant Information [20] Given the exponential growth of papers and the language barrier between different disciplines, scientists need effective ways to retrieve relevant papers. Specifically, we will provide real-world examples of information retrieval (IR) in the Covid-19 (Wang et al., 2020a). Then, we will comprehensively introduce the tasks in scientific information retrieval. Further, we will cover existing methods and applications of scientific information retrieval by categorizing them into four major types, including scientific paper retrieval (Hongwimol et al., 2021), paper relationship discovery (Luu et al., 2021), scientific evidence extraction (Li et al., 2021), and scientific dataset recommendation (Viswanathan et al., 2023). Finally, we will discuss how information retrieval can be used for downstream tasks related to the paper lifecycle, including scientific idea discovery (Hope et al., 2020), and scientific fact-checking (Wang et al., 2023). We will also discuss the potential risks of incorrect information retrieval results.

3.3. Hypothesis Generation and Experiments [25]

Generating Research Directions [20] Since we have built the knowledge base and retrieved relevant papers based on certain topics, we will then present automatic scientific hypotheses generation, the goal of which is to suggest potential research directions for researchers. We will start by showing drug repurposing for COVID-19 as a real-world application of scientific hypothesis generation (Hope et al., 2020; Zhang et al., 2021a; Wang et al., 2021b). We will then give an overview of literature-based research direction discovery (Henry and McInnes, 2017; Hope et al., 2023). After that, we will show how to effectively utilize existing literature and a knowledge base to discover new scientific directions (Wang et al., 2019; Krenn et al., 2023). Lastly, we will discuss the ethical considerations for scientific hypothesis discovery, including usage requirements, potential risks, and system performance limitations.

LLMs as Experimental Agents [5] In this paragraph, we will discuss several real-world applications of using LLMs for experimental agents, including experimental planning and scientific reasoning techniques. By integrating external knowledge bases and domain-specific tools, LLMs can help experts by formulating synthesis procedures (Bran et al., 2023), editing drugs (Liu et al., 2023), analyzing prediction results (Kumar et al., 2023), or even automating experiments (Wierenga et al., 2023). Currently, this direction remains highly exploratory.

3.4. Hands-on Paper Draft Assistant [50]

We will lead a hands-on exercise session using Google Colab, an important component of our tutorial. We will start by providing attendees with a group of seed terms as starting topics and their background knowledge (i.e., background sentences, knowledge graphs, and citation networks). The goal of this practice is first to generate new research ideas about these seed terms and finally to generate key elements of a paper, including a title, an abstract, and a related work section for these topics. Every attendee will initially brainstorm the most effective strategies to generate new hypotheses from the given input. They will later design a pipeline to write key elements of the paper, given the generated hypotheses and background knowledge. We will also ask participants to evaluate the generation quality from multiple perspectives including automatic and human evaluation.

Because writing code from scratch is time-consuming, we will let participants choose from pre-installed state-of-the-art hypotheses and paper generation frameworks. We will also provide them with prepaid accounts and corresponding datasets. By the end of this session, audiences will understand how to build systems for hypothesis generation and paper writing, be familiar with methods prevalent in the realm of automatic scientific paper writing, and know evaluation methods for paper generation. We will release a toolkit on GitHub.

3.5. Drafting a Paper [20]

In this part, we will divide the process of scientific paper writing into several components. We will first review available related work generation frameworks which utilize pretrained language models and graph neural networks (Lu et al., 2020; Ge et al., 2021). Next, we will dive into a more challenging aspect of paper writing: generating paper abstracts based on titles and knowledge graphs (Koncel-Kedziorski et al., 2019; Wang et al., 2019). We will also explore the generation of other paper components, including claim generation (Wright et al., 2022), definition generation (August et al., 2022), table captioning (Chen et al., 2021), and figure captioning (Hsu et al., 2021). Lastly, we will discuss human-AI collaborative writing (Lee et al., 2022).

3.6. Paper Review and Ethics (45)

Automatic Scientific Reviewing [15] An important step in the process of scientific writing is evaluating paper quality to prevent distorted scientific dissemination. Due to the rapid growth in the number of paper submissions, the quality of peer reviews has become a widely discussed topic, as shown in Section 5.3 of Rogers et al. (2023). Therefore, we will present an automatic scientific review assistant to alleviate this issue. We will first demonstrate current progress in automatic scientific review (Yuan et al., 2022). We will then divide the scientific review process into two tasks: peer-review score prediction (Kang et al., 2018) and review comment generation (Wang et al., 2020b). We will also focus on knowledge-guided review score prediction and review comment generation (Yuan and Liu, 2022). Finally, we will discuss automatic peer review in the era of LLMs (Liu and Shah, 2023; Zeng et al., 2023), which includes error detection, checklist verification, paper recommendation, and corpus comparison (Zhong et al., 2023).

Scientific Fact-Checking [15] We will start this section by introducing the danger of misinformation in scientific publications during the COVID-19 pandemic (Nelson et al., 2020). Additionally, language models tend to generate non-factual content (Maynez et al., 2020). We will also outline the importance of scientific fact-checking and highlight its difference from general fact-checking. Then, we will cover current scientific fact-checking datasets (Wadden et al., 2020; Sarrouti et al., 2021) and potential approaches (Zhang et al., 2021b; Yu et al., 2022) for this task. Finally, we will focus on the existing papers on human-centered fact-checking (Glockner et al., 2022; Juneja and Mitra, 2022) and try to adapt them to the scientific domain.

Ethics Concerns in the LLM Era [15] We will recap the increasing trend of using LLMs in academic writing. We will discuss the benefits of LLMs for scholarly publishing, including performing straightforward but time-consuming tasks (Conroy, 2023c) and improving equity in science (Lund et al., 2023). We will then address its risks and ethical concerns by showing a paper (Ayache and Omand, 2022) generated by GPT3 (Brown et al., 2020) as an example. Based on that paper, we will highlight potential issues, including incorrect reference (Conroy, 2023b), extensive plagiarism (Anderson et al., 2023), accuracy concerns (Hosseini et al., 2023), and equity concerns due to its subscription fee. Further, we will show the current challenges in AI-generated research paper detection (Gao et al., 2023). We will also include potential solutions for detecting AI-generated text (Crothers et al., 2023), such as watermarking LLMs (Kirchenbauer et al., 2023), writing style analysis (Ma et al., 2023).

3.7. Open Questions [15]

At the end of the tutorial, we will first discuss recent exploratory work. We will discuss making scientific ideas more accessible to the general public with text style transfer (Dangovski et al., 2021; Goldsack et al., 2022; Fatima and Strube, 2023). We will conclude the tutorial by presenting the remaining challenges and future directions, including 1) multimodal analysis of formulas, tables, figures, and citation networks, 2) multimodal scientific hypothesis generation, and 3) automatic verification of the new hypothesis.

4. Diversity Considerations

The methods introduced in this tutorial can help mitigate the language barrier in interdisciplinary science communication. We will cover a broad diversity of methods and applications in different domains. The methods we introduced are mostly domain/language-agnostic. Therefore, they can apply to different domains with various languages. We estimate that only 15-20% of the work will involve one of the four presenters. The papers we discussed in the tutorial are produced by authors from a variety of backgrounds. Our diverse tutorial team represents two universities (UIUC and HUJI) and originates from three geographically distant countries (across China, Israel, and the U.S.). Their seniority varies, ranging from junior/senior Ph.D. students to assistant/full professors, and the team includes a female researcher. Our presenters will promote our tutorial on social media to help diversify our audience participation.

5. Reading List

- Related Tutorials (Jiang and Shang, 2020; Chen et al., 2022; Asai et al., 2023)
- General Guideline (Gil, 2022; Yuan et al., 2022; Birhane et al., 2023; Lund et al., 2023)
- Survey Papers (Li and Ouyang, 2022; Vladika and Matthes, 2023; Hope et al., 2023)
- Scientific IE (Luan et al., 2018; Jain et al., 2020; Shen et al., 2022; Song et al., 2023)
- Scientific IR (Wang et al., 2020c)
- Review Generation (Yuan and Liu, 2022)
- Hypothesis Generation (Krenn et al., 2023)
- Paper Draft Generation(Wang et al., 2021a)

6. Presenters

Qingyun Wang is a Ph.D. student in the Computer Science Department at UIUC. His research lies in controllable knowledge-driven natural language generation, focusing on NLP for scientific discovery. He served as a PC member for multiple conferences including ICML, ACL, ICLR, NeurIPS, etc. He previously entered the finalist of the first Alexa Prize competition. He received the NAACL-HLT 2021 Best Demo Reward. He has experience presenting a tutorial at EMNLP 2021.

Carl Edwards is a Ph.D. student in the Computer Science Department at UIUC. Broadly, he is interested in information extraction, information retrieval, text mining, representation learning, and multimodality. Particularly, he is interested in applying these to the scientific domain to accelerate scientific discovery. His current work focuses on integrating natural language and molecules, especially using multimodal representations.

Heng Ji is a professor at the Computer Science Department of UIUC, and Amazon Scholar. She is a leading expert on multimodal multilingual information extraction. She has coordinated the NIST TAC Knowledge Base Population task since 2010. She has served as the PC Co-Chair of many conferences including NAACL-HLT2018 and AACL-IJCNLP2022 and has presented many tutorials. She is elected as NAACL secretary 2020-2023. Her research interests broadly cover information extraction and NLP for Science, particularly in leveraging NLP for drug discovery.

Tom Hope is an assistant professor at the School of Computer Science and Engineering of HUJI, and a research scientist at AI2. He develops artificial intelligence methods that augment and scale scientific knowledge discovery by harnessing vast repositories of scientific knowledge. His work has received four best paper awards, appeared in top venues, and received coverage from Nature and Science. He was awarded the 2022 Azrieli Early Career Faculty Fellowship, and was a member of the KDD 2020 Best Paper Selection Committee.

7. Other Tutorial Information

All tutorial materials are publicly available at `https://sites.google.com/view/coling2024-paper-lifecycle/`.

8. Ethics Statement

The methods we introduce in the tutorial aim to provide investigative leads for a scientific domain. The final results are not intended to be used without human review. We emphasize that the tools introduced in tutorials are designed to assist human scientists. The identified research directions and the process should be evaluated by trained researchers to ensure ethical outcomes. Because many methods are built on top of pretrained large language models, those systems may exhibit bias due to their pretraining dataset. This tutorial also provides opportunities to discuss the ethical considerations when designing and using those methods and provides a specific section to discuss ethical considerations related to LLMs. Most training sets for these methods are written in English, which might alienate readers historically underrepresented in the NLP domain.

Acknowledgements

This work is supported by the Molecule Maker Lab Institute: an AI research institute program supported by NSF under award No. 2019897, by DOE Center for Advanced Bioenergy and Bioproducts Innovation U.S. Department of Energy, Office of Science, Office of Biological and Environmental Research under Award Number DESC0018420, by U.S. the AI Research Institutes program by National Science Foundation and the Institute of Education Sciences, Department of Education through Award No. 2229873 - AI Institute for Transforming Education for Children with Speech and Language Processing Challenges, and by AI Agriculture: the Agriculture and Food Research Initiative (AFRI) grant no. 2020-67021- 32799/project accession no.1024178 from the USDA National Institute of Food and Agriculture. The views and conclusions contained herein are those of the authors and should not be interpreted as necessarily representing the official policies, either expressed or implied of, the National Science Foundation, the U.S. Department of Energy, and the U.S. Government. The U.S. Government is authorized to reproduce and distribute reprints for governmental purposes notwithstanding any copyright annotation therein.

9. Bibliographical References

2023. Overcoming the language barrier in science communication. *Nature Reviews Bioengineering*, 1(5):305–305.

Alfred V. Aho and Jeffrey D. Ullman. 1972. *The Theory of Parsing, Translation and Compiling*, volume 1. Prentice-Hall, Englewood Cliffs, NJ.

American Psychological Association. 1983. *Publications Manual*. American Psychological Association, Washington, DC.

Nash Anderson, Daniel L Belavy, Stephen M Perle, Sharief Hendricks, Luiz Hespanhol, Evert Verhagen, and Aamir R Memon. 2023. Ai did not write this manuscript, or did it? can we trick the ai text detector into generated texts? the potential future of chatgpt and ai in sports & exercise medicine manuscript generation.

Rie Kubota Ando and Tong Zhang. 2005. A framework for learning predictive structures from multiple tasks and unlabeled data. *Journal of Machine Learning Research*, 6:1817–1853.

Galen Andrew and Jianfeng Gao. 2007. Scalable training of L1-regularized log-linear models. In *Proceedings of the 24th International Conference on Machine Learning*, pages 33–40.

Akari Asai, Sewon Min, Zexuan Zhong, and Danqi Chen. 2023. Retrieval-based language models and applications. In *Proceedings of the 61st Annual Meeting of the Association for Computational Linguistics (Volume 6: Tutorial Abstracts)*, pages 41–46, Toronto, Canada. Association for Computational Linguistics.

Tal August, Katharina Reinecke, and Noah A. Smith. 2022. Generating scientific definitions with controllable complexity. In *Proceedings of the 60th Annual Meeting of the Association for Computational Linguistics (Volume 1: Long Papers)*, pages 8298–8317, Dublin, Ireland. Association for Computational Linguistics.

Eliot H Ayache and Conor Omand. 2022. Generating scientific articles with machine learning. *Machine Learning Repository*, arXiv:2203.16569.

Abeba Birhane, Atoosa Kasirzadeh, David Leslie, and Sandra Wachter. 2023. Science in the age of large language models. *Nature Reviews Physics*, 5(5):277–280.

Daniil A Boiko, Robert MacKnight, and Gabe Gomes. 2023. Emergent autonomous scientific research capabilities of large language models. *Chemical Physics Repository*, arXiv:2304.05332.

Andres M Bran, Sam Cox, Andrew D White, and Philippe Schwaller. 2023. Chemcrow: Augmenting large-language models with chemistry tools. *Chemical Physics Repository*, arXiv:2304.05376.

Tom Brown, Benjamin Mann, Nick Ryder, Melanie Subbiah, Jared D Kaplan, Prafulla Dhariwal, Arvind Neelakantan, Pranav Shyam, Girish Sastry, Amanda Askell, Sandhini Agarwal, Ariel Herbert-Voss, Gretchen Krueger, Tom Henighan, Rewon Child, Aditya Ramesh, Daniel Ziegler, Jeffrey Wu, Clemens Winter, Chris Hesse, Mark Chen, Eric Sigler, Mateusz Litwin, Scott Gray, Benjamin Chess, Jack Clark, Christopher Berner, Sam McCandlish, Alec Radford, Ilya Sutskever, and Dario Amodei. 2020. Language models are few-shot learners. In *Advances in Neural Information Processing Systems*, volume 33, pages 1877–1901. Curran Associates, Inc.

Isabel Cachola, Kyle Lo, Arman Cohan, and Daniel Weld. 2020. TLDR: Extreme summarization of scientific documents. In *Findings of the Association for Computational Linguistics: EMNLP 2020*, pages 4766–4777, Online. Association for Computational Linguistics.

Virginia Casigliani, Francesca De Nard, Erica De Vita, Guglielmo Arzilli, Francesca Maria Grosso, Filippo Quattrone, Lara Tavoschi, and Pierluigi Lopalco. 2020. Too much information, too little evidence: is waste in research fuelling the covid-19 infodemic? *BMJ*, 370.

Arie Cattan, Sophie Johnson, Daniel S Weld, Ido Dagan, Iz Beltagy, Doug Downey, and Tom Hope. 2021. Scico: Hierarchical cross-document coreference for scientific concepts. In *3rd Conference on Automated Knowledge Base Construction*.

Ashok K. Chandra, Dexter C. Kozen, and Larry J. Stockmeyer. 1981. Alternation. *Journal of the Association for Computing Machinery*, 28(1):114–133.

Hong Chen, Hiroya Takamura, and Hideki Nakayama. 2021. SciXGen: A scientific paper dataset for context-aware text generation. In *Findings of the Association for Computational Linguistics: EMNLP 2021*, pages 1483–1492, Punta Cana, Dominican Republic. Association for Computational Linguistics.

Muhao Chen, Lifu Huang, Manling Li, Ben Zhou, Heng Ji, and Dan Roth. 2022. New frontiers of information extraction. In *Proceedings of the 2022 Conference of the North American Chapter of the Association for Computational Linguistics: Human Language Technologies: Tutorial Abstracts*, pages 14–25, Seattle, United States. Association for Computational Linguistics.

Dimitrios Christofidellis, Giorgio Giannone, Jannis Born, Ole Winther, Teodoro Laino, and Matteo Manica. 2023. Unifying molecular and textual representations via multi-task language modelling. In *International Conference on Machine Learning, ICML 2023, 23-29 July 2023, Honolulu, Hawaii, USA*, volume 202 of *Proceedings of Machine Learning Research*, pages 6140–6157. PMLR.

Arman Cohan, Iz Beltagy, Daniel King, Bhavana Dalvi, and Dan Weld. 2019. Pretrained language models for sequential sentence classification. In *Proceedings of the 2019 Conference on Empirical Methods in Natural Language Processing and the 9th International Joint Conference on Natural Language Processing (EMNLP-IJCNLP)*, pages 3693–3699, Hong Kong, China. Association for Computational Linguistics.

Gemma Conroy. 2023a. How chatgpt and other ai tools could disrupt scientific publishing. *Nature*, 622(7982):234–236.

Gemma Conroy. 2023b. Scientific sleuths spot dishonest chatgpt use in papers. *Nature*.

Gemma Conroy. 2023c. Scientists used chatgpt to generate an entire paper from scratch—but is it any good? *Nature*, 619(7970):443–444.

Evan N. Crothers, Nathalie Japkowicz, and Herna L. Viktor. 2023. Machine-generated text: A comprehensive survey of threat models and detection methods. *IEEE Access*, 11:70977–71002.

Tamara Czinczoll, Helen Yannakoudakis, Pushkar Mishra, and Ekaterina Shutova. 2022. Scientific and creative analogies in pretrained language models. In *Findings of the Association for Computational Linguistics: EMNLP 2022*, pages 2094–2100, Abu Dhabi, United Arab Emirates. Association for Computational Linguistics.

Rumen Dangovski, Michelle Shen, Dawson Byrd, Li Jing, Desislava Tsvetkova, Preslav Nakov, and Marin Soljačić. 2021. We can explain your research in layman's terms: Towards automating science journalism at scale. In *Proceedings of the AAAI Conference on Artificial Intelligence*, volume 35, pages 12728–12737.

Luigi De Angelis, Francesco Baglivo, Guglielmo Arzilli, Gaetano Pierpaolo Privitera, Paolo Ferragina, Alberto Eugenio Tozzi, and Caterina Rizzo. 2023. Chatgpt and the rise of large language models: the new ai-driven infodemic threat in public health. *Frontiers in Public Health*, 11:1166120.

Carl Edwards, Tuan Lai, Kevin Ros, Garrett Honke, Kyunghyun Cho, and Heng Ji. 2022. Translation between molecules and natural language. In *Proceedings of the 2022 Conference on Empirical Methods in Natural Language Processing*, pages 375–413, Abu Dhabi, United Arab Emirates. Association for Computational Linguistics.

Mehwish Fatima and Michael Strube. 2023. Cross-lingual science journalism: Select, simplify and rewrite summaries for non-expert readers. In *Proceedings of the 61st Annual Meeting of the Association for Computational Linguistics (Volume 1: Long Papers)*, pages 1843–1861, Toronto, Canada. Association for Computational Linguistics.

Raymond Fok, Hita Kambhamettu, Luca Soldaini, Jonathan Bragg, Kyle Lo, Marti Hearst, Andrew Head, and Daniel S Weld. 2023. Scim: Intelligent skimming support for scientific papers. In *Proceedings of the 28th International Conference on Intelligent User Interfaces*, IUI '23, page 476–490, New York, NY, USA. Association for Computing Machinery.

Jacob G. Foster, Andrey Rzhetsky, and James A. Evans. 2015. Tradition and innovation in scientists' research strategies. *American Sociological Review*.

Giacomo Frisoni, Miki Mizutani, Gianluca Moro, and Lorenzo Valgimigli. 2022. BioReader: a retrieval-enhanced text-to-text transformer for biomedical literature. In *Proceedings of the 2022 Conference on Empirical Methods in Natural Language Processing*, pages 5770–5793, Abu Dhabi, United Arab Emirates. Association for Computational Linguistics.

Catherine A Gao, Frederick M Howard, Nikolay S Markov, Emma C Dyer, Siddhi Ramesh, Yuan Luo, and Alexander T Pearson. 2023. Comparing scientific abstracts generated by chatgpt to real abstracts with detectors and blinded human reviewers. *NPJ Digital Medicine*, 6(1):75.

Yubin Ge, Ly Dinh, Xiaofeng Liu, Jinsong Su, Ziyao Lu, Ante Wang, and Jana Diesner. 2021. BACO: A background knowledge- and content-based framework for citing sentence generation. In *Proceedings of the 59th Annual Meeting of the Association for Computational Linguistics and the 11th International Joint Conference on Natural Language Processing (Volume 1: Long Papers)*, pages 1466–1478, Online. Association for Computational Linguistics.

Yolanda Gil. 2022. Will ai write scientific papers in the future? *AI Magazine*, 42(4):3–15.

Paul P Glasziou, Sharon Sanders, and Tammy Hoffmann. 2020. Waste in covid-19 research. *BMJ*, 369.

Max Glockner, Yufang Hou, and Iryna Gurevych. 2022. Missing counter-evidence renders NLP fact-checking unrealistic for misinformation. In *Proceedings of the 2022 Conference on Empirical Methods in Natural Language Processing*, pages 5916–5936, Abu Dhabi, United Arab Emirates. Association for Computational Linguistics.

Tomas Goldsack, Zhihao Zhang, Chenghua Lin, and Carolina Scarton. 2022. Making science simple: Corpora for the lay summarisation of scientific literature. In *Proceedings of the 2022 Conference on Empirical Methods in Natural Language Processing*, pages 10589–10604, Abu Dhabi, United Arab Emirates. Association for Computational Linguistics.

Dan Gusfield. 1997. *Algorithms on Strings, Trees and Sequences*. Cambridge University Press, Cambridge, UK.

Chi Han, Qifan Wang, Wenhan Xiong, Yu Chen, Heng Ji, and Sinong Wang. 2023. Lm-infinite: Simple on-the-fly length generalization for large language models. *Machine Learning Repository*, arXiv:2308.16137.

Paul KJ Han, Brian J Zikmund-Fisher, Christine W Duarte, Megan Knaus, Adam Black, Aaron M Scherer, and Angela Fagerlin. 2018. Communication of scientific uncertainty about a novel pandemic health threat: ambiguity aversion and its mechanisms. *Journal of health communication*, 23(5):435–444.

Sam Henry and Bridget T McInnes. 2017. Literature based discovery: models, methods, and trends. *Journal of biomedical informatics*, 74:20–32.

Zhi Hong, Aswathy Ajith, James Pauloski, Eamon Duede, Kyle Chard, and Ian Foster. 2023. The diminishing returns of masked language models to science. In *Findings of the Association for Computational Linguistics: ACL 2023*, pages 1270–1283, Toronto, Canada. Association for Computational Linguistics.

Pollawat Hongwimol, Peeranuth Kehasukcharoen, Pasit Laohawarutchai, Piyawat Lertvittayakumjorn, Aik Beng Ng, Zhangsheng Lai, Timothy Liu, and Peerapon Vateekul. 2021. ESRA: Explainable scientific research assistant. In *Proceedings of the 59th Annual Meeting of the Association for Computational Linguistics and the 11th International Joint Conference on Natural Language Processing: System Demonstrations*, pages 114–121, Online. Association for Computational Linguistics.

Tom Hope, Doug Downey, Daniel S Weld, Oren Etzioni, and Eric Horvitz. 2023. A computational inflection for scientific discovery. *Communications of the ACM*, 66(8):62–73.

Tom Hope, Jason Portenoy, Kishore Vasan, Jonathan Borchardt, Eric Horvitz, Daniel Weld, Marti Hearst, and Jevin West. 2020. SciSight: Combining faceted navigation and research group detection for COVID-19 exploratory scientific search. In *Proceedings of the 2020 Conference on Empirical Methods in Natural Language Processing: System Demonstrations*, pages 135–143, Online. Association for Computational Linguistics.

Mohammad Hosseini, Lisa M Rasmussen, and David B Resnik. 2023. Using ai to write scholarly publications.

Yufang Hou, Charles Jochim, Martin Gleize, Francesca Bonin, and Debasis Ganguly. 2019. Identification of tasks, datasets, evaluation metrics, and numeric scores for scientific leaderboards construction. In *Proceedings of the 57th Annual Meeting of the Association for Computational Linguistics*, pages 5203–5213, Florence, Italy. Association for Computational Linguistics.

Ting-Yao Hsu, C Lee Giles, and Ting-Hao Huang. 2021. SciCap: Generating captions for scientific figures. In *Findings of the Association for*

Computational Linguistics: EMNLP 2021*, pages 3258–3264, Punta Cana, Dominican Republic. Association for Computational Linguistics.

Yue Hu and Xiaojun Wan. 2014. Automatic generation of related work sections in scientific papers: An optimization approach. In *Proceedings of the 2014 Conference on Empirical Methods in Natural Language Processing (EMNLP)*, pages 1624–1633, Doha, Qatar. Association for Computational Linguistics.

Sarthak Jain, Madeleine van Zuylen, Hannaneh Hajishirzi, and Iz Beltagy. 2020. SciREX: A challenge dataset for document-level information extraction. In *Proceedings of the 58th Annual Meeting of the Association for Computational Linguistics*, pages 7506–7516, Online. Association for Computational Linguistics.

Meng Jiang and Jingbo Shang. 2020. Scientific text mining and knowledge graphs. In *Proceedings of the 26th ACM SIGKDD International Conference on Knowledge Discovery & Data Mining*, KDD '20, page 3537–3538, New York, NY, USA. Association for Computing Machinery.

Prerna Juneja and Tanushree Mitra. 2022. Human and technological infrastructures of fact-checking. *Proc. ACM Hum.-Comput. Interact.*, 6(CSCW2).

David Jurgens, Srijan Kumar, Raine Hoover, Dan McFarland, and Dan Jurafsky. 2018. Measuring the evolution of a scientific field through citation frames. *Transactions of the Association for Computational Linguistics*, 6:391–406.

Dongyeop Kang, Waleed Ammar, Bhavana Dalvi, Madeleine van Zuylen, Sebastian Kohlmeier, Eduard Hovy, and Roy Schwartz. 2018. A dataset of peer reviews (PeerRead): Collection, insights and NLP applications. In *Proceedings of the 2018 Conference of the North American Chapter of the Association for Computational Linguistics: Human Language Technologies, Volume 1 (Long Papers)*, pages 1647–1661, New Orleans, Louisiana. Association for Computational Linguistics.

John Kirchenbauer, Jonas Geiping, Yuxin Wen, Jonathan Katz, Ian Miers, and Tom Goldstein. 2023. A watermark for large language models. In *Proceedings of the 40th International Conference on Machine Learning*, volume 202 of *Proceedings of Machine Learning Research*, pages 17061–17084. PMLR.

Rik Koncel-Kedziorski, Dhanush Bekal, Yi Luan, Mirella Lapata, and Hannaneh Hajishirzi. 2019. Text Generation from Knowledge Graphs with Graph Transformers. In *Proceedings of the 2019 Conference of the North American Chapter of the Association for Computational Linguistics: Human Language Technologies, Volume 1 (Long and Short Papers)*, pages 2284–2293, Minneapolis, Minnesota. Association for Computational Linguistics.

Mario Krenn, Lorenzo Buffoni, Bruno Coutinho, Sagi Eppel, Jacob Gates Foster, Andrew Gritsevskiy, Harlin Lee, Yichao Lu, João P. Moutinho, Nima Sanjabi, Rishi Sonthalia, Ngoc Mai Tran, Francisco Valente, Yangxinyu Xie, Rose Yu, and Michael Kopp. 2023. Forecasting the future of artificial intelligence with machine learning-based link prediction in an exponentially growing knowledge network. *Nature Machine Intelligence*.

Varun Kumar, Leonard Gleyzer, Adar Kahana, Khemraj Shukla, and George Em Karniadakis. 2023. Mycrunchgpt: A chatgpt assisted framework for scientific machine learning. *Machine Learning Repository*, arXiv:2306.15551.

Esther Landhuis. 2016. Scientific literature: Information overload. *Nature*, 535(7612):457–458.

Mina Lee, Percy Liang, and Qian Yang. 2022. Coauthor: Designing a human-ai collaborative writing dataset for exploring language model capabilities. In *Proceedings of the 2022 CHI Conference on Human Factors in Computing Systems*, CHI '22, New York, NY, USA. Association for Computing Machinery.

Xiangci Li, Gully Burns, and Nanyun Peng. 2021. Scientific discourse tagging for evidence extraction. In *Proceedings of the 16th Conference of the European Chapter of the Association for Computational Linguistics: Main Volume*, pages 2550–2562, Online. Association for Computational Linguistics.

Xiangci Li and Jessica Ouyang. 2022. Automatic related work generation: A meta study. *Computation and Language Repository*, arXiv:2201.01880.

Ryan Liu and Nihar B Shah. 2023. Reviewergpt? an exploratory study on using large language models for paper reviewing. *Computation and Language Repository*, arXiv:2306.00622.

Shengchao Liu, Jiongxiao Wang, Yijin Yang, Chengpeng Wang, Ling Liu, Hongyu Guo, and Chaowei Xiao. 2023. Chatgpt-powered conversational drug editing using retrieval and domain feedback. *Chemical Physics Repository*, arXiv:2305.18090.

Kyle Lo, Lucy Lu Wang, Mark Neumann, Rodney Kinney, and Daniel Weld. 2020. S2ORC: The semantic scholar open research corpus. In *Proceedings of the 58th Annual Meeting of the Association for Computational Linguistics*, pages 4969–4983, Online. Association for Computational Linguistics.

Yao Lu, Yue Dong, and Laurent Charlin. 2020. Multi-XScience: A large-scale dataset for extreme multi-document summarization of scientific articles. In *Proceedings of the 2020 Conference on Empirical Methods in Natural Language Processing (EMNLP)*, pages 8068–8074, Online. Association for Computational Linguistics.

Yi Luan, Luheng He, Mari Ostendorf, and Hannaneh Hajishirzi. 2018. Multi-task identification of entities, relations, and coreference for scientific knowledge graph construction. In *Proceedings of the 2018 Conference on Empirical Methods in Natural Language Processing*, pages 3219–3232, Brussels, Belgium. Association for Computational Linguistics.

Li Lucy, Jesse Dodge, David Bamman, and Katherine Keith. 2023. Words as gatekeepers: Measuring discipline-specific terms and meanings in scholarly publications. In *Findings of the Association for Computational Linguistics: ACL 2023*, pages 6929–6947, Toronto, Canada. Association for Computational Linguistics.

Brady D Lund, Ting Wang, Nishith Reddy Mannuru, Bing Nie, Somipam Shimray, and Ziang Wang. 2023. Chatgpt and a new academic reality: Artificial intelligence-written research papers and the ethics of the large language models in scholarly publishing. *Journal of the Association for Information Science and Technology*, 74(5):570–581.

Kelvin Luu, Xinyi Wu, Rik Koncel-Kedziorski, Kyle Lo, Isabel Cachola, and Noah A. Smith. 2021. Explaining relationships between scientific documents. In *Proceedings of the 59th Annual Meeting of the Association for Computational Linguistics and the 11th International Joint Conference on Natural Language Processing (Volume 1: Long Papers)*, pages 2130–2144, Online. Association for Computational Linguistics.

Yongqiang Ma, Jiawei Liu, Fan Yi, Qikai Cheng, Yong Huang, Wei Lu, and Xiaozhong Liu. 2023. Ai vs. human–differentiation analysis of scientific content generation. *Computation and Language Repository*, arXiv:2301.10416.

Joshua Maynez, Shashi Narayan, Bernd Bohnet, and Ryan McDonald. 2020. On faithfulness and factuality in abstractive summarization. In *Proceedings of the 58th Annual Meeting of the Association for Computational Linguistics*, pages 1906–1919, Online. Association for Computational Linguistics.

Taylor Nelson, Nicole Kagan, Claire Critchlow, Alan Hillard, and Albert Hsu. 2020. The danger of misinformation in the covid-19 crisis. *Missouri Medicine*, 117(6):510.

Linda Nordling. 2023. How chatgpt is transforming the postdoc experience. *Nature*, 622:655 – 657.

OpenAI. 2023. Gpt-4 technical report. *ArXiv*, abs/2303.08774.

Gihan Panapitiya, Fred Parks, Jonathan Sepulveda, and Emily Saldanha. 2021. Extracting material property measurement data from scientific articles. In *Proceedings of the 2021 Conference on Empirical Methods in Natural Language Processing*, pages 5393–5402, Online and Punta Cana, Dominican Republic. Association for Computational Linguistics.

Joo-Young Park. 2023. Could chatgpt help you to write your next scientific paper?: concerns on research ethics related to usage of artificial intelligence tools. *Journal of the Korean Association of Oral and Maxillofacial Surgeons*, 49(3):105–106.

Juan Manuel Parrilla. 2023. Chatgpt use shows that the grant-application system is broken. *Nature*.

Long N Phan, James T Anibal, Hieu Tran, Shaurya Chanana, Erol Bahadroglu, Alec Peltekian, and Grégoire Altan-Bonnet. 2021. Scifive: a text-to-text transformer model for biomedical literature. *Computation and Language Repository*, arXiv:2106.03598.

Mohammad Sadegh Rasooli and Joel R. Tetreault. 2015. Yara parser: A fast and accurate dependency parser. *Computing Research Repository*, arXiv:1503.06733. Version 2.

Anna Rogers, Marzena Karpinska, Jordan Boyd-Graber, and Naoaki Okazaki. 2023. Program chairs' report on peer review at acl 2023. In *Proceedings of the 61st Annual Meeting of the Association for Computational Linguistics (Volume 1: Long Papers)*, pages xl–lxxv, Toronto, Canada. Association for Computational Linguistics.

Frank Rosenblatt. 1958. The perceptron: a probabilistic model for information storage and organization in the brain. *Psychological review*, 65(6):386.

Mobashir Sadat and Cornelia Caragea. 2022. SciNLI: A corpus for natural language inference on scientific text. In *Proceedings of the 60th Annual Meeting of the Association for Computational Linguistics (Volume 1: Long Papers)*, pages 7399–7409, Dublin, Ireland. Association for Computational Linguistics.

Mourad Sarrouti, Asma Ben Abacha, Yassine Mrabet, and Dina Demner-Fushman. 2021. Evidence-based fact-checking of health-related claims. In *Findings of the Association for Computational Linguistics: EMNLP 2021*, pages 3499–3512, Punta Cana, Dominican Republic. Association for Computational Linguistics.

Teven Le Scao, Angela Fan, Christopher Akiki, Ellie Pavlick, Suzana Ilić, Daniel Hesslow, Roman Castagné, Alexandra Sasha Luccioni, François Yvon, Matthias Gallé, et al. 2022. Bloom: A 176b-parameter open-access multilingual language model. *Computation and Language Repository*, arXiv:2211.05100.

Zejiang Shen, Kyle Lo, Lucy Lu Wang, Bailey Kuehl, Daniel S. Weld, and Doug Downey. 2022. VILA: Improving structured content extraction from scientific PDFs using visual layout groups. *Transactions of the Association for Computational Linguistics*, 10:376–392.

Yu Song, Santiago Miret, and Bang Liu. 2023. MatSci-NLP: Evaluating scientific language models on materials science language tasks using text-to-schema modeling. In *Proceedings of the 61st Annual Meeting of the Association for Computational Linguistics (Volume 1: Long Papers)*, pages 3621–3639, Toronto, Canada. Association for Computational Linguistics.

C Stokel-Walker. 2022. Ai bot chatgpt writes smart essays—should professors worry?[published online ahead of print december 9, 2022]. *Nature News*.

Chris Stokel-Walker. 2023. Chatgpt listed as author on research papers: many scientists disapprove. *Nature*, 613(7945):620–621.

Ross Taylor, Marcin Kardas, Guillem Cucurull, Thomas Scialom, Anthony Hartshorn, Elvis Saravia, Andrew Poulton, Viktor Kerkez, and Robert Stojnic. 2022. Galactica: A large language model for science. *Computation and Language Repository*, arXiv:2211.09085.

Ana Sabina Uban, Cornelia Caragea, and Liviu P. Dinu. 2021. Studying the evolution of scientific topics and their relationships. In *Findings of the Association for Computational Linguistics: ACL-IJCNLP 2021*, pages 1908–1922, Online. Association for Computational Linguistics.

Richard Van Noorden. 2014. Scientists may be reaching a peak in reading habits. *Nature*.

Ashish Vaswani, Noam Shazeer, Niki Parmar, Jakob Uszkoreit, Llion Jones, Aidan N Gomez, Ł ukasz Kaiser, and Illia Polosukhin. 2017. Attention is all you need. In *Advances in Neural Information Processing Systems (Neruips)*. Curran Associates, Inc.

Vijay Viswanathan, Luyu Gao, Tongshuang Wu, Pengfei Liu, and Graham Neubig. 2023. DataFinder: Scientific dataset recommendation from natural language descriptions. In *Proceedings of the 61st Annual Meeting of the Association for Computational Linguistics (Volume 1: Long Papers)*, pages 10288–10303, Toronto, Canada. Association for Computational Linguistics.

Vijay Viswanathan, Graham Neubig, and Pengfei Liu. 2021. CitationIE: Leveraging the citation graph for scientific information extraction. In *Proceedings of the 59th Annual Meeting of the Association for Computational Linguistics and the 11th International Joint Conference on Natural Language Processing (Volume 1: Long Papers)*, pages 719–731, Online. Association for Computational Linguistics.

Juraj Vladika and Florian Matthes. 2023. Scientific fact-checking: A survey of resources and approaches. In *Findings of the Association for Computational Linguistics: ACL 2023*, pages 6215–6230, Toronto, Canada. Association for Computational Linguistics.

David Wadden, Shanchuan Lin, Kyle Lo, Lucy Lu Wang, Madeleine van Zuylen, Arman Cohan, and Hannaneh Hajishirzi. 2020. Fact or fiction: Verifying scientific claims. In *Proceedings of the 2020 Conference on Empirical Methods in Natural Language Processing (EMNLP)*, pages 7534–7550, Online. Association for Computational Linguistics.

David Wadden, Kyle Lo, Bailey Kuehl, Arman Cohan, Iz Beltagy, Lucy Lu Wang, and Hannaneh Hajishirzi. 2022. SciFact-open: Towards open-domain scientific claim verification. In *Findings of the Association for Computational Linguistics: EMNLP 2022*, pages 4719–4734, Abu Dhabi, United Arab Emirates. Association for Computational Linguistics.

Gengyu Wang, Kate Harwood, Lawrence Chillrud, Amith Ananthram, Melanie Subbiah, and Kathleen McKeown. 2023. Check-COVID: Fact-checking COVID-19 news claims with scientific evidence. In *Findings of the Association for Computational Linguistics: ACL 2023*, pages 14114–14127, Toronto, Canada. Association for Computational Linguistics.

Lucy Lu Wang, Kyle Lo, Yoganand Chandrasekhar, Russell Reas, Jiangjiang Yang, Doug Burdick, Darrin Eide, Kathryn Funk, Yannis Katsis, Rodney Michael Kinney, Yunyao Li, Ziyang Liu,

William Merrill, Paul Mooney, Dewey A. Murdick, Devvret Rishi, Jerry Sheehan, Zhihong Shen, Brandon Stilson, Alex D. Wade, Kuansan Wang, Nancy Xin Ru Wang, Christopher Wilhelm, Boya Xie, Douglas M. Raymond, Daniel S. Weld, Oren Etzioni, and Sebastian Kohlmeier. 2020a. CORD-19: The COVID-19 open research dataset. In *Proceedings of the 1st Workshop on NLP for COVID-19 at ACL 2020*, Online. Association for Computational Linguistics.

Qingqin Wang, Yun Xiong, Yao Zhang, Jiawei Zhang, and Yangyong Zhu. 2021a. Autocite: Multi-modal representation fusion for contextual citation generation. In *Proceedings of the 14th ACM International Conference on Web Search and Data Mining*, WSDM '21, page 788–796, New York, NY, USA. Association for Computing Machinery.

Qingyun Wang, Lifu Huang, Zhiying Jiang, Kevin Knight, Heng Ji, Mohit Bansal, and Yi Luan. 2019. PaperRobot: Incremental draft generation of scientific ideas. In *Proceedings of the 57th Annual Meeting of the Association for Computational Linguistics*, pages 1980–1991, Florence, Italy. Association for Computational Linguistics.

Qingyun Wang, Manling Li, Xuan Wang, Nikolaus Parulian, Guangxing Han, Jiawei Ma, Jingxuan Tu, Ying Lin, Ranran Haoran Zhang, Weili Liu, Aabhas Chauhan, Yingjun Guan, Bangzheng Li, Ruisong Li, Xiangchen Song, Yi Fung, Heng Ji, Jiawei Han, Shih-Fu Chang, James Pustejovsky, Jasmine Rah, David Liem, Ahmed ELsayed, Martha Palmer, Clare Voss, Cynthia Schneider, and Boyan Onyshkevych. 2021b. COVID-19 literature knowledge graph construction and drug repurposing report generation. In *Proceedings of the 2021 Conference of the North American Chapter of the Association for Computational Linguistics: Human Language Technologies: Demonstrations*, pages 66–77, Online. Association for Computational Linguistics.

Qingyun Wang, Qi Zeng, Lifu Huang, Kevin Knight, Heng Ji, and Nazneen Fatema Rajani. 2020b. ReviewRobot: Explainable paper review generation based on knowledge synthesis. In *Proceedings of the 13th International Conference on Natural Language Generation*, pages 384–397, Dublin, Ireland. Association for Computational Linguistics.

Xuan Wang, Yingjun Guan, Weili Liu, Aabhas Chauhan, Enyi Jiang, Qi Li, David Liem, Dibakar Sigdel, John Caufield, Peipei Ping, and Jiawei Han. 2020c. EVIDENCEMINER: Textual evidence discovery for life sciences. In *Proceedings of the 58th Annual Meeting of the Association for Computational Linguistics: System Demonstrations*, pages 56–62, Online. Association for Computational Linguistics.

Rick P. Wierenga, Stefan M. Golas, Wilson Ho, Connor W. Coley, and Kevin M. Esvelt. 2023. Pylabrobot: An open-source, hardware-agnostic interface for liquid-handling robots and accessories. *Device*, 1(4):100111.

Dustin Wright, David Wadden, Kyle Lo, Bailey Kuehl, Arman Cohan, Isabelle Augenstein, and Lucy Lu Wang. 2022. Generating scientific claims for zero-shot scientific fact checking. In *Proceedings of the 60th Annual Meeting of the Association for Computational Linguistics (Volume 1: Long Papers)*, pages 2448–2460, Dublin, Ireland. Association for Computational Linguistics.

Xinyu Xing, Xiaosheng Fan, and Xiaojun Wan. 2020. Automatic generation of citation texts in scholarly papers: A pilot study. In *Proceedings of the 58th Annual Meeting of the Association for Computational Linguistics*, pages 6181–6190, Online. Association for Computational Linguistics.

Michihiro Yasunaga, Jungo Kasai, Rui Zhang, Alexander R Fabbri, Irene Li, Dan Friedman, and Dragomir R Radev. 2019. Scisummnet: A large annotated corpus and content-impact models for scientific paper summarization with citation networks. In *Proceedings of the AAAI conference on artificial intelligence*, volume 33, pages 7386–7393.

Michihiro Yasunaga, Jure Leskovec, and Percy Liang. 2022. LinkBERT: Pretraining language models with document links. In *Proceedings of the 60th Annual Meeting of the Association for Computational Linguistics (Volume 1: Long Papers)*, pages 8003–8016, Dublin, Ireland. Association for Computational Linguistics.

Yue Yu, Chenyan Xiong, Si Sun, Chao Zhang, and Arnold Overwijk. 2022. COCO-DR: Combating distribution shift in zero-shot dense retrieval with contrastive and distributionally robust learning. In *Proceedings of the 2022 Conference on Empirical Methods in Natural Language Processing*, pages 1462–1479, Abu Dhabi, United Arab Emirates. Association for Computational Linguistics.

Weizhe Yuan and Pengfei Liu. 2022. Kid-review: Knowledge-guided scientific review generation with oracle pre-training. In *Proceedings of the AAAI Conference on Artificial Intelligence*, volume 36, pages 11639–11647.

Weizhe Yuan, Pengfei Liu, and Graham Neubig. 2022. Can we automate scientific reviewing? *Journal of Artificial Intelligence Research*, 75:171–212.

Qi Zeng, Mankeerat Sidhu, Hou Pong Chan, Lu Wang, and Heng Ji. 2023. Meta-review generation with checklist-guided iterative introspection. *Computation and Language Repository*, arXiv:2305.14647.

Rui Zhang, Dimitar Hristovski, Dalton Schutte, Andrej Kastrin, Marcelo Fiszman, and Halil Kilicoglu. 2021a. Drug repurposing for covid-19 via knowledge graph completion. *Journal of Biomedical Informatics*, 115:103696.

Zhiwei Zhang, Jiyi Li, Fumiyo Fukumoto, and Yanming Ye. 2021b. Abstract, rationale, stance: A joint model for scientific claim verification. In *Proceedings of the 2021 Conference on Empirical Methods in Natural Language Processing*, pages 3580–3586, Online and Punta Cana, Dominican Republic. Association for Computational Linguistics.

Ruiqi Zhong, Peter Zhang, Steve Li, Jinwoo Ahn, Dan Klein, and Jacob Steinhardt. 2023. Goal driven discovery of distributional differences via language descriptions. *Computation and Language Repository*, arXiv:2302.14233.

Chenguang Zhu, Yichong Xu, Xiang Ren, Bill Yuchen Lin, Meng Jiang, and Wenhao Yu. 2022. Knowledge-augmented methods for natural language processing. In *Proceedings of the 60th Annual Meeting of the Association for Computational Linguistics: Tutorial Abstracts*, pages 12–20, Dublin, Ireland. Association for Computational Linguistics.

Tutorial Proposal: Hallucination in Large Language Models

Vipula Rawte[1*], Aman Chadha[2,3†], Amit Sheth[1], Amitava Das[1]
[1]AI Institute, University of South Carolina, USA
[2]Stanford University, USA, [3]Amazon Science, USA
vrawte@mailbox.sc.edu

Abstract

In the fast-paced domain of Large Language Models (LLMs), the issue of hallucination is a prominent challenge. Despite continuous endeavors to address this concern, it remains a highly active area of research within the LLM landscape. Grasping the intricacies of this problem can be daunting, especially for those new to the field. This tutorial aims to bridge this knowledge gap by introducing the emerging realm of hallucination in LLMs. It will comprehensively explore the key aspects of hallucination, including benchmarking, detection, and mitigation techniques. Furthermore, we will delve into the specific constraints and shortcomings of current approaches, providing valuable insights to guide future research efforts for participants.

Keywords: large language models, hallucination, detection, mitigation

1. Hallucination - the emerging adversity of LLM

In the context of LLMs, hallucination refers to a phenomenon where the model generates or outputs information that is not accurate or factual. Instead of producing factually correct responses, the LLM may create content that is entirely fabricated or diverges significantly from reality. This can include the generation of fictional events, incorrect details, or imaginative content that did not exist in the source text or dataset. For example, Bard committed an error while responding to a query about the new findings from the James Webb Space Telescope (Reuters, 2023). In particular, when asked *"What recent discoveries could be shared with a 9-year-old"*, Bard provided various answers, one of which incorrectly suggested that the telescope had captured the initial images of a planet beyond our solar system, also known as exoplanets. In reality, the initial images of exoplanets were captured by the European Southern Observatory's Very Large Telescope (VLT) in 2004, a fact that has been verified by NASA.

Hallucination is a significant challenge in LLMs, as it can lead to the dissemination of misinformation and undermine the reliability and trustworthiness of the model's output. Researchers and developers have been working on detecting and mitigating hallucinations in LLMs to improve their accuracy and reliability for various applications. Our tutorial website: `https://vr25.github.io/lrec-coling-hallucination-tutorial/`.

*corresponding author
†Work does not relate to position at Amazon.

2. Outline

1. Introduction to hallucination in LLMs (see Section 3) (45 mins)
2. Categories of Hallucination (see Section 3.1) (45 mins)
3. Detection, Hallucination Benchmark and metric (see Section 3.2) (45 mins)
4. Mitigation techniques (see Section 3.3) (45 mins)
   (a) Black-box
   (b) Gray-box
   (c) Prompt-based

3. Hallucination Spectrum: Types and Scales

All LLMs, such as OpenAI's ChatGPT to Google's Bard, encounter a common issue: they generate fabricated information! Language models with generative capabilities lack genuine intelligence; they are statistical models that predict words. By training on vast datasets, often derived from the public web, these models acquire the ability to assess the likelihood of data occurrences through pattern recognition, considering the context of surrounding data. Thus, this probability-driven method is far from generating factually correct content. This problem is generally known as *hallucination* in LLMs. This section of the tutorial will cover the background, fundamentals of LLMs, and various causes of hallucination.

3.1. Categories of hallucination

Different categories of hallucination are highlighted in Figs. 1 to 3. Additionally, two primary orientations of hallucination are: (i) Factual Mirage (FM) and (ii) Silver Lining (SL), defined and exemplified below (Rawte et al., 2023a).

LREC-COLING 2024 Tutorials, pages 68–72
20-25 May, 2024.

Article: Jung Lee is a well-known **French** writer who was **born in Paris**. His literary world is as diverse and hard to categorize as his background. He has lived in both urban and rural areas, deep in the mountains and in the seaside towns and has developed a wide range of interests from the tradition of Confucian culture to advertising.

Generated Summary: Jung Lee is one of South Korea's best-known writers.

Figure 1: Entity "Jung Lee" is associated with "South Korea". Name-Nationality problem identified in (Ladhak et al., 2023).

[Factual Prompt] One of lung cancer's symptoms is shortness of breath.

[Greedy] The American Cancer Society estimates that more than 228,000 people will be diagnosed with lung cancer in the United States this year.\n\n ~~The American Cancer Society estimates that more than 228,000 people will be diagnosed with lung cancer in the United States this year.\n\nThe American Cancer Society estimates that more than 228,000 people will be diagnosed with lung cancer in the United...~~

[p=0.9] That would make an oxygen mask one of the more popular treatments for this devastating disease. It helps ease breathing and give patients back their strength. **Learn more here.<|endoftext|>"**

[Ours] Other symptoms include coughing (including coughing up blood), chest pain, hoarseness, weight loss, and loss of appetite. The symptoms of lung cancer may resemble those of a bad cold or pneumonia. A chest x - ray is necessary to confirm the diagnosis. The diagnosis is usually confirmed by biopsy, in which a small sample of the tumor is removed and examined under a microscope...

[Non-Factual Prompt] Cancer can be prevented by drinking too much alcohol.

[Greedy] \nCancer can be prevented by eating too much red meat.\n\n~~Cancer can be prevented by eating too much sugar.\n\nCancer can be prevented by eating too much fat.\n\nCancer can be prevented by eating~~ too much processed food.\n\nCancer can be...

[p=0.9] More than 90% of hepatocellular carcinoma is associated with alcohol use.\n\nAbout 9 percent of cancers can be prevented if we don't eat more than 1.5 ounces of processed meat each day.\n\nDiet is believed to play a role in 7% of cancers and...

[Ours] Cancer is often treated with some combination of radiation therapy, surgery, chemotherapy and targeted therapy. Pain and symptom management are an important part of care. Palliative care is particularly important in people with advanced disease. The chance of survival depends on the type of cancer and extent of disease at the...

Figure 2: Example of factual and non-factual prompts (Lee et al., 2022)

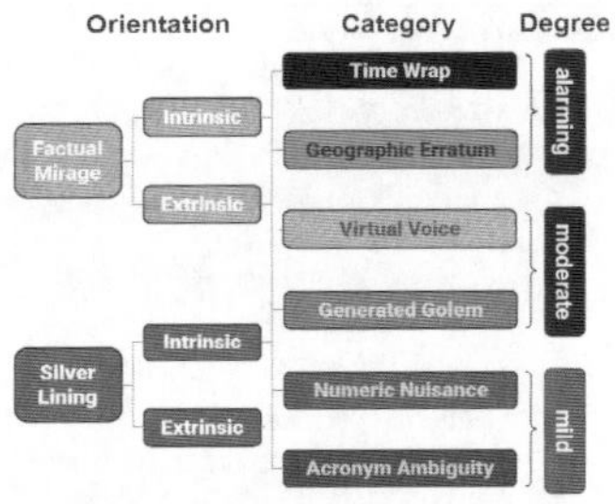

Figure 3: Hallucination: orientation, category, and degree (decreasing level of difficulty from top to bottom) (Rawte et al., 2023a).

3.1.1. Factual Mirage

Factual mirage (FM) is defined as the phenomenon wherein an LLM engages in hallucination or distortion of a given prompt that is factually correct. FM can potentially be subdivided into two distinct sub-categories.

Intrinsic factual mirage (IFM) occurs when the LLM is providing a correct response while adding additional supplementary facts such as "*the world fashion capital,*" resulting in distortion or hallucination, has also been described in (Cao et al., 2022).

Extrinsic factual mirage (EFM) refers to the phenomenon where an LLM deviates from factual accuracy.

3.1.2. Silver Lining (SL)

Silver lining (SL) is defined as the phenomenon in which an LLM indulges in hallucination by conjuring an elaborate and captivating narrative based on a given prompt that is factually incorrect.

Intrinsic silver lining (ISL) is the category when in some cases LLM does not generate a convincing story.

Extrinsic silver lining (ESL) occurs when an LLM generates a highly detailed and persuasive narrative in response to a factually incorrect prompt, it falls under the category of Extrinsic Silver Lining.

Furthermore, six distinct categories of hallucination are defined and exemplified in (Rawte et al., 2023a). **Numeric Nuisance (NN)** (Fig. 5) occurs when an LLM generates numeric values related to past events, such as dates, ages, or monetary amounts, that are inconsistent with the actual facts; **Acronym Ambiguity (AA)** (Fig. 6) pertains to instances in which LLMs generate an imprecise expansion for an acronym; **Generated Golem (GG)** (Fig. 7) arises when an LLM fabricates an imaginary personality in relation to a past event, without concrete evidence; **Virtual Voice (VV)** (Fig. 8) refers to situations where LLMs generate quotations attributed to either fictional or real characters without sufficient evidence to verify the authenticity of such statements; **Geographic Erratum (GE)** (Fig. 9) occurs when LLMs generate an incorrect location associated with an event; **Time Wrap (TW)** (Fig. 10) entails LLMs generating text that exhibits a mashed fusion of events from different timelines. In the example - U.S. president during the Ukraine-Russia war is Joe Biden, not Barack Obama, thus contradicting the factual reality.

3.2. Detection, Benchmarks and Metrics

Several works discuss hallucination detection techniques involving self-contradiction or others (Manakul et al., 2023; Mündler et al., 2023; Zhang et al., 2023a). Some recent works such as (Li et al., 2023; Rawte et al., 2023a) have constructed large-scale hallucination benchmarks. Furthermore, a metric to evaluate LLM hallucination called *Hallucination Vulnerability Index (HVI)* is introduced in (Rawte et al., 2023a).

3.3. Mitigation techniques

Up to this point, two main strategies have been suggested to tackle hallucination: (i) preventing LLMs from hallucinating through the implementation of strategies during training and generation; (ii) mitigating hallucination after generation. Two categories called black-box and gray-box techniques are introduced in (Manakul et al., 2023). Factuality checks conducted during or after generation without external resources fall under black-box methods, whereas those using external resources are categorized as gray-box methods.

While completely eliminating hallucination poses a complex challenge, (Rawte et al., 2023a) investigates two potential mitigation avenues (refer to Fig. 4): (i) automatic and (ii) human-in-the-loop. The former, a black-box method, $\text{ENTROPY}_{\text{BB}}$ (see row 2 in Fig. 4), entails identifying high-entropy words within a hallucinated text (generated by a high-HVI LLM) and substi-

Prompt	*USA's stance on Ukraine Russia war*
Hallucinated text	The official stance of the United States on the Russia-Ukraine war has been consistent in supporting Ukraine's sovereignty, territorial integrity, and the peaceful resolution of the conflict. The U.S. has condemned Russia's actions in annexing Crimea and its support for separatist movements in eastern Ukraine. Despite maintaining a diplomatic stance, the U.S. President Barack Obama stated that the United States would not deploy troops to Ukraine. Additionally, this lack of support extends to the withholding of financial and military assistance, including military equipment, training, and advisory support. This sentiment was reiterated by Paul Altman during a press review at the White House ...
Mitigated text ENTROPY$_{BB}$	The official stance of the government on the ongoing war has been consistent in supporting resolution of the conflict. The government has condemned Russia in country and its support for separatist movements in eastern country. Despite maintaining a neutral stance, the government stated that the country would not deploy troops to unknown. Additionally, this lack of support extends to the withholding of financial and resources, including administrative, technical, and legal. This sentiment was echoed by minister during a press review at the conference ...
Edit Suggestions FACTUALITY$_{GB}$	The official stance of the United States on the Russia-Ukraine war has been consistent in supporting Ukraine's sovereignty, territorial integrity, and the peaceful resolution of the conflict. The U.S. has condemned Russia's actions in annexing Crimea and its support for separatist movements in eastern Ukraine. Despite maintaining a diplomatic stance, U.S. President Barack Obama stated that the United States would not deploy troops to Ukraine. Additionally, this lack of support extends to the withholding of financial and military assistance, including military equipment, training, and advisory support. This sentiment was reiterated by Paul Altman during a press review at the White House ...

Figure 4: A hallucination example pre- and post-mitigation. A - hallucinated fragments, B - high entropy fragments, C - replaced text, D - highlighted text for no information found, and E - refuted text fragments by textual entailment.

moderate

Prompt: *Twitter is said to have laid off more workers.*

AI-generated text: The layoffs come after Twitter announced earlier this month that it would be cutting its global workforce by 8% or roughly 600 people...

Fact: Twitter laid off 200 people which is roughly 10%

Figure 5: Numeric Nuisance

moderate

Prompt: *RLHF in reinforcement learning*

AI-generated text: ...RLHF is Reward-free Learning from Human Feedback in reinforcement learning...

Fact: RLHF stands for *"Reinforcement Learning from Human Feedback"*

Figure 6: Acronym Ambiguity

moderate

Prompt: *Earthquake in Turkey*

AI-generated text: ...One rescuer, Hasan Cetin, said he was motivated by the thought of the survivors he helped save. "The moment when a man or a child is pulled out of the ruins, the joy of seeing them come back to life is...

Fact: There is no evidence that the person Hasan Cetin exists.

Figure 7: Generated Golem

alarming

Prompt: *Pfizer Press Release on COVID-19 vaccine*

AI-generated text: ...Pfizer emphasized that their vaccine demonstrated an impressive efficacy rate... Pfizer CEO said, "This is a giant leap for humanity.."...

Fact: Pfizer CEO never said this.

Figure 8: Virtual Voice

alarming

Prompt: *Prime Minister of the United Kingdom visiting India*

AI-generated text: ...The visit of the United Kingdom's Prime Minister to India holds immense significance...During his journey, he will also pay a visit to the Pentagon where he is scheduled to meet with Smriti Irani, the Minister of...

Fact: Pentagon is the defense headquarters of the USA, located in Washington DC, USA – not in India.

Figure 9: Geographic Erratum

alarming

Prompt: *USA on Ukraine war*

AI-generated text: ...U.S. President Barack Obama says the U.S. will not put troops in Ukraine...

Fact: The actual U.S. president during the Ukraine-Russia war is Joe Biden.

Figure 10: Time Wrap

tuting them with predictions from another LLM (with lower HVI). The latter, a gray-box method, FACTUALITY$_{GB}$ (see row 3 in Fig. 4), involves sentence-level fact-checking using textual entailment techniques, flagging sentences for human review if they are deemed susceptible.

3.3.1. Black-box approaches

Although the detection of high-entropy words may appear technically viable, a fundamental challenge arises from the fact that numerous contemporary LLMs are not open-source (their APIs are subscription-based). (Rawte et al., 2023a) proposed viable solution involves leveraging open-source LLMs for the identification of high-entropy words, followed by their replacement using a lower HVI-based LLM. Their findings revealed that `albert-large-v2` (Lan et al., 2020) effectively detects high-entropy words in GPT-3-generated content. Conversely, `distilroberta-base` (Sanh et al., 2019) exhibits superior performance in substituting high-entropy words, resulting in reduced hallucination. An important aspect of their approach involves treating consecutive high-entropy words as a single entity, masking them collectively before replacement. This strategy proves particularly effective in addressing hallucinations linked to Generated Golem or Acronym Ambiguity.

3.3.2. Gray-box approaches

The Google Search API (Search) is employed to search a given prompt, enabling text generation and retrieval of the top 20 documents. Each sentence of the AI-generated text is then assessed using `RoBERTa-Large` (Liu et al., 2019), a cutting-edge textual entailment model trained on SNLI (Bowman et al., 2015), classified as *support*, *refute*, or *not enough information*. Sentences with higher scores in the *refute* and *not enough information* categories are inevitably flagged for additional human verification. Empirically, it is observed that there is an overall alert rate of 26% on sentences generated by an LLM, indicating that 26% of the text required modification to alleviate concerns. Besides methods using textual entailment, other gray-box methods involve utilizing Retrieval-augmented generation (RAG) to address the hallucination issue (Elaraby et al., 2023; Varshney et al., 2023).

3.3.3. Prompt-based approaches

When given an appropriate prompt, an LLM can generate and implement a plan for self-verification to assess its own output quality. Subsequently, it can integrate this analysis to enhance its responses, thereby mitigating hallucination as shown in Fig. 11.

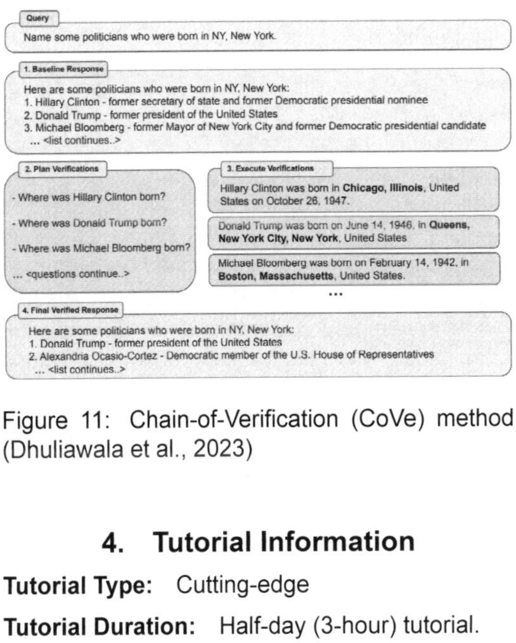

Figure 11: Chain-of-Verification (CoVe) method (Dhuliawala et al., 2023)

4. Tutorial Information

Tutorial Type: Cutting-edge

Tutorial Duration: Half-day (3-hour) tutorial.

Target audience and pre-requisites: Our goal is to connect with individuals in both academic and industry circles who are passionate about generative AI models. **Approximate count:** 30-50. We expect participants to have a foundational understanding of core linguistic principles, statistical NLP, and a basic grasp of machine learning and neural networks.

Diversity considerations The techniques discussed in our tutorial have the potential to be applied across different languages and domains. Moreover, this tutorial was collaboratively created by a team of researchers from two different universities and one industry (AI Institute at the University of South Carolina, Stanford, Amazon, USA). Regarding gender diversity, the tutorial comprises one female presenter and three male presenters. This tutorial proposers consist of a mix of senior, mid-career, and early-career researchers.

Reading list. Apart from the papers referenced in this proposal, a comprehensive list of survey papers can be accessed here:

- Hallucination in Large Language Models: (Zhang et al., 2023b), (Ye et al., 2023)
- Hallucination in Large Foundation Models: (Rawte et al., 2023b)

Sharing of Tutorial Materials: All the tutorial resources will be made publicly available.

Ethics Statement

The tutorial will feature cutting-edge research on hallucination in LLMs, encompassing detection, mitigation, and evaluation strategies. It will address the safety implications associated with contemporary LLMs and the responsible deployment of these models in real-world applications.

5. Presenters

Vipula Rawte is a Ph.D. student at AIISC, UofSC, USA, advised by Dr. Amit Sheth. Her primary research interests are in Generative AI and Large Language Models. Her email is `vrawte@mailbox.sc.edu`

Aman Chadha heads GenAI R&D at AWS and is a Researcher at Stanford AI. His main research interests are Multimodal AI, On-device AI, and Human-Centered AI. His email is `hi@aman.ai`

Dr. Amit Sheth is the founding Director of the Artificial Intelligence Institute and NCR Chair & Professor at the University of South Carolina. His research interests are Neurosymbolic AI, Social Media Analysis/AI & Social Good. He has organized several activities and given keynotes such as Cysoc2021 @ ICWSM2021, Emoji2021 @ICWSM2021, KiLKGC 2021 @KGC21. His email is `amit@sc.edu`

Dr. Amitava Das is a Research Associate Professor at AIISC, UofSC, USA, and an advisory scientist at Wipro AI Labs, Bangalore, India. He has previously organized several successful workshops such as Memotion @SemEval2020, SentiMix @SemEval2020, Computational Approaches to Linguistic Code-Switching @ LREC 2020, CONSTRAINT @AAAI2021, Defactify 2.0 @AAAI2023. His email is `amitava@mailbox.sc.edu`

6. Bibliographical References

Samuel R Bowman, Gabor Angeli, Christopher Potts, and Christopher D Manning. 2015. The snli corpus.

Meng Cao, Yue Dong, and Jackie Chi Kit Cheung. 2022. Hallucinated but factual! inspecting the factuality of hallucinations in abstractive summarization. In *Proceedings of the 60th Annual Meeting of the Association for Computational Linguistics (Volume 1: Long Papers)*, pages 3340–3354.

Shehzaad Dhuliawala, Mojtaba Komeili, Jing Xu, Roberta Raileanu, Xian Li, Asli Celikyilmaz, and Jason Weston. 2023. Chain-of-verification reduces hallucination in large language models. *arXiv preprint arXiv:2309.11495*.

Mohamed Elaraby, Mengyin Lu, Jacob Dunn, Xueying Zhang, Yu Wang, and Shizhu Liu. 2023. Halo: Estimation and reduction of hallucinations in open-source weak large language models. *arXiv preprint arXiv:2308.11764*.

Faisal Ladhak, Esin Durmus, Mirac Suzgun, Tianyi Zhang, Dan Jurafsky, Kathleen Mckeown, and Tatsunori B Hashimoto. 2023. When do pretraining biases propagate to downstream tasks? a case study in text summarization. In *Proceedings of the 17th Conference of the European Chapter of the Association for Computational Linguistics*, pages 3198–3211.

Zhenzhong Lan, Mingda Chen, Sebastian Goodman, Kevin Gimpel, Piyush Sharma, and Radu Soricut. 2020. Albert: A lite bert for self-supervised learning of language representations.

Nayeon Lee, Wei Ping, Peng Xu, Mostofa Patwary, Pascale N Fung, Mohammad Shoeybi, and Bryan Catanzaro. 2022. Factuality enhanced language models for open-ended text generation. *Advances in Neural Information Processing Systems*, 35:34586–34599.

Junyi Li, Xiaoxue Cheng, Wayne Xin Zhao, Jian-Yun Nie, and Ji-Rong Wen. 2023. Halueval: A large-scale hallucination evaluation benchmark for large language models.

Yinhan Liu, Myle Ott, Naman Goyal, Jingfei Du, Mandar Joshi, Danqi Chen, Omer Levy, Mike Lewis, Luke Zettlemoyer, and Veselin Stoyanov. 2019. Roberta: A robustly optimized bert pretraining approach. *arXiv preprint arXiv:1907.11692*.

Potsawee Manakul, Adian Liusie, and Mark J. F. Gales. 2023. Selfcheckgpt: Zero-resource black-box hallucination detection for generative large language models.

Niels Mündler, Jingxuan He, Slobodan Jenko, and Martin Vechev. 2023. Self-contradictory hallucinations of large language models: Evaluation, detection and mitigation.

Vipula Rawte, Swagata Chakraborty, Agnibh Pathak, Anubhav Sarkar, S.M Towhidul Islam Tonmoy, Aman Chadha, Amit Sheth, and Amitava Das. 2023a. The troubling emergence of hallucination in large language models - an extensive definition, quantification, and prescriptive remediations. In *Proceedings of the 2023 Conference on Empirical Methods in Natural Language Processing*, pages 2541–2573, Singapore. Association for Computational Linguistics.

Vipula Rawte, Amit Sheth, and Amitava Das. 2023b. A survey of hallucination in large foundation models. *arXiv preprint arXiv:2309.05922*.

Reuters. 2023. Alphabet shares dive after google ai chatbot bard flubs answer in ad.

Victor Sanh, Lysandre Debut, Julien Chaumond, and Thomas Wolf. 2019. Distilbert, a distilled version of bert: smaller, faster, cheaper and lighter. *ArXiv*, abs/1910.01108.

Google Search. Google search api.

Neeraj Varshney, Wenlin Yao, Hongming Zhang, Jianshu Chen, and Dong Yu. 2023. A stitch in time saves nine: Detecting and mitigating hallucinations of llms by validating low-confidence generation. *arXiv preprint arXiv:2307.03987*.

Hongbin Ye, Tong Liu, Aijia Zhang, Wei Hua, and Weiqiang Jia. 2023. Cognitive mirage: A review of hallucinations in large language models. *arXiv preprint arXiv:2309.06794*.

Muru Zhang, Ofir Press, William Merrill, Alisa Liu, and Noah A. Smith. 2023a. How language model hallucinations can snowball.

Yue Zhang, Yafu Li, Leyang Cui, Deng Cai, Lemao Liu, Tingchen Fu, Xinting Huang, Enbo Zhao, Yu Zhang, Yulong Chen, et al. 2023b. Siren's song in the ai ocean: A survey on hallucination in large language models. *arXiv preprint arXiv:2309.01219*.

Addressing Bias and Hallucination in Large Language Models

Nihar Sahoo*, Ashita Saxena*, Kishan Maharaj*, Arif Ahmad*, Abhijit Mishra†, Pushpak Bhattacharyya*
*CFILT, Indian Institute of Technology Bombay, India,
† University of Texas at Austin, Texas, USA
{nihar, ashitasaxena, kishan, pb}@cse.iitb.ac.in, arifahmadpeace@gmail.com,
abhijitmishra@utexas.edu

Abstract

In the landscape of natural language processing (NLP), addressing the challenges of bias and hallucination is paramount to ensuring the ethical and unbiased development of Large Language Models (LLMs). This tutorial delves into the intricate dimensions of LLMs, shedding light on the critical importance of understanding and mitigating the profound impacts of bias and hallucination. The tutorial begins with discussions on the complexity of bias propagation in LLM development, where we dissect its origins and far-reaching impacts along with the automatic evaluation metrics for bias measurement. We then present innovative methodologies for mitigating diverse forms of bias, including both static and contextualized word embeddings and robust benchmarking strategies. In addition, the tutorial explores the interlinkage between hallucination and bias in LLMs by shedding light on how bias can be perceived as a hallucination problem. Furthermore, we also talk about cognitively-inspired deep learning frameworks for hallucination detection which leverages human gaze behavior. Ultimately, this cutting-edge tutorial serves as a guiding light, equipping participants with indispensable tools and insights to navigate the ethical complexities of LLMs, thus paving the way for the development of unbiased and ethically robust NLP systems.

1. Introduction

Large Language Models (LLMs) represent a cutting-edge class of AI models guided by specific prompts to generate tailored outputs, revolutionizing diverse sectors worldwide. These models, exemplified by ChatGPT and Google Bard, alongside open-source counterparts like Dolly 2.0 and LLaMa2.0, have garnered immense popularity. LLMs are poised to underpin transformative advancements across developed and developing societies, including facilitating cross-language communication, personalizing education, propelling healthcare innovations, ultimately ensuring broader accessibility to digital content and services for diverse audiences. However, amidst their astounding capabilities, LLMs are not without their challenges. This tutorial provides a comprehensive overview of two critical aspects of LLMs: *bias* and *hallucination*, with a predominant focus on *bias*.

We begin the tutorial with a primer on Language Models (LLMs), providing an overview of their training methods, variations, and historical development. We also highlight the ethical considerations pertinent to their deployment in practical contexts.

Given the significant impact of bias in LLMs, we then proceed to the first segment where, we define bias formally, outlining its types and the rationale behind its study. Subsequently, we explore the origins of bias in NLP pipelines, with a particular emphasis on the role of hallucination in the propagation of biased content and its implications in different domains. To address and alleviate bias, we then present several approaches, focusing on methods for both static and contextualized word embeddings. The importance of benchmarking datasets in the identification of bias is underscored, alongside an introduction to specific benchmarks tailored for quantifying bias, including the extraction of social bias from hate speech.

We then discuss bias from the lens of hallucination, which highlights the parallel between the presence of bias and hallucination. We conclude this discussion with a glimpse of cognitively inspired hallucination detection.

We hope this tutorial acts as a beacon, providing participants with essential resources and knowledge to navigate the ethical intricacies of LLMs, thereby facilitating the creation of impartial and morally sound NLP systems. We have made all the materials of this tutorial publicly available [1].

2. Target Audience

The target audiences include researchers and industry practitioners working on NLP tasks who extensively use LLMs for research or applications. This tutorial will give them an in-depth understanding of how to develop and fine-tune efficient yet ethically sound LLMs. We will also provide application-based demos and code walkthroughs for programming enthusiasts interested in the internal workings of these techniques.

[1] Tutorial Website

LREC-COLING 2024 Tutorials, pages 73–79

3. Outline

Duration: Half Day

3.1. Introduction to LLMs

[Duration: 20 mins]

1. Language modeling: Task and Types
2. LLM paradigms: Dataset, training, evaluation
3. Evolution of LLMs
4. Ethical concerns

3.2. Understanding of Bias in LLMs

[Duration: 15 mins]

1. Bias definition and its types
2. Sources of bias in LLM development pipelines
3. Hallucination as a reason for bias
4. Downstream impact

3.3. Approaches for Bias detection

[Duration: 40 mins]

1. Bias Metrics: WEAT, SEAT, and MAC
2. Bias assessment in static word embeddings: Using PCA and Nullspace projection
3. Identifying Undesirable associations in Transformers: multi-headed attention Layer analysis
4. Intersectional biases across social axes: Gender and Race, Gender and Religion
5. Datasets and source of biases within data
6. Popular multilingual approaches: Few-shot, continuous pretraining, and prompting

Tea Break

3.4. Approaches for bias mitigation

[Duration: 40 mins]

1. Word embeddings: Soft and Hard debiasing
2. Debiasing context-representations
3. Designing Fairness-oriented loss functions
4. Counter-narratives based Debasing
5. Debiasing using prompting

3.5. Bias benchmarking Datasets

[Duration: 25 mins]

1. Importance of benchmarking datasets
2. Benchmarks for bias quantification: Stereoset, Crows-Pairs, BBQ, BIOS, and IndiBias

3.6. Bias from the lens of Hallucination

[Duration: 10 mins]

1. Parallels between the presence of bias and hallucination in machine-generated text
2. Possible causes of biases in hallucinated content

3.7. Cognitively inspired approaches for Hallucination detection

[Duration: 10 mins]

1. Basics of cognitively inspired deep learning methods
2. Behavioural insights related to hallucination and attention bias
3. Cognitively inspired deep learning architecture for hallucination detection

3.8. Open Problems and Future scope

[Duration: 10 mins]

3.9. Conclusion and Closing Remarks

[Duration: 10 mins]

4. Outline Description

4.1. Introduction to LLMs

The introduction section, spanning 20 minutes, outlines the fundamental aspects of Language Models (LLMs) by discussing language modeling as a task and the various types of such models. It further highlights the key paradigms governing LLMs, including dataset, training, and evaluation, while tracing their evolutionary trajectory. Lastly, the segment underscores the ethical considerations associated with the use of LLMs.

4.2. Understanding of Bias in LMs

In this section, spanning 30 minutes, the focus is on comprehending bias in Language Models (LMs). The discussion includes an elucidation of bias and its various types, such as gender, racial, and cultural biases (Singh et al., 2022; Crawford, 2017). We will also discuss data-bias, algorithmic and user-interaction driven biases (Hovy and Spruit, 2016; Vig et al., 2020) and highlight the role of hallucination as a contributing factor, followed by the downstream impacts of bias across various sensitive domains such as healthcare.

4.3. Approaches for Bias Detection

This section of 45 minutes covers NLP-based bias detection methods. Initially, we discuss the methodologies that quantify text data bias using WEAT (Caliskan et al., 2017), SEAT (Liang et al., 2020), and MAC (Manzini et al., 2019) metrics. Then we discuss the methods for detecting biases at various levels of text-processing, *e.g.,* word-embeddings (Bolukbasi et al., 2016) followed by contextualized sentence embeddings (Zhao et al., 2019; Garimella et al., 2021). The section also discusses intersectional biases (Tan and Celis, 2019; Lalor et al.,

2022) in different languages and cultures. The importance of dataset biases and bias detection methods for multilingual LLMs (Sahoo et al., 2023), including few-shot and continuous pretraining, will also be highlighted.

4.4. Approaches for bias mitigation

This segment covers various techniques for mitigating bias, including strategies such as soft and hard debiasing in word embeddings (Bolukbasi et al., 2016), and debiasing context-representations in Transformer based models. We will also delve into modern zero-shot techniques such as debiasing via prompts that guide models to produce unbiased results at inference time (Guo et al., 2022; Schick et al., 2021). Some other relevant topics such as Fairness-oriented Loss Functions (Zhang et al., 2018), counter-narratives (Sahoo et al., 2024a) based language rectification and debiasing (Sahoo et al., 2022) will also be highlighted.

4.5. Bias benchmarking datasets

In this section, we will discuss the significance of benchmarking datasets for bias evaluation. Several benchmarking datasets, such as Stereoset (Nadeem et al., 2021), Crows-Pairs (Nangia et al., 2020), BBQ (Parrish et al., 2022), BIOS (De-Arteaga et al., 2019), and IndiBias (Sahoo et al., 2024b), have emerged as valuable tools for measuring and assessing bias in language models. These benchmarks facilitate a standardized approach to assessing and comparing the performance of models in terms of bias mitigation and awareness.

Then we will discuss the biased behavior of the model from the lens of hallucination and conclude the overall tutorial with open questions, Q&A with audience followed by closing remarks.

4.6. Bias from the lens of Hallucination

In this section, we will highlight the presence of bias in hallucinated content. Hallucination is a challenging problem in this era of LLMs. The hallucinated content often contain biases. We will talk about the causes of biases and hallucinations and their similarities in this section.

4.7. Cognitively inspired approaches for Hallucination detection

In this section, we will draw parallels between human cognitive behaviour and deep learning methodologies for addressing the problem of hallucination detection (Mahowald et al., 2023; Maharaj et al., 2023). We will delve into the diverse cognitive insights and advantages that arise from integrating cognitive signals such as human eye-tracking data into deep learning-based architectures for hallucination assessment.

5. Diversity Considerations

We acknowledge the critical importance of incorporating diverse perspectives in the discussion of bias and hallucination within LLMs. This tutorial emphasizes the significance of including voices from underrepresented communities and diverse backgrounds, recognizing the nuanced impact of cultural and linguistic diversity on the understanding and mitigation of bias and hallucination. Notably, all presenters hail from different regions of India and the USA, representing a rich tapestry of language and cultural backgrounds, fostering a comprehensive exploration of these intricate NLP challenges from various global viewpoints.

6. Reading List

We intend to make the tutorial self-contained. The tutorial materials such as the slides and video recordings will published for later reference. Further reading materials beyond the content of this tutorial will be provided in the slides itself.

7. Presenters

Nihar Sahoo is a PhD student in the Computer Science department of IIT Bombay, supervised by Prof. Pushpak Bhattacharyya. His research interest lies in Ethical AI, social biases/toxicity in languages, and explainability in NLP. He has given a tutorial on *social bias detection and mitigation in NLP* at ICON. He has published papers on bias detection at conferences such as BMVC, LREC, CoNLL, NAACL, AAAI, ACL.

Ashita Saxena is a 3rd year MS by Research (CSE) student at IIT Bombay guided by Prof. Pushpak Bhattacharyya. Her research focuses on hallucination detection and mitigation in NLP tasks and her work is published in EMNLP. She has worked as a Research Intern at IBM Research on Natural Language Generation (NLG).

Kishan Maharaj is an MS (by Research) student at IIT Bombay (CSE), guided by Prof. Pushpak Bhattacharyya. His research focuses on cognitively inspired natural language processing, specifically hallucination detection and mitigation. His work was published in EMNLP. He is currently working with IBM research on prompt-based hallucination mitigation. Formerly, he worked with Turtle Mint and TATA Sons on various data science problems.

Arif Ahmad is currently in the final year of a BTech/MTech dual degree in Electrical Engineering and AI at IIT Bombay. He is working in the area of Fairness and Bias in NLP systems and

Models, under the supervision of Prof. Pushpak Bhattacharyya at the CFILT Lab in IIT Bombay.

Dr. Abhijit Mishra an Assistant Professor of Practice at the School of Information, University of Texas at Austin, boasts extensive experience in ML and NLP, spanning over a decade. Formerly a Research Scientist at Apple Inc. and IBM Research, his contributions to NLP-based products like Siri and Watson are noteworthy. With notable publications at key AI and NLP conferences such as ACL, EMNLP, and AAAI, he has demonstrated expertise in various NLP domains, including multilingual and multimodal Natural Language Understanding and Generation, Sentiment Analysis, and Cognitive NLP with eye-tracking. Dr. Mishra's recent focus on ethical LLM development aligns closely with the theme of the tutorial.

Prof. Pushpak Bhattacharyya is a Professor of Computer Science and Engineering at IIT Bombay. Educated in the IIT System (B.Tech IIT Kharagpur, M.Tech IIT Kanpur, PhD IIT Bombay), Dr. Bhattacharyya has done extensive research in Natural Language Processing and Machine Learning. He has published more than 350 research papers, has authored/co-authored 6 books including a textbook on machine translation, and has guided more than 350 students for their PhD, Masters and Undergraduate thesis. He has received many Research Excellence Awards- Manthan award from Ministry of IT, H.H. Mathur and P.K.Patwardhan awards from IIT Bombay, VNMM award from IIT Roorkee, and substantial research grants from Government and industry. Prof. Bhattacharyya holds the Bhagat Singh Rekhi Chair Professorship of IIT Bombay, is a Fellow of National Academy of Engineering, Abdul Kalam National Fellow, Distinguished Alumnus of IIT Kharagpur, past Director of IIT Patna and past President of ACL.

8. Other Information

We anticipate the active participation of approximately 100 individuals, estimated based on the past engagement with similar tutorials and the current outreach efforts. This estimate takes into account the projected interest within the NLP community, specifically on responsible LLM development and aligns with our preparation for interactive sessions and engaging discussions.

9. Ethics Statement

At the core of our tutorial on "Addressing Bias and Hallucinations in Large Language Models" lies a commitment to addressing the ethical concerns of NLP. We recognize that NLP technologies have profound societal impacts, and as educators and researchers, we have a responsibility to raise awareness about potential issues, promote ethical practices, and foster a deeper understanding of bias and hallucination in NLP systems.

10. Bibliographical References

Ayush Agrawal, Lester Mackey, and Adam Tauman Kalai. 2023. Do language models know when they're hallucinating references? *arXiv preprint arXiv:2305.18248*.

Afra Feyza Akyürek, Sejin Paik, Muhammed Yusuf Kocyigit, Seda Akbiyik, Şerife Leman Runyun, and Derry Wijaya. 2022. On measuring social biases in prompt-based multi-task learning.

Md Abdul Aowal, Maliha T Islam, Priyanka Mary Mammen, and Sandesh Shetty. 2023. Detecting natural language biases with prompt-based learning.

Simran Arora, Avanika Narayan, Mayee F Chen, Laurel Orr, Neel Guha, Kush Bhatia, Ines Chami, Frederic Sala, and Christopher Ré. 2022. Ask me anything: A simple strategy for prompting language models. *arXiv preprint arXiv:2210.02441*.

Tolga Bolukbasi, Kai-Wei Chang, James Y Zou, Venkatesh Saligrama, and Adam T Kalai. 2016. Man is to computer programmer as woman is to homemaker? debiasing word embeddings. *Advances in neural information processing systems*, 29.

Helena Bonaldi, Sara Dellantonio, Serra Sinem Tekiroglu, and Marco Guerini. 2022. Human-machine collaboration approaches to build a dialogue dataset for hate speech countering. In *Proceedings of the 2022 Conference on Empirical Methods in Natural Language Processing*, pages 8031–8049. Association for Computational Linguistics.

Marc-Etienne Brunet, Colleen Alkalay-Houlihan, Ashton Anderson, and Richard Zemel. 2019. Understanding the origins of bias in word embeddings. In *International conference on machine learning*, pages 803–811. PMLR.

Aylin Caliskan, Joanna J Bryson, and Arvind Narayanan. 2017. Semantics derived automatically from language corpora contain human-like biases. *Science*, 356(6334):183–186.

Yi-Ling Chung, Elizaveta Kuzmenko, Serra Sinem Tekiroglu, and Marco Guerini. 2019. CONAN - COunter NArratives through nichesourcing: a multilingual dataset of responses to fight online hate speech. In *Proceedings of the 57th Annual*

Meeting of the Association for Computational Linguistics, pages 2819–2829, Florence, Italy. Association for Computational Linguistics.

Kate Crawford. 2017. The trouble with bias.

Maria De-Arteaga, Alexey Romanov, Hanna Wallach, Jennifer Chayes, Christian Borgs, Alexandra Chouldechova, Sahin Geyik, Krishnaram Kenthapadi, and Adam Tauman Kalai. 2019. Bias in bios. In *Proceedings of the Conference on Fairness, Accountability, and Transparency*. ACM.

Bhuwan Dhingra, Manaal Faruqui, Ankur Parikh, Ming-Wei Chang, Dipanjan Das, and William W Cohen. 2019. Handling divergent reference texts when evaluating table-to-text generation. *arXiv preprint arXiv:1906.01081*.

Shehzaad Dhuliawala, Mojtaba Komeili, Jing Xu, Roberta Raileanu, Xian Li, Asli Celikyilmaz, and Jason Weston. 2023. Chain-of-verification reduces hallucination in large language models. *arXiv preprint arXiv:2309.11495*.

Esin Durmus, He He, and Mona Diab. 2020. Feqa: A question answering evaluation framework for faithfulness assessment in abstractive summarization. *arXiv preprint arXiv:2005.03754*.

Ondřej Dušek and Zdeněk Kasner. 2020. Evaluating semantic accuracy of data-to-text generation with natural language inference. *arXiv preprint arXiv:2011.10819*.

Nouha Dziri, Andrea Madotto, Osmar Zaiane, and Avishek Joey Bose. 2021. Neural path hunter: Reducing hallucination in dialogue systems via path grounding. *arXiv preprint arXiv:2104.08455*.

Oliver Eberle, Stephanie Brandl, Jonas Pilot, and Anders Søgaard. 2022. Do transformer models show similar attention patterns to task-specific human gaze? In *Proceedings of the 60th Annual Meeting of the Association for Computational Linguistics (Volume 1: Long Papers)*, pages 4295–4309.

Fanton, Margherita. 2021. Human-in-the-Loop for Data Collection: a Multi-Target Counter Narrative Dataset to Fight Online Hate Speech. In *Proceedings of the 59th Annual Meeting of the Association for Computational Linguistics*. Association for Computational Linguistics.

Shangbin Feng, Chan Young Park, Yuhan Liu, and Yulia Tsvetkov. 2023. From pretraining data to language models to downstream tasks: Tracking the trails of political biases leading to unfair NLP models. In *Proceedings of the 61st Annual Meeting of the Association for Computational Linguistics (Volume 1: Long Papers)*, pages 11737–11762, Toronto, Canada. Association for Computational Linguistics.

Katja Filippova. 2020. Controlled hallucinations: Learning to generate faithfully from noisy data. In *Findings of the Association for Computational Linguistics: EMNLP 2020*, pages 864–870.

Aparna Garimella, Akhash Amarnath, Kiran Kumar, Akash Pramod Yalla, Anandhavelu N, Niyati Chhaya, and Balaji Vasan Srinivasan. 2021. He is very intelligent, she is very beautiful? On Mitigating Social Biases in Language Modelling and Generation. In *Findings of the Association for Computational Linguistics: ACL-IJCNLP 2021*, pages 4534–4545, Online. Association for Computational Linguistics.

Zhibin Gou, Zhihong Shao, Yeyun Gong, Yelong Shen, Yujiu Yang, Nan Duan, and Weizhu Chen. 2023. Critic: Large language models can self-correct with tool-interactive critiquing. *arXiv preprint arXiv:2305.11738*.

Tanya Goyal and Greg Durrett. 2020. Evaluating factuality in generation with dependency-level entailment. *arXiv preprint arXiv:2010.05478*.

Yue Guo, Yi Yang, and Ahmed Abbasi. 2022. Autodebias: Debiasing masked language models with automated biased prompts. In *Proceedings of the 60th Annual Meeting of the Association for Computational Linguistics (Volume 1: Long Papers)*, pages 1012–1023, Dublin, Ireland. Association for Computational Linguistics.

Tianxing He, Jingzhao Zhang, Zhiming Zhou, and James Glass. 2019. Exposure bias versus self-recovery: Are distortions really incremental for autoregressive text generation? *arXiv preprint arXiv:1905.10617*.

Dirk Hovy and Shannon L. Spruit. 2016. The social impact of natural language processing. In *Proceedings of the 54th Annual Meeting of the Association for Computational Linguistics (Volume 2: Short Papers)*, pages 591–598, Berlin, Germany. Association for Computational Linguistics.

Jie Huang and Kevin Chen-Chuan Chang. 2023. Citation: A key to building responsible and accountable large language models. *arXiv preprint arXiv:2307.02185*.

Yichong Huang, Xiachong Feng, Xiaocheng Feng, and Bing Qin. 2021. The factual inconsistency problem in abstractive text summarization: A survey. *arXiv preprint arXiv:2104.14839*.

Masahiro Kaneko and Danushka Bollegala. 2021. Dictionary-based debiasing of pre-trained word embeddings. *ArXiv*, abs/2101.09525.

Wojciech Kryściński, Bryan McCann, Caiming Xiong, and Richard Socher. 2019. Evaluating the factual consistency of abstractive text summarization. *arXiv preprint arXiv:1910.12840*.

Philippe Laban, Tobias Schnabel, Paul N Bennett, and Marti A Hearst. 2022. Summac: Re-visiting nli-based models for inconsistency detection in summarization. *Transactions of the Association for Computational Linguistics*, 10:163–177.

Faisal Ladhak, Esin Durmus, Mirac Suzgun, Tianyi Zhang, Dan Jurafsky, Kathleen McKeown, and Tatsunori Hashimoto. 2023. When do pre-training biases propagate to downstream tasks? a case study in text summarization. In *Proceedings of the 17th Conference of the European Chapter of the Association for Computational Linguistics*, pages 3206–3219, Dubrovnik, Croatia. Association for Computational Linguistics.

John Lalor, Yi Yang, Kendall Smith, Nicole Forsgren, and Ahmed Abbasi. 2022. Benchmarking intersectional biases in NLP. In *Proceedings of the 2022 Conference of the North American Chapter of the Association for Computational Linguistics: Human Language Technologies*, pages 3598–3609, Seattle, United States. Association for Computational Linguistics.

Paul Pu Liang, Irene Mengze Li, Emily Zheng, Yao Chong Lim, Ruslan Salakhutdinov, and Louis-Philippe Morency. 2020. Towards debiasing sentence representations.

Shayne Longpre, Kartik Perisetla, Anthony Chen, Nikhil Ramesh, Chris DuBois, and Sameer Singh. 2021. Entity-based knowledge conflicts in question answering. *arXiv preprint arXiv:2109.05052*.

Kishan Maharaj, Ashita Saxena, Raja Kumar, Abhijit Mishra, and Pushpak Bhattacharyya. 2023. Eyes show the way: Modelling gaze behaviour for hallucination detection. In *Findings of the Association for Computational Linguistics: EMNLP 2023*, pages 11424–11438, Singapore. Association for Computational Linguistics.

Kyle Mahowald, Anna A Ivanova, Idan A Blank, Nancy Kanwisher, Joshua B Tenenbaum, and Evelina Fedorenko. 2023. Dissociating language and thought in large language models: a cognitive perspective. *arXiv preprint arXiv:2301.06627*.

Potsawee Manakul, Adian Liusie, and Mark JF Gales. 2023. Selfcheckgpt: Zero-resource black-box hallucination detection for generative large language models. *arXiv preprint arXiv:2303.08896*.

Thomas Manzini, Lim Yao Chong, Alan W Black, and Yulia Tsvetkov. 2019. Black is to criminal as Caucasian is to police: Detecting and removing multiclass bias in word embeddings. In *Proceedings of the 2019 Conference of the North American Chapter of the Association for Computational Linguistics: Human Language Technologies, Volume 1 (Long and Short Papers)*, pages 615–621, Minneapolis, Minnesota. Association for Computational Linguistics.

Marianna Martindale, Marine Carpuat, Kevin Duh, and Paul McNamee. 2019. Identifying fluently inadequate output in neural and statistical machine translation. In *Proceedings of Machine Translation Summit XVII: Research Track*, pages 233–243.

Joshua Maynez, Shashi Narayan, Bernd Bohnet, and Ryan McDonald. 2020. On faithfulness and factuality in abstractive summarization. *arXiv preprint arXiv:2005.00661*.

Anshuman Mishra, Dhruvesh Patel, Aparna Vijayakumar, Xiang Lorraine Li, Pavan Kapanipathi, and Kartik Talamadupula. 2021. Looking beyond sentence-level natural language inference for question answering and text summarization. In *Proceedings of the 2021 Conference of the North American Chapter of the Association for Computational Linguistics: Human Language Technologies*, pages 1322–1336.

Moin Nadeem, Anna Bethke, and Siva Reddy. 2021. StereoSet: Measuring stereotypical bias in pretrained language models. In *Proceedings of the 59th Annual Meeting of the Association for Computational Linguistics and the 11th International Joint Conference on Natural Language Processing (Volume 1: Long Papers)*, pages 5356–5371, Online. Association for Computational Linguistics.

Nikita Nangia, Clara Vania, Rasika Bhalerao, and Samuel R. Bowman. 2020. CrowS-pairs: A challenge dataset for measuring social biases in masked language models. In *Proceedings of the 2020 Conference on Empirical Methods in Natural Language Processing (EMNLP)*, pages 1953–1967, Online. Association for Computational Linguistics.

Alicia Parrish, Angelica Chen, Nikita Nangia, Vishakh Padmakumar, Jason Phang, Jana Thompson, Phu Mon Htut, and Samuel R. Bowman. 2022. Bbq: A hand-built bias benchmark for question answering.

Clément Rebuffel, Thomas Scialom, Laure Soulier, Benjamin Piwowarski, Sylvain Lamprier, Jacopo

Staiano, Geoffrey Scoutheeten, and Patrick Gallinari. 2021. Data-questeval: A referenceless metric for data-to-text semantic evaluation. *arXiv preprint arXiv:2104.07555*.

Nihar Sahoo, Himanshu Gupta, and Pushpak Bhattacharyya. 2022. Detecting unintended social bias in toxic language datasets. In *Proceedings of the 26th Conference on Computational Natural Language Learning (CoNLL)*, pages 132–143, Abu Dhabi, United Arab Emirates (Hybrid). Association for Computational Linguistics.

Nihar Sahoo, Niteesh Mallela, and Pushpak Bhattacharyya. 2023. With prejudice to none: A few-shot, multilingual transfer learning approach to detect social bias in low resource languages. In *Findings of the Association for Computational Linguistics: ACL 2023*, pages 13316–13330, Toronto, Canada. Association for Computational Linguistics.

Nihar Ranja Sahoo, Gyana Prakash Beria, and Pushpak Bhattacharyya. 2024a. IndicCONAN: A multilingual dataset for combating hate speech in indian context. *Proceedings of the AAAI Conference on Artificial Intelligence*, 38(20):22313–22321.

Nihar Ranjan Sahoo, Pranamya Prashant Kulkarni, Narjis Asad, Arif Ahmad, Tanu Goyal, Aparna Garimella, and Pushpak Bhattacharyya. 2024b. IndiBias: A benchmark dataset to measure social biases in language models for indian context.

Timo Schick, Sahana Udupa, and Hinrich Schütze. 2021. Self-diagnosis and self-debiasing: A proposal for reducing corpus-based bias in nlp.

Thomas Scialom, Paul-Alexis Dray, Patrick Gallinari, Sylvain Lamprier, Benjamin Piwowarski, Jacopo Staiano, and Alex Wang. 2021. Questeval: Summarization asks for fact-based evaluation. *arXiv preprint arXiv:2103.12693*.

Emily Sheng, Kai-Wei Chang, Premkumar Natarajan, and Nanyun Peng. 2019. The woman worked as a babysitter: On biases in language generation. *arXiv preprint arXiv:1909.01326*.

Kurt Shuster, Spencer Poff, Moya Chen, Douwe Kiela, and Jason Weston. 2021. Retrieval augmentation reduces hallucination in conversation. *arXiv preprint arXiv:2104.07567*.

Sandhya Singh, Prapti Roy, Nihar Sahoo, Niteesh Mallela, Himanshu Gupta, Pushpak Bhattacharyya, Milind Savagaonkar, Nidhi, Roshni Ramnani, Anutosh Maitra, and Shubhashis Sengupta. 2022. Hollywood identity bias dataset: A context oriented bias analysis of movie dialogues.

Yi Chern Tan and L. Elisa Celis. 2019. Assessing social and intersectional biases in contextualized word representations.

Ran Tian, Shashi Narayan, Thibault Sellam, and Ankur P Parikh. 2019. Sticking to the facts: Confident decoding for faithful data-to-text generation. *arXiv preprint arXiv:1910.08684*.

Jesse Vig, Sebastian Gehrmann, Yonatan Belinkov, Sharon Qian, Daniel Nevo, Yaron Singer, and Stuart Shieber. 2020. Investigating gender bias in language models using causal mediation analysis. In *Advances in Neural Information Processing Systems*, volume 33, pages 12388–12401. Curran Associates, Inc.

Alex Wang, Kyunghyun Cho, and Mike Lewis. 2020a. Asking and answering questions to evaluate the factual consistency of summaries. *arXiv preprint arXiv:2004.04228*.

Yuhang Wang, Dongyuan Lu, Chao Kong, and Jitao Sang. 2023. Towards alleviating the object bias in prompt tuning-based factual knowledge extraction. In *Findings of the Association for Computational Linguistics: ACL 2023*, pages 4420–4432, Toronto, Canada. Association for Computational Linguistics.

Zhenyi Wang, Xiaoyang Wang, Bang An, Dong Yu, and Changyou Chen. 2020b. Towards faithful neural table-to-text generation with content-matching constraints. *arXiv preprint arXiv:2005.00969*.

Pengfei Yu and Heng Ji. 2023. Self information update for large language models through mitigating exposure bias. *arXiv preprint arXiv:2305.18582*.

Brian Hu Zhang, Blake Lemoine, and Margaret Mitchell. 2018. Mitigating unwanted biases with adversarial learning. In *Proceedings of the 2018 AAAI/ACM Conference on AI, Ethics, and Society*, pages 335–340.

Jieyu Zhao, Tianlu Wang, Mark Yatskar, Ryan Cotterell, Vicente Ordonez, and Kai-Wei Chang. 2019. Gender bias in contextualized word embeddings. *arXiv preprint arXiv:1904.03310*.

Knowledge-enhanced Response Generation in Dialogue Systems: Current Advancements and Emerging Horizons

Priyanshu Priya[1], **Deeksha Varshney**[1], **Mauajama Firdaus**[2], **Asif Ekbal**[1]
[1]Indian Institute of Technology Patna, India
[2]University of Alberta, Edmonton, Canada
(priyanshu_2021cs26@iitp.ac.in, 1821cs13@iitp.ac.in, mauzama.03@gmail.com, asif@iitp.ac.in)

Abstract

This tutorial provides an in-depth exploration of Knowledge-enhanced Dialogue Systems (KEDS), diving into their foundational aspects, methodologies, advantages, and practical applications. Topics include the distinction between internal and external knowledge integration, diverse methodologies employed in grounding dialogues, and innovative approaches to leveraging knowledge graphs for enhanced conversation quality. Furthermore, the tutorial touches upon the rise of biomedical text mining, the advent of domain-specific language models, and the challenges and strategies specific to medical dialogue generation. The primary objective is to give attendees a comprehensive understanding of KEDS. By delineating the nuances of these systems, the tutorial aims to elucidate their significance, highlight advancements made using deep learning, and pinpoint the current challenges. Special emphasis is placed on showcasing how KEDS can be fine-tuned for domain-specific requirements, with a spotlight on the healthcare sector. The tutorial is crafted for both beginners and intermediate researchers in the dialogue systems domain, with a focus on those keen on advancing research in KEDS. It will also be valuable for practitioners in sectors like healthcare, seeking to integrate advanced dialogue systems.

1. Introduction

In the realm of artificial intelligence, dialogue systems have evolved as crucial interfaces facilitating human-machine interaction through natural language conversations. These systems are broadly categorized into task-oriented and open-domain dialogue systems. While task-oriented systems are designed to assist users in specific tasks like restaurant booking (Firdaus et al., 2020d, 2021c; Varshney and Singh, 2021), open-domain systems engage in a broader spectrum of conversational topics without a defined objective (Firdaus et al., 2020a; Varshney et al., 2020). The integration of deep learning, particularly neural language models, has significantly elevated the performance of these systems, yet challenges like understanding user opinions, integrating visual data, and ambiguity in open-domain interactions persist (Chen et al., 2017). In addressing the limitation of generating bland or generic responses common in traditional dialogue systems, Knowledge Enhanced Dialogue Systems (KEDS) have emerged as a prominent solution. The crux of KEDS lies in grounding the dialogues in external or internal knowledge, thereby enriching the conversation with insightful and contextually relevant responses. This tutorial provides an in-depth examination of KEDS, shedding light on its integral components, various approaches, and the benefits derived from such systems.

In this tutorial, we first introduce the foundational frameworks of Knowledge-enhanced Dialogue Systems (KEDS), establishing a solid understanding of how they augment dialogue systems. Following this, we explore the diverse methodologies employed to incorporate both internal and external knowledge sources, thereby enriching the conversational experience. We delve into internal knowledge sources embedded in the input text, such as topics, keywords, and internal graph structures, as discussed in (Ahmad et al., 2023; Mishra et al., 2022b; Firdaus et al., 2021a; Xie and Pu, 2021; Priya et al., 2023a). Concurrently, we investigate external knowledge acquisition from resources like uni-and-multi-modal knowledge bases, knowledge graphs, and grounded text such as persona information, Wikipedia information as elucidated in (Dinan et al., 2018; Zhou et al., 2018b; Firdaus et al., 2020f; Varshney and Singh, 2021; Ghazvininejad et al., 2018; Varshney et al., 2022a).

The discourse further extends to domain-specific applications, particularly in the healthcare sector. In the healthcare domain, having a thorough understanding of a person's medical history, mental state, symptoms, and treatment plan is crucial. Studies have indicated that the integration of extensive knowledge resources into healthcare dialogue systems presents multiple significant benefits. These include improving the system's understanding of medical terminology and concepts, equipping the system with the ability to reason and make inferences, grasping the emotional nuances within conversations, and discerning beneficial response patterns that contribute to emotional alleviation (Varshney et al., 2023b; Liang et al., 2021). Motivated by these insights, this tutorial session aims to explore various research endeavors that incorporate external knowledge into healthcare dialogue systems, thereby facilitating personalized and effective support (Shen et al., 2022; Deng et al., 2023; Varshney

LREC-COLING 2024 Tutorials, pages 80–87

et al., 2022c, 2023b,c; Liu et al., 2021).

In the conclusion section, we highlight the shortcomings of conventional dialogue systems to provide a clearer pathway for newcomers to further research in KEDS systems.

2. Target Audience

We believe that the potential target audience could be the students at all levels (Doctorals, Masters, Bachelors), and anyone who is associated with healthcare, customer care, & related application areas, and researchers. We would assume an acquaintance with basic concepts about chatbots and neural networks, such as those included in most introductory Machine Learning (ML), Deep Learning (DL) and Natural Language Processing (NLP) courses. We expect an audience size of about 25-30 participants.

3. Outline

This tutorial is organized as follows:

- **Introduction (15 minutes)** We will briefly introduce dialogue systems, including the different types of dialogue systems and limitations of traditional dialogue systems (Chen et al., 2017). Afterward, we will discuss the notion of knowledge-enhanced response generation in dialogue systems and the different categories of knowledge sources, *viz.* internal knowledge and external knowledge. Precisely, we will delve into the concepts of (i) Internal knowledge sources embedded in the input text, including but not limited to topic, keyword, and internal graph structure (Xing et al., 2017; Xu et al., 2020; Li and Sun, 2018; Chen and Yang, 2023), and (ii) External knowledge acquisition, including but not limited to the multimodal information, persona, knowledge base, external knowledge graph, and grounded text (Firdaus et al., 2020b, 2022d; Dinan et al., 2018; Zhou et al., 2018b; Ghazvininejad et al., 2018).
- **Need and Challenges of Knowledge-enhanced Response Generation in Dialogues (15 minutes)**
  An effective dialogue system should be able to generate coherent, contextually relevant, user-centric, and informative responses. To achieve this, these systems require diverse information sources, including textual and structured data from external sources, user attributes (like sentiment, emotions, politeness, personal profile information - age, gender, persona, etc.), and contextual information (Wang et al., 2023a). Integrating the knowledge into the generated responses poses challenges concerning the retrieval or selection of pertinent knowledge and effective comprehension and utilization of the acquired knowledge to facilitate response generation (Wang et al., 2023b).
  In this section, we will discuss how the varied knowledge resources enhance response generation and improve the interpretability of dialogue systems by incorporating explicit semantics. Subsequently, we will address the challenges inherent in knowledge-enhanced response generation within dialogue systems.
- **Internal Knowledge-enhanced Response Generation in Dialogue Systems (60 minutes)**
  In this part of the tutorial, we aim to delineate the internal knowledge-enhanced response generation methods and applications. The information from internal knowledge sources helps enlighten and drive the generated responses to be informative and avoids generating universally relevant replies with little semantics. The internal knowledge can be obtained from topical information, keywords, and internal graph structures. We will point out the works that incorporate these knowledge sources for response generation.
  (i) *Response enhanced by Topic*: A dialogue system frequently employing responses such as *"I don't know"*, *"Okay"* *"I see"* may appear repetitive and uninformative. While these off-topic replies are generally harmless for addressing various inquiries, they lack engagement and are likely to prematurely conclude conversations, significantly diminishing the overall user experience (Xing et al., 2017; Ahmad et al., 2023). Consequently, there is a pressing demand for on-topic response generation. This part of the tutorial delves into the works that have incorporated topical knowledge to guide the informative response generation (Xing et al., 2017; Xu et al., 2020).
  (ii) *Response enhanced by Keywords*: Recent research has incorporated personalized data into the dialogue generation process to enhance the quality of dialogue responses, particularly concerning emotional aspects, *viz.* emotion (Rashkin et al., 2019), sentiment (Chen and Nakamura, 2021), and politeness (Mishra et al., 2022b; Wang et al., 2020). We will discuss the works that attempt to integrate emotion (Zhou et al., 2018a; Firdaus et al., 2021a; Madasu et al., 2022; Majumder et al., 2022; Mishra et al., 2022c; Samad et al., 2022), sentiment (Firdaus et al., 2021b, 2022a), politeness (Golchha et al., 2019; Firdaus et al., 2020c; Mishra et al., 2022a; Firdaus et al., 2022a; Mishra et al., 2023a,c,b; Priya et al., 2023b), and intent (Xie and Pu, 2021) into the generated responses to make them personalized and engaging.

(iii) ***Response enhanced by Internal Knowledge Graph***: Internal knowledge graphs are valuable for comprehending lengthy input sequences. They serve as intermediaries to consolidate or eliminate redundant data, resulting in a concise representation of the input document (Fan et al., 2019; Priya et al., 2023a). Furthermore, KG representations enable the creation of structured summaries and emphasize the connections between related concepts, particularly in cases where complex events associated with a single entity extend across multiple sentences (Huang et al., 2020). In this part of the tutorial, we will present works integrating an internal knowledge graph to enhance response generation capabilities (Liang et al., 2022; Firdaus et al., 2020e).

- **External Knowledge-enhanced Response Generation in Dialogue Systems (60 minutes)**
  (i) *Persona Information*. Research focused on personas in dialogue systems requires that the agent adopts a specific character when engaging with users. This persona is closely linked to personality, which influences the emotional and personal aspects of users. In this section of the tutorial, we discuss studies that have employed persona-aware techniques to enhance the efficacy of response generation in dialogue systems (Firdaus et al., 2020f; Saha and Ananiadou, 2022; Firdaus et al., 2022d,b; Zhong et al., 2022). Findings from these studies suggest that persona information drives empathetic and personalized conversations more than non-empathetic ones.
  (ii) *Multimodal Information*. Lately, the utilization of multimodal information has witnessed a surge in popularity in the field of dialogue systems. This approach is instrumental in comprehensively understanding users' emotional and mental states, as it leverages textual and non-textual attributes (Firdaus et al., 2023). In this part of the tutorial, we aim to discuss several notable studies in the literature that have harnessed multimodal data to enhance response generation within dialogue systems (Tavabi et al., 2019; Firdaus et al., 2020a, 2022c).
  (iii) *External Knowledge Bases.* Knowledge-grounded systems utilize external resources such as Wikipedia documents to enhance response generation. (Dinan et al., 2018) released the first Wikipedia knowledge-grounded conversation dataset. (Varshney et al., 2023a) utilized the knowledge on various topics such as politics, and movies using the Topical Chat (Gopalakrishnan et al., 2019) and CMU_DoG (Zhou et al., 2018c) dataset to propose a knowledge-emotion enabled conversational model. (Lin et al., 2020) introduced a model that combined knowledge decoders with a pointer network to effectively handle out-of-vocabulary words. Experts suggest converting unstructured knowledge into organized knowledge graphs, composed of triplets (entity, relation, entity/item). Models, such as CCM, retrieve subgraphs from these graphs, especially using knowledge bases like ConceptNet (Speer and Havasi, 2012), and employ attention mechanisms to blend this knowledge into conversations (Zhou et al., 2018b). Concept Flow expands this by including extended subgraph ranges, integrating knowledge from two sources (Zhang et al., 2019). (Varshney et al., 2022a) utilizes both knowledge graphs and Wikipedia documents with a coreference-based knowledge graph augmenting method to improve factual accuracy in dialogue systems.
- **Knowledge-grounded Dialogue Systems in Healthcare (20 minutes)** In healthcare, background knowledge is vital in understanding an individual's medical history, mental condition, symptoms, and treatment plan. Research has shown that integrating comprehensive knowledge resources in the healthcare dialogue systems offers several key advantages, such as enhancing the system's grasp of medical concepts and terminology, empowering the system with reasoning and inference capabilities, comprehending emotional dynamics in conversations, and identifying useful response patterns leading to emotional relief (Varshney et al., 2022b; Liang et al., 2021). Driven by these considerations, in this tutorial session, we will discuss the studies that infuse external knowledge in healthcare dialogue systems for providing personalized and effective support (Shen et al., 2022; Deng et al., 2023; Varshney et al., 2022c, 2023b,c; Liu et al., 2021).
- **Hands-on Session (50 minutes)**
  1. Setting up a basic knowledge-enhanced dialogue system for healthcare domain (Varshney et al., 2023c,b).
  2. Integrating a sample knowledge base (e.g., Unified Medical Language System).
  3. Evaluating the performance of the dialogue using automated metrics such as BLEU, F1, and embedding-based metrics.
- **Conclusion and Future Perspectives (20 minutes)**
  This tutorial explores notable studies on knowledge-enhanced dialogue generation, showcasing how leveraging diverse information sources can enhance dialogue model efficacy. Despite advancements, several challenges remain, highlighting exciting future re-

search avenues. We'll delve into four key research directions: (i) Knowledge Acquisition from Pre-trained Language Models: Pre-trained models harbor vast implicit knowledge without external memory reliance (Lewis et al., 2020), opening avenues for efficient knowledge extraction methods like knowledge distillation, data augmentation using pre-trained models as knowledge sources (Petroni et al., 2019), and prompting of language models (Li and Liang, 2021). (ii) Knowledge Acquisition from Limited Resources: In real-world scenarios, new domains often have scarce examples, necessitating rapid adaptation of knowledge-enhanced dialogue models via efficient meta-learning algorithms that minimize task-specific fine-tuning. (iii) Continuous Knowledge Acquisition: A noteworthy exploration is done in (Mazumder et al., 2018), where authors devised a knowledge acquisition engine for chatbots, enabling continuous learning from diverse information sources during interactions. (iv) Leveraging Emotional Knowledge through External Sources: Utilizing emotional knowledge bases like SenticNet aids in discerning user emotional states and background, thus generating emotionally coherent responses, crucial in healthcare and social good applications like persuasion and negotiation.

4. Proposed Length of the tutorial

Half-day (4h long including a coffee break (30m long))

5. Diversity Considerations

This tutorial on Knowledge-enhanced Dialogue Systems (KEDS) emphasizes inclusivity and diversity in three ways: (i) Enhancing Fairness: It educates on designing less biased, more inclusive dialogue systems, promoting equity in healthcare communication tools. (ii) Addressing Unique Needs: It's relevant to underrepresented groups like healthcare professionals and researchers from certain countries, offering tailored insights. (iii) Diverse Presenters: The presenters, originating from an underrepresented country, embody the commitment to diversity and inclusivity in computational linguistics.

6. Reading List

Extensive reading list is available at Reading List for Knowledge-enhanced Dialogue Systems.

7. Presenters

1. Priyanshu Priya, Indian Institute of Technology Patna, India (priyanshu_2021cs26@iitp.ac.in; priyanshu528priya@gmail.com; LinkedIn)
2. Deeksha Varshney, Indian Institute of Technology Patna, India (deeksha_1821cs13@iitp.ac.in; deeksha.varshney2695@gmail.com; LinkedIn)
3. Mauajama Firdaus, University of Alberta, Canada (mauzama.03@gmail.com; LinkedIn)
4. Asif EKbal, Indian Institute of Technology Patna, India. (asif@iitp.ac.in; asif.ekabl@gmail.com); Webpage: http://www.iitp.ac.in/ asif/; LinkedIn.

8. Other Information

While we are dedicated to accommodate a flexible number of participants, we anticipate an audience of 25-30 people. Our estimate is based on the previous attendance at the tutorial delivered on the topic "Empathetic Conversational Artificial Intelligence Systems: Recent Advances and New Frontiers" was presented at the 32nd International Joint Conference on Artificial Intelligence, held from 19-25 August, 2023 at Macao, S.A.R, China., as well as the outreach efforts we have undertaken to promote the tutorial.

We would appreciate access to standard audio-visual equipment, such as microphones, projectors, and screens, to guarantee the tutorial's success. Furthermore, a high-speed internet connection is essential to ensure a seamless hands-on session during the tutorial, and an interactive whiteboard might be useful during the presentation for explanatory reasons. This configuration will assist us in facilitating interesting and informative discussions.

9. Ethics Statement

Dialogue systems are becoming ubiquitous in daily applications like healthcare and customer care, necessitating ethical considerations in development and usage. Key considerations include: (i) Knowledge-enhanced dialogue systems can collect sensitive user information, including personal and health data. To safeguard users' privacy, the data used in the research presented here has been anonymized, and personal details have been protected; (ii) In the context of knowledge-enhanced dialogue systems, user-centric design is essential, ensuring that users have control over the conversation and information sharing. Respecting user autonomy, these systems should offer options to conclude the conversation or seek further assistance. The datasets created for various research topics covered in this tutorial have been crafted to preserve user autonomy.

10. Bibliographical References

Zishan Ahmad, Kshitij Mishra, Asif Ekbal, and Pushpak Bhattacharyya. 2023. RPTCS: A reinforced persona-aware topic-guiding conversational system. In *Proceedings of the 17th Conference of the European Chapter of the Association for Computational Linguistics*, pages 3482–3494, Dubrovnik, Croatia. Association for Computational Linguistics.

Hongshen Chen, Xiaorui Liu, Dawei Yin, and Jiliang Tang. 2017. A survey on dialogue systems: Recent advances and new frontiers. *Acm Sigkdd Explorations Newsletter*, 19(2):25–35.

Jiaao Chen and Diyi Yang. 2023. Controllable conversation generation with conversation structures via diffusion models. In *Findings of the Association for Computational Linguistics: ACL 2023*, pages 7238–7251.

Sinan Chen and Masahide Nakamura. 2021. Generating personalized dialogues based on conversation log summarization and sentiment analysis. In *The 23rd International Conference on Information Integration and Web Intelligence*, pages 217–222.

Yang Deng, Wenxuan Zhang, Yifei Yuan, and Wai Lam. 2023. Knowledge-enhanced mixed-initiative dialogue system for emotional support conversations. *arXiv preprint arXiv:2305.10172*.

Emily Dinan, Stephen Roller, Kurt Shuster, Angela Fan, Michael Auli, and Jason Weston. 2018. Wizard of wikipedia: Knowledge-powered conversational agents. In *International Conference on Learning Representations*.

Angela Fan, Claire Gardent, Chloé Braud, and Antoine Bordes. 2019. Using local knowledge graph construction to scale seq2seq models to multi-document inputs. *arXiv preprint arXiv:1910.08435*.

Mauajama Firdaus, Hardik Chauhan, Asif Ekbal, and Pushpak Bhattacharyya. 2020a. Emosen: Generating sentiment and emotion controlled responses in a multimodal dialogue system. *IEEE Transactions on Affective Computing*, 13(3):1555–1566.

Mauajama Firdaus, Hardik Chauhan, Asif Ekbal, and Pushpak Bhattacharyya. 2020b. Meisd: A multimodal multi-label emotion, intensity and sentiment dialogue dataset for emotion recognition and sentiment analysis in conversations. In *Proceedings of the 28th International Conference on Computational Linguistics*, pages 4441–4453.

Mauajama Firdaus, Hardik Chauhan, Asif Ekbal, and Pushpak Bhattacharyya. 2021a. More the merrier: Towards multi-emotion and intensity controllable response generation. In *Proceedings of the AAAI Conference on Artificial Intelligence*, volume 35, pages 12821–12829.

Mauajama Firdaus, Asif Ekbal, and Pushpak Bhattacharyya. 2020c. Incorporating politeness across languages in customer care responses: Towards building a multi-lingual empathetic dialogue agent. In *Proceedings of the Twelfth Language Resources and Evaluation Conference*, pages 4172–4182.

Mauajama Firdaus, Asif Ekbal, and Pushpak Bhattacharyya. 2022a. Polise: Reinforcing politeness using user sentiment for customer care response generation. In *Proceedings of the 29th International Conference on Computational Linguistics*, pages 6165–6175.

Mauajama Firdaus, Umang Jain, Asif Ekbal, and Pushpak Bhattacharyya. 2021b. Seprg: sentiment aware emotion controlled personalized response generation. In *Proceedings of the 14th International Conference on Natural Language Generation*, pages 353–363.

Mauajama Firdaus, Arunav Shandilya, Asif Ekbal, and Pushpak Bhattacharyya. 2022b. Being polite: Modeling politeness variation in a personalized dialog agent. *IEEE Transactions on Computational Social Systems*.

Mauajama Firdaus, Gopendra Vikram Singh, Asif Ekbal, and Pushpak Bhattacharyya. 2023. Affectgcn: a multimodal graph convolutional network for multi-emotion with intensity recognition and sentiment analysis in dialogues. *Multimedia Tools and Applications*, pages 1–22.

Mauajama Firdaus, Nidhi Thakur, and Asif Ekbal. 2020d. MultiDM-GCN: Aspect-guided response generation in multi-domain multi-modal dialogue system using graph convolutional network. In *Findings of the Association for Computational Linguistics: EMNLP 2020*, pages 2318–2328, Online. Association for Computational Linguistics.

Mauajama Firdaus, Nidhi Thakur, and Asif Ekbal. 2020e. Multidm-gcn: Aspect-guided response generation in multi-domain multi-modal dialogue system using graph convolutional network. In *Findings of the Association for Computational Linguistics: EMNLP 2020*, pages 2318–2328.

Mauajama Firdaus, Nidhi Thakur, and Asif Ekbal. 2021c. Aspect-aware response generation for multimodal dialogue system. *ACM Transactions on Intelligent Systems and Technology (TIST)*, 12(2):1–33.

Mauajama Firdaus, Nidhi Thakur, and Asif Ekbal. 2022c. Sentiment guided aspect conditioned dialogue generation in a multimodal system. In *Advances in Information Retrieval: 44th European Conference on IR Research, ECIR 2022, Stavanger, Norway, April 10–14, 2022, Proceedings, Part I*, pages 199–214. Springer.

Mauajama Firdaus, Naveen Thangavelu, Asif Ekba, and Pushpak Bhattacharyya. 2020f. Persona aware response generation with emotions. In *2020 International Joint Conference on Neural Networks (IJCNN)*, pages 1–8. IEEE.

Mauajama Firdaus, Naveen Thangavelu, Asif Ekbal, and Pushpak Bhattacharyya. 2022d. I enjoy writing and playing, do you: A personalized and emotion grounded dialogue agent using generative adversarial network. *IEEE Transactions on Affective Computing*.

Marjan Ghazvininejad, Chris Brockett, Ming-Wei Chang, Bill Dolan, Jianfeng Gao, Wen-tau Yih, and Michel Galley. 2018. A knowledge-grounded neural conversation model. In *Thirty-Second AAAI Conference on Artificial Intelligence*.

Hitesh Golchha, Mauajama Firdaus, Asif Ekbal, and Pushpak Bhattacharyya. 2019. Courteously yours: Inducing courteous behavior in customer care responses using reinforced pointer generator network. In *Proceedings of the 2019 Conference of the North American Chapter of the Association for Computational Linguistics: Human Language Technologies, Volume 1 (Long and Short Papers)*, pages 851–860.

Karthik Gopalakrishnan, Behnam Hedayatnia, Qinglang Chen, Anna Gottardi, Sanjeev Kwatra, Anu Venkatesh, Raefer Gabriel, Dilek Hakkani-Tür, and Amazon Alexa AI. 2019. Topical-chat: Towards knowledge-grounded open-domain conversations. In *INTERSPEECH*, pages 1891–1895.

Luyang Huang, Lingfei Wu, and Lu Wang. 2020. Knowledge graph-augmented abstractive summarization with semantic-driven cloze reward. *arXiv preprint arXiv:2005.01159*.

Patrick Lewis, Ethan Perez, Aleksandra Piktus, Fabio Petroni, Vladimir Karpukhin, Naman Goyal, Heinrich Küttler, Mike Lewis, Wen-tau Yih, Tim Rocktäschel, et al. 2020. Retrieval-augmented generation for knowledge-intensive nlp tasks. *Advances in Neural Information Processing Systems*, 33:9459–9474.

Jingyuan Li and Xiao Sun. 2018. A syntactically constrained bidirectional-asynchronous approach for emotional conversation generation. In *Proceedings of the 2018 Conference on Empirical Methods in Natural Language Processing*, pages 678–683.

Xiang Lisa Li and Percy Liang. 2021. Prefix-tuning: Optimizing continuous prompts for generation. *arXiv preprint arXiv:2101.00190*.

Yunlong Liang, Fandong Meng, Ying Zhang, Yufeng Chen, Jinan Xu, and Jie Zhou. 2021. Infusing multi-source knowledge with heterogeneous graph neural network for emotional conversation generation. In *Proceedings of the AAAI Conference on Artificial Intelligence*, volume 35, pages 13343–13352.

Yunlong Liang, Fandong Meng, Ying Zhang, Yufeng Chen, Jinan Xu, and Jie Zhou. 2022. Emotional conversation generation with heterogeneous graph neural network. *Artificial Intelligence*, 308:103714.

Xiexiong Lin, Weiyu Jian, Jianshan He, Taifeng Wang, and Wei Chu. 2020. Generating informative conversational response using recurrent knowledge-interaction and knowledge-copy. In *Proceedings of the 58th annual meeting of the association for computational linguistics*, pages 41–52.

Wenge Liu, Jianheng Tang, Xiaodan Liang, and Qingling Cai. 2021. Heterogeneous graph reasoning for knowledge-grounded medical dialogue system. *Neurocomputing*, 442:260–268.

Avinash Madasu, Mauajama Firdaus, and Asif Eqbal. 2022. A unified framework for emotion identification and generation in dialogues. *arXiv preprint arXiv:2205.15513*.

Navonil Majumder, Deepanway Ghosal, Devamanyu Hazarika, Alexander Gelbukh, Rada Mihalcea, and Soujanya Poria. 2022. Exemplars-guided empathetic response generation controlled by the elements of human communication. *IEEE Access*, 10:77176–77190.

Sahisnu Mazumder, Nianzu Ma, and Bing Liu. 2018. Towards a continuous knowledge learning engine for chatbots. *arXiv preprint arXiv:1802.06024*.

Kshitij Mishra, Mauajama Firdaus, and Asif Ekbal. 2022a. Please be polite: Towards building a politeness adaptive dialogue system for goal-oriented conversations. *Neurocomputing*, 494:242–254.

Kshitij Mishra, Mauajama Firdaus, and Asif Ekbal. 2022b. Predicting politeness variations in goal-oriented conversations. *IEEE Transactions on Computational Social Systems*.

Kshitij Mishra, Mauajama Firdaus, and Asif Ekbal. 2023a. Genpads: Reinforcing politeness in an end-to-end dialogue system. *Plos one*, 18(1):e0278323.

Kshitij Mishra, Priyanshu Priya, and Asif Ekbal. 2023b. Help me heal: A reinforced polite and empathetic mental health and legal counseling dialogue system for crime victims. In *Proceedings of the AAAI Conference on Artificial Intelligence*, volume 37, pages 14408–14416.

Kshitij Mishra, Priyanshu Priya, and Asif Ekbal. 2023c. Pal to lend a helping hand: Towards building an emotion adaptive polite and empathetic counseling conversational agent. In *Proceedings of the 61st Annual Meeting of the Association for Computational Linguistics (Volume 1: Long Papers)*, pages 12254–12271.

Kshitij Mishra, Azlaan Mustafa Samad, Palak Totala, and Asif Ekbal. 2022c. Pepds: A polite and empathetic persuasive dialogue system for charity donation. In *Proceedings of the 29th International Conference on Computational Linguistics*, pages 424–440.

Fabio Petroni, Tim Rocktäschel, Patrick Lewis, Anton Bakhtin, Yuxiang Wu, Alexander H Miller, and Sebastian Riedel. 2019. Language models as knowledge bases? *arXiv preprint arXiv:1909.01066*.

Priyanshu Priya, Mauajama Firdaus, and Asif Ekbal. 2023a. A multi-task learning framework for politeness and emotion detection in dialogues for mental health counselling and legal aid. *Expert Systems with Applications*, 224:120025.

Priyanshu Priya, Kshitij Mishra, Palak Totala, and Asif Ekbal. 2023b. Partner: A persuasive mental health and legal counselling dialogue system for women and children crime victims. In *Proceedings of the Thirty-Second International Joint Conference on Artificial Intelligence, IJCAI-23*, pages 6183–6191. International Joint Conferences on Artificial Intelligence Organization. AI for Good.

Hannah Rashkin, Eric Michael Smith, Margaret Li, and Y-Lan Boureau. 2019. Towards empathetic open-domain conversation models: A new benchmark and dataset. In *Proceedings of the 57th Annual Meeting of the Association for Computational Linguistics*, pages 5370–5381, Florence, Italy. Association for Computational Linguistics.

Tulika Saha and Sophia Ananiadou. 2022. Emotion-aware and intent-controlled empathetic response generation using hierarchical transformer network. In *2022 International Joint Conference on Neural Networks (IJCNN)*, pages 1–8. IEEE.

Azlaan Mustafa Samad, Kshitij Mishra, Mauajama Firdaus, and Asif Ekbal. 2022. Empathetic persuasion: Reinforcing empathy and persuasiveness in dialogue systems. In *Findings of the Association for Computational Linguistics: NAACL 2022*, pages 844–856.

Siqi Shen, Verónica Pérez-Rosas, Charles Welch, Soujanya Poria, and Rada Mihalcea. 2022. Knowledge enhanced reflection generation for counseling dialogues. In *Proceedings of the 60th Annual Meeting of the Association for Computational Linguistics (Volume 1: Long Papers)*, pages 3096–3107.

Robyn Speer and Catherine Havasi. 2012. Representing general relational knowledge in ConceptNet 5. In *Proceedings of the Eighth International Conference on Language Resources and Evaluation (LREC'12)*, pages 3679–3686, Istanbul, Turkey. European Language Resources Association (ELRA).

Leili Tavabi, Kalin Stefanov, Setareh Nasihati Gilani, David Traum, and Mohammad Soleymani. 2019. Multimodal learning for identifying opportunities for empathetic responses. In *2019 International Conference on Multimodal Interaction*, pages 95–104.

Deeksha Varshney, Asif Ekbal, Ganesh Prasad Nagaraja, Mrigank Tiwari, Abhijith Athreya Mysore Gopinath, and Pushpak Bhattacharyya. 2020. Natural language generation using transformer network in an open-domain setting. In *Natural Language Processing and Information Systems: 25th International Conference on Applications of Natural Language to Information Systems, NLDB 2020, Saarbrücken, Germany, June 24–26, 2020, Proceedings 25*, pages 82–93. Springer.

Deeksha Varshney, Asif Ekbal, Mrigank Tiwari, and Ganesh Prasad Nagaraja. 2023a. Emokbgan: Emotion controlled response generation using generative adversarial network for knowledge grounded conversation. *PloS one*, 18(2):e0280458.

Deeksha Varshney, Akshara Prabhakar, and Asif Ekbal. 2022a. Commonsense and named entity aware knowledge grounded dialogue generation. In *Proceedings of the 2022 Conference of the North American Chapter of the Association for Computational Linguistics: Human Language Technologies*, pages 1322–1335, Seattle, United

States. Association for Computational Linguistics.

Deeksha Varshney, Akshara Prabhakar, and Asif Ekbal. 2022b. Commonsense and named entity aware knowledge grounded dialogue generation. *arXiv preprint arXiv:2205.13928*.

Deeksha Varshney and Asif Ekbal Anushkha Singh. 2021. Knowledge grounded multimodal dialog generation in task-oriented settings. In *Proceedings of the 35th Pacific Asia Conference on Language, Information and Computation*, pages 425–435.

Deeksha Varshney, Aizan Zafar, Niranshu Kumar Behera, and Asif Ekbal. 2023b. Knowledge graph assisted end-to-end medical dialog generation. *Artificial Intelligence in Medicine*, 139:102535.

Deeksha Varshney, Aizan Zafar, Niranshu Kumar Behera, and Asif Ekbal. 2023c. Knowledge grounded medical dialogue generation using augmented graphs. *Scientific Reports*, 13(1):3310.

Deeksha Varshney, Aizan Zafar, Niranshu Kumar Behra, and Asif Ekbal. 2022c. Cdialog: A multi-turn covid-19 conversation dataset for entity-aware dialog generation. *arXiv preprint arXiv:2212.06049*.

Ming Wang, Bo Ning, and Bin Zhao. 2023a. A review of knowledge-grounded dialogue systems. In *2023 8th International Conference on Image, Vision and Computing (ICIVC)*, pages 819–824. IEEE.

Xintao Wang, Qianwen Yang, Yongting Qiu, Jiaqing Liang, Qianyu He, Zhouhong Gu, Yanghua Xiao, and Wei Wang. 2023b. Knowledgpt: Enhancing large language models with retrieval and storage access on knowledge bases. *arXiv preprint arXiv:2308.11761*.

Yi-Chia Wang, Alexandros Papangelis, Runze Wang, Zhaleh Feizollahi, Gokhan Tur, and Robert Kraut. 2020. Can you be more social? injecting politeness and positivity into task-oriented conversational agents. *arXiv preprint arXiv:2012.14653*.

Yubo Xie and Pearl Pu. 2021. Empathetic dialog generation with fine-grained intents. In *Proceedings of the 25th Conference on Computational Natural Language Learning*, pages 133–147.

Chen Xing, Wei Wu, Yu Wu, Jie Liu, Yalou Huang, Ming Zhou, and Wei-Ying Ma. 2017. Topic aware neural response generation. In *Proceedings of the AAAI Conference on Artificial Intelligence*, volume 31.

Minghong Xu, Piji Li, Haoran Yang, Pengjie Ren, Zhaochun Ren, Zhumin Chen, and Jun Ma. 2020. A neural topical expansion framework for unstructured persona-oriented dialogue generation. *arXiv preprint arXiv:2002.02153*.

Houyu Zhang, Zhenghao Liu, Chenyan Xiong, and Zhiyuan Liu. 2019. Grounded conversation generation as guided traverses in commonsense knowledge graphs. *arXiv preprint arXiv:1911.02707*.

Hanxun Zhong, Zhicheng Dou, Yutao Zhu, Hongjin Qian, and Ji-Rong Wen. 2022. Less is more: Learning to refine dialogue history for personalized dialogue generation. *arXiv preprint arXiv:2204.08128*.

Hao Zhou, Minlie Huang, Tianyang Zhang, Xiaoyan Zhu, and Bing Liu. 2018a. Emotional chatting machine: Emotional conversation generation with internal and external memory. In *Thirty-Second AAAI Conference on Artificial Intelligence*.

Hao Zhou, Tom Young, Minlie Huang, Haizhou Zhao, Jingfang Xu, and Xiaoyan Zhu. 2018b. Commonsense knowledge aware conversation generation with graph attention. In *Proceedings of the 27th International Joint Conference on Artificial Intelligence*, pages 4623–4629.

Kangyan Zhou, Shrimai Prabhumoye, and Alan W Black. 2018c. A dataset for document grounded conversations. In *Proceedings of the 2018 Conference on Empirical Methods in Natural Language Processing*, pages 708–713, Brussels, Belgium. Association for Computational Linguistics.

Author Index

Association for Computational Linguistics
209 N. Eighth Street
Stroudsburg, Pennsylvania 18360

ISBN 978-1-7138-9761-3

CURRAN ASSOCIATES INC.
proceedings.com